Lingua Mater
Americana

Margot Davidson

Lingua Mater Americana

Margot Davidson

Hillside Education
475 Bidwell Hill Road
Lake Ariel, PA 18436

©Margot Davidson, Hillside Education, 2009

ISBN: 978-0-9906720-9-8

Cover design by Mary Jo Loboda

Sentences used for correct grammar imitation practice in Unit 3 attributed to
Mr. Thomas Longua, adapted

Put it before them briefly so they will read it, clearly so they will appreciate it, picturesquely so they will remember it, and above all, accurately so they will be guided by its light.

—Joseph Pulitzer

Table of Contents

Unit 1

Unit Two

Unit Three – Expository Style

Unit Four – Short Story Unit

Unit One

Week 1
Review of Parts of Speech,
Subject and Predicate

Day 1

Read this description from a story and think about it.

His eyes fell on the still, upright, and rigid form of the Indian runner, who had borne to the camp the unwelcome tidings of the preceding evening. Although in a state of perfect repose, and apparently disregarding, with characteristic stoicism, the excitement and bustle around him, there was a sullen fierceness mingled with the quiet of the savage, that was likely to arrest the attention of much more experienced eyes than those which now scanned him, in unconcealed amazement. The native bore both the tomahawk and knife of his tribe; and yet his appearance was not altogether that of a warrior. On the contrary, there was an air of neglect about his person, like that which might have proceeded from great and recent exertion, which he had not yet found leisure to repair. The colors of the war-paint had blended in dark confusion about his fierce countenance, and rendered his swarthy lineaments still more savage and repulsive than if art had attempted an effect which had been thus produced by chance. His eye, alone, which glistened like a fiery star amid lowering clouds, was to be seen in its state of native wildness. For a single instant his searching and yet wary glance met the wondering look of the other, and then changing its direction, partly in cunning, and partly in disdain, it remained fixed, as if penetrating the distant air.

—From *Last of the Mohicans* by James Fenimore Cooper

Write your first impressions of this short description. For example, what did you like, what didn't you like? What questions came to your mind as you read it?

Be sure you know the meaning of these words:
stoicism
sullen
proceeded
swarthy

Grammar Study

Review and Analysis of Parts of Speech

Find an example of each of the following parts of speech in the description on the previous page. Tell how you can tell what part of speech it is. (Pronoun- it is taking the place of such and such a noun.) See the Appendix for definitions and samples of the parts of speech.

1. Noun; indicate number and gender
2. Pronoun
3. Adjective
4. Action verb; indicate past or present tense
5. Intransitive verb; transitive verb (how can you tell the difference)
6. Adverb
7. Conjunction
8. Preposition

The Last of the Mohicans by Newell Convers Wyeth

Day 2

Guided Response

Reread the selection from Day 1 and think about the following questions.
Discuss them with your teacher or takes notes for each one in your notebook.

1. What impression of the Indian does the author give through his description?
    What is the overall tone of the description?

2. Is this an Indian to be trusted? What in the description helps you decide?

3. In the context of the description, what do the following phrases tell you
    about the Indian:

    a. characteristic stoicism
    b. sullen fierceness
    c. swarthy lineaments
    d. [glance changing direction] partly in cunning, partly in disdain

4. Look at every sentence in the passage and underline the action verbs. What is the
    effect of these action verbs in the description?

5. Without looking back at Cooper's description, reproduce this description of this
    Indian in your notebook.

Grammar

Practice with Parts of Speech

**Identify the part of speech of each of the underlined words below. Indicate if the verbs
are transitive or intransitive.**

<u>On</u> that day, two men were lingering on the banks of a small but rapid stream, within an
hour's journey of the encampment of Webb, like those who awaited the <u>appearance</u> of an
absent person, or the approach of some expected event. The <u>vast</u> canopy of woods spread
<u>itself</u> to the margin of the river, overhanging the water, and shadowing <u>its</u> dark current with
a deeper <u>hue</u>. The rays of the sun <u>were beginning</u> to grow <u>less</u> fierce, and the <u>intense</u> heat
of the day was lessened, as the cooler vapors of the springs and fountains <u>rose</u> above their
leafy beds, and <u>rested</u> in the atmosphere. Still that breathing silence, which marks the drowsy
sultriness of an American landscape in July, <u>pervaded</u> the secluded spot, <u>interrupted</u> only by
the low voices of the men, the occasional and lazy tap of a woodpecker, the discordant cry <u>of</u>
some gaudy jay, <u>or</u> a swelling on the ear, from the dull roar of a distant waterfall.

—From *Last of the Mohicans*, Chapter 3

Day 3

Reread the passage from Last of the Mohicans printed on Day 1.
Reread your reproduction of this description from Day 2.

Writing

Today you will write a rough draft of your *own* description of a person. In Cooper's description you get a sense of the attitude, personality, and character of the Indian. The Indian doesn't do much in this passage, but you can tell a lot about him.

1. Select a person to describe. Choose someone you know well. Think about that person's character and personality. You will want your description to convey the personality to the reader.

2. Jot down several incidents that show the personality of your selected person. Make a list of telling phrases and action verbs. (See questions 3 and 4 from Guided Response on Day 2.)

3. Begin the writing phase by "free writing" about this person. Write for an extended period of time in your notebook without worry about spelling, form, or punctuation. Just let your ideas flow; write whatever you think about your selected person. Write about several different incidents or different perspectives of your selected person.

4. Reread your "free-write." Chose one incident that will portray this person in the way you think best shows his/her personality. See if you make the actions of the person show his attitude or personality.

5. Write your rough/first draft of a description of a person using one incident.

Grammar Study

Review of Parts of the Sentence

There are two parts to every sentence: a subject and a predicate. The subject tells you what is being spoken of, and the predicate tells you what is said about the subject. All the words that go with the simple noun subject, like adjectives and prepositional phrases that modify it, are called the *subject* of the sentence. All the words that go with the simple verb of the sentence, including adverbs and modifying prepositional phrases are called the *predicate* of the sentence. In simple sentences, the subject is usually right at the beginning of the sentence like this sample:

The dog gamboled down the road after the boys.

The dog is the complete subject and *gamboled down the road after the boys* is the complete predicate.

So when you are asked to divide a sentence into its subject and predicate parts, you could just draw a line between the simple subject *dog* and the simple predicate *gamboled.*

However, in more complex sentences, parts of the predicate can appear near the beginning of the sentence like this sample:

> After the boys left on their bicycles, the dog gamboled down the road.

The dog is still the subject. *After the boys left on their bicycles* modifies *gamboled* by telling when. You could ask yourself: Does *after the boys left on their bicycles* modify the dog? No, it does not; so it belongs with the predicate.

Exercises

In each of the following sentences, underline the complete predicate.

1. The industry and movements of the rider were not less remarkable than those of the ridden.

2. A young man, in the dress of an officer, conducted to their steeds two females, who, as it was apparent by their dresses, were prepared to encounter the fatigues of a journey in the woods.

3. The flush which still lingered above the pines in the western sky was not more bright nor delicate than the bloom on her cheek.

4. The frown which had gathered around the handsome, open, and manly brow of Heyward, gradually relaxed, and his lips curled into a slight smile, as he regarded the stranger. (This is a compound sentence so it will have 2 subjects and 2 predicates.)

5. The delivery of these skillful rhymes was accompanied, on the part of the stranger, by a regular rise and fall of his right hand, which terminated at the descent, by suffering the fingers to dwell a moment on the leaves of the little volume.

6. A gleam of exultation shot across the darkly-painted lineaments of the inhabitant of the forest, as he traced the route of his intended victims, who rode unconsciously onward.

7. The shapeless person of the singing master was concealed behind the numberless trunks of trees, that rose, in dark lines, in the intermediate space.
    —From Last of the Mohicans, Chapter 2

Day 4

Reread the passage from *Last of the Mohicans* printed on Day 1.

Writing

A. Read the following description of a person written by an 8th grade student.

> He stood a little ways off from the fire under the shadow of a nearby tent. The dancing flames reflected in his eyes as he silently observed the other scouts idly chatting and goofing on the logs and benches. His arms were folded in a proud yet calm gesture. His back, as straight as a flag staff, suggested physical and spiritual strength. Judging the time was right, he rose slowly to call for attention.

B. Answer the following questions about this brief description.

1. What do you think the author wanted to show about the character of the person by this description? How well does the description show the character?

2. What parts of the description best show the character?

3. What do you think the author should add to make this description better?

4. Notice the sentence variety that the author uses. Some sentences are short, some are longer with phrases. What effect does this give to the reading?

C. Reread the rough draft of your description of a person that *you* wrote on Day 3. Ask yourself these same four questions. After reflecting on them, make any changes in your paper to make it a stronger description.

Grammar Study

Look at the description you wrote and divide each sentence into its subject and predicate parts. You will be amazed at the complex sentences you wrote!

In your writing find one of each of the parts of speech listed on Day 1 and list them in your notebook. (An interjection is also a part of speech, but it is not listed on Day 1. If you used an interjection, please identify it.)

File your description of a person in the drafts folder.

Week 2
Complements

Day 1
Read this personal narrative and reflect upon it.

The Whistle

When I was a child of seven years old, my friends, on a holiday, filled my pocket with coppers. I went directly to a shop where they sold toys for children; and being charmed with the sound of a *whistle,* that I met by the way in the hands of another boy, I voluntarily offered and gave all my money for one. I then came home, and went whistling all over the house, much pleased with my *whistle,* but disturbing all the family. My brothers, and sisters, and cousins, understanding the bargain I had made, told me I had given four times as much for

BENJAMIN FRANKLIN

it as it was worth; put me in mind what good things I might have bought with the rest of the money; and laughed at me so much for my folly, that I cried with vexation; and the reflection gave me more chagrin than the *whistle* gave me pleasure.

This, however, was afterwards of use to me, the impression continuing on my mind; so that often, when I was tempted to buy some unnecessary thing, I said to myself, *Don't give too much for the whistle;* and I saved my money.

As I grew up, came into the world, and observed the actions of men, I thought I met with many, very many, *who gave too much for the whistle.*

When I saw one too ambitious of court favor, sacrificing his time in attendance on levees, his repose, his liberty, his virtue, and perhaps his friends, to attain it, I have said to myself, *This man gives too much for his whistle.*

When I saw another fond of popularity, constantly employing himself in political bustles, neglecting his own affairs, and ruining them by that neglect, *He pays, indeed,* said I, *too much for his whistle.*

If I knew a miser, who gave up every kind of comfortable living, all the pleasure of doing good to others, all the esteem of his fellow-citizens, and the joys of benevolent friendship, for the sake of accumulating wealth, *Poor man,* said I, *you pay too much for your whistle.*

When I met with a man of pleasure, sacrificing every laudable improvement of the mind, or of his fortune, to mere corporeal sensations, and ruining his health in their pursuit, *Mistaken man,* said I, *you are providing pain for yourself, instead of pleasure; you give too much for your whistle.*

If I see one fond of appearance, or fine clothes, fine houses, fine furniture, fine equipages, all above his fortune, for which he contracts debts, and ends his career in a prison, *Alas!* say I, *he has paid dear, very dear, for his whistle.*

When I see a beautiful sweet-tempered girl married to an ill-natured brute of a husband, *What a pity,* say I, *that she should pay so much for a whistle!*

In short, I conceive that great part of the miseries of mankind are brought upon them by the false estimates they have made of the value of things, and by their *giving too much for their whistles.*

Yet I ought to have charity for these unhappy people, when I consider that, with all this wisdom of which I am boasting, there are certain things in the world so tempting, for example, the apples of King John, which happily are not to be bought; for if they were put to sale by auction, I might very easily be led to ruin myself in the purchase, and find that I had once more given too much for the whistle.

Benjamin Franklin

Write your first impressions of this personal narrative. For example, what did you like, what didn't you like? What questions came to your mind as you read it? What do you think Mr. Franklin's main point is?

Declaration of Independence by John Turnbull

Grammar Study

Parts of Sentences

In the last lesson, you divided a sentence into two parts, the complete subject and the complete predicate. The complete subject contains a noun about which the sentence is written. It also contains any words (modifiers), phrases, or clauses that describe that noun. The subject noun is called the *simple subject*.

The complete predicate contains a verb, known as the *simple predicate*, which asserts something about the simple subject. It also includes modifiers, phrases, or clauses that tell more about the verb.

Sometimes a subject and predicate need a little more to complete the thought of the sentence. If you see the sentence *Snow melts,* you know that it is a complete statement because the verb *melts* makes a complete assertion about the subject *snow*, and there is no need of any other words to express the basic idea. However, if you read the sentence *The snow is* or *The snow seems* or *The snow makes*, it seems as if the thought is incomplete. The reader wants to ask *The snow is what? The snow makes what?* And yet, each expression consists of a noun and verb, which ought to make a complete sentence.

So in some cases, a noun and a verb are not sufficient to make a complete statement, some other word being necessary to fill our or complete the assertion of the verb. Words of this kind are called *complements*.

	Subject	Predicate	
	noun	verb	complement
Example:	The snow	is	beautiful.
	The snow	seems	deep
	The snow	makes	drifts

The complement may be modified by other words, but they are not considered complements.

> A complement is the part of the sentence necessary to complete
> the assertion of the verb.

Exercise A
Make sentences of the following groups of words by adding an appropriate complement. You may do this orally with your teacher. Please notice whether you add a noun or an adjective to complete the sentence.

1. The sky became _____
2. The sun gives _____
3. The water looks _____
4. Tomorrow will be _____
5. These flowers smell _____
6. The boy threw _____
7. She has been _____
8. My friend lost _____

Exercise B

Identify the simple subject, simple predicate, and complement of each of the following sentences. Say whether the complement is an adjective or a noun.

1. Hiawatha aimed his arrow.
2. Every man must educate himself.
3. March brings breezes loud and shrill.
4. Each of us has his faults.
5. The Lord is merciful to His people.
6. Fresh winds purify the air.

Exercise C

Write sentences of your own, using the following verbs. Underline the complement in each of your sentences.

sell   build   tastes   take   know   seems

Day 2

Guided Response

Reread the narrative by Benjamin Franklin.

1. Explain how this incident in Mr. Franklin's childhood influenced his life.

2. Make a list of the things for which Franklin thinks people gave too much.

3. Think of the example of the girl with the brutish husband. How is it that she paid too much for the whistle? What did she pay?

4. Which of Franklin's examples do you think is the most important thing to have made a mistake and paid too much for? Which one would cause the most grief to the "creature" as Franklin calls him or her?

5. Can you think of anything in our times that shows this maxim Franklin learned as a child? Think of as many as you can.

Grammar Study

Predicate Nominative and Predicate Adjective

When the simple predicate is a linking verb, sometimes called a *copulative*, the verb complement is either a *predicate nominative* or a *predicate adjective*. Other nouns, such as *seems* and *becomes* also serve as linking verbs. The predicate nominative is a noun that renames the simple subject and the predicate adjective is an adjective that describes the simple subject.

Examplse: The boy is courteous. (predicate adjective)
            The boy is a scout. (predicate nominative)
            She seems happy. (predicate adjective)
            He became king. (predicate nominative)

> A **predicate adjective** is an adjective that is used to predicate an attribute of the subject.
>
> A **predicate nominative** is a *noun* or *pronoun* which follows the verb and describes or renames the subject.

Exercise A
Review the sentences in Exercise B on Day 1. Say which, if any, contain a predicate nominative and which, if any, contain a predicate adjective.

Exercise B
Identify the complements in the following sentences and say whether they are predicate adjectives or predicate nominatives.

1. The sunset colors are brilliant.
2. Washington and Lincoln were true patriots.
3. A book is a good companion.
4. November woods are bare and still.
5. Sally will be the winner after all.
6. His faith was strong, and all marveled at his fortitude.
7. Beggars cannot be choosers.

Exercise C
Write two sentences of your own, each of which contains a predicate adjective.
Write two sentences of your own, each of which contains a predicate nominative.

Day 3

Writing

Mr. Franklin's story of the whistle he bought at so dear a price is a good example of a personal narrative. Personal or autobiographical narratives are sometimes the easiest kind of papers to write since we know the subject—our self—so well and can speak authentically about it.

In this case, Mr. Franklin tells about an experience he had as a youth and what he learned from it. You will write a personal narrative in which you describe an experience *you* have had and what you learned from it.

Here is the general outline of a personal narrative:

Introduction: Anecdote or dialogue to set the stage for the incident. Sometimes it is just the beginning of the story, as in "The Whistle" by Ben Franklin. Sometimes the writer gives the reader a hint or foreshadowing of what lesson was learned.

Body: The story is told in chronological order, using lots of details and descriptive language to bring the scene to life for the reader.

Conclusion: The author reflects on the significance of the event to his/her life.

Prewriting:
Think of an event in your life that you remember well and that you may have often reflected upon. (Please see the sample personal narrative in the Appendix.) Since you will have to tell the story in chronological order, begin by listing what happened. Then close your eyes and visualize the scene. Think of details that would help a reader visualize it as you do. Make a list of sensory details (sharp colors, smells, sounds, etc.). Draw a chart like the one below on your paper to record your lists.

Events in order: 1. 2. 3. 4. 5. 6.				
Sounds	Smells	Visual	Taste	Texture

Then chart or outline your essay. (Draw a chart or outline like this on your paper and note in each section what you will include in your paper.)

Chart

Introduction:
Conclusion: (Reflect on the significance of the event.)

Outline

I. Introduction:

    A.

    B.

II. Body (Narration)

    A.
    B.
    C.
    D.

III. Conclusion:

    A.

    B. (Reflect on what it means to you or why you remember it so well.)

Set your prewriting aside until Day 4

Grammar Study

Direct and Indirect Object

Sometimes the complement of the verb receives the action of the verb. In that case, the verb is said to be *transitive* (the action transfers to an object) and the complement is a noun called the *direct object*. If a verb does not transfer its action to an object it is said to be *intransitive*.

Transitive: *Sam threw the ball.*
"Ball" is the *direct object* of the verb "threw."

An *indirect object* precedes the direct object and tells to whom or for whom the action of the verb is done and who is receiving the direct object. *There must be a direct object to have an indirect object.* The indirect object is a noun or pronoun.

*Sam gave the **door** a kick.*
*Sam gave **me** a dollar.*

"Door" is the *indirect object* of the verb "gave."
"Me" is the indirect object of the verb "gave." ("Dollar" is the direct object of the verb.)

Exercise A
Identify the direct and indirect objects in the following sentences.

1. Give me liberty or give me death.
2. Every failure should teach a man something.
3. You can't teach an old dog new tricks.
4. God grant us peace!
5. Diligence will bring you great rewards in life.
6. Our forefathers gave us liberty by their blood.

Exercise B
Find two transitive and two intransitive verbs in "The Whistle."

Exercise C
Write three sentences that contain both a direct and an indirect object.

Day 4

Writing

Review the notes you made for the personal narrative about an event in your life.

Writing: Using the chart or outline you made, write your paper.

Sharing: Ask someone to read your draft and ask him or her the following questions about it:

Was the narrative clear?
Was it descriptive enough? If not, where should more description language be included?
What questions remain in his or her mind after hearing the paper?
Does the conclusion give a good reflection on what this event meant to the writer?

Revising: Make changes in your paper based on the conversation you have with your reader.

*File this paper in your **drafts** folder.*

Grammar Study

Review – Complements

Review the four kinds of verb complements discussed in this chapter. Be able to explain what a verb complement is and when each one would be used.

Exercise A

Analyze each of the following sentences. Decide what kind of complement is used in each one. Label the following items in each sentence: simple subject (SS), simple predicate (SP), predicate adjective (PA), predicate nominative (PN), direct object (DO), indirect object (IO). Then say whether each verb is a transitive or intransitive verb.

1. The raccoon is a most courageous little fellow. He never shows the white flag. On one occasion my dog attacked a raccoon. The raccoon was small and my dog was big and fierce. The little fellow faced the odds with perfect composure. He never betrayed a sign of fear. He never for a moment lost his head. His coolness saved his life. I never saw a finer example of grit.

2. It was the most extraordinary looking gentleman he had ever seen in his life. He had a very large nose, slightly brass-colored; his cheeks were very round, and very red, and might have warranted a supposition that he had been blowing a refractory fire for the last eight-and-forty hours; his eyes twinkled merrily through long silky eyelashes, his mustaches curled twice round like a corkscrew on each side of his mouth, and his hair, of a curious mixed pepper-and-salt color, descended far over his shoulders.

From King of the Golden River by John Ruskin

3. The gulls are the children of the winds and the waves. Their home is a bare cliff or a sandy bar within sight and sound of the sea. Here they rear their young, and the pounding surf sings the babies' lullaby. They wrest their livelihood from the waters, defying cold and storm. These sailor birds lead wandering and restless lives, now seeking the watery solitudes of mid-ocean, and again some busy river course or inland lake close to the haunts of men.

Exercise B

Read the sentences you wrote for Exercise C on Day 1 and say whether you used a predicate nominative, a predicate adjective, a direct object, or an indirect object in each one.

Week 3
Prepositional and Infinitive Phrases

Day 1
Look carefully at the painting below.

The Historian by E. Irving Couse

Write your first impressions of the image. What do you think is happening?

Grammar Study

A phrase is a group of words that go together but do not make a complete sentence. This is sometimes called a *syntactic unit*. The use of phrases will bring more detail and sophistication to your writing.

Prepositional Phrases

> A *prepositional phrase* is a group of words made up of the preposition, its object, and the object's modifiers.
>
> Matt set the book *on the low table*.
>
> "On" is the preposition, "the" and "low" modify *table*, and "table" is the object of the preposition.

NOTE: A preposition *always* has an object. If you see a word that you think is a preposition (such as "up," "down," "around") and it has no object, then it is most likely an adverb, not a preposition. If you haven't done so yet, you should memorize the list of prepositions so that you can recognize them immediately.

Exercise
On your paper write the prepositional phrases that you find in the text below. Label the preposition, its object, and adjectives (you may identify the articles separately).

WIGWAM LEGEND OF HIAWATHA

The first day he listened with attentive gravity to the plans of the different speakers; on the next day he arose and said: "My friends and brothers; you are members of many tribes, and have come from a great distance. We have come to promote the common interest, and our mutual safety. How shall it be accomplished? To oppose these Northern hordes in tribes singly, while we are at variance often with each other, is impossible. By uniting in a common band of brotherhood we may hope to succeed.

"Let this be done, and we shall drive the enemy from our land. Listen to me by tribes. You, the Mohawks, who are sitting under the shadow of the great tree, whose branches spread wide around, and whose roots sink deep into the earth, shall be the first nation, because you are warlike and mighty. You, the Oneidas, who recline your bodies against the everlasting stone that cannot be moved, shall be the second nation, because you always give wise counsel. You, the Onondagas, who have your habitation at the foot of the great hills, and are overshadowed by their crags, shall be the third nation, because you are greatly gifted in speech. You, the Senecas, whose dwelling is in the dark forest, and whose home is all over the land, shall be the fourth nation, because your hunting is cunning and superior. And you, the Cayugas, the people who live in the open country and possess much wisdom, shall be the fifth nation, because you understand better the raising of corn and beans, and making lodges.

"Unite, ye five nations, and have one common interest, and no foe shall disturb and subdue you. You, the people who are the feeble bushes, and you who are a fishing people, may place yourselves under our protection, and we will defend you. And you of the South and West may do the same, and we will protect you. We earnestly desire the alliance and friendship of you all. Brothers, if we unite in this great bond, the Great Spirit will smile upon us, and we shall be free, prosperous, and happy; but if we remain as we are, we shall receive his frown. We shall be enslaved, ruined, perhaps annihilated. We may perish under the war-storm, and our names be no longer remembered by good men, nor be repeated in the dance and song. Brothers, those are the words of Hiawatha. I have spoken. I am done."

From *Legends Every Child Should Know* by Hamilton Wright Mabie

Day 2

Guided Response

Examine the painting *The Historian* carefully and discuss these questions with your teacher.

1. Why do you think the painting is called *The Historian*?

2. What history is he telling?

3. What do you think the older man is saying to the younger?

4. What are they using to record the event?

5. Look at each of the images he has drawn and make a guess as to what each one is. Give the reasons for your guesses.

6. Think of some questions that the boy might ask.

7. Using your story from Week 2, make a picture history of it.

31

Grammar Study

Infinitive Phrases

An infinitive construction is one of three kinds of *verbals*, that is, a verb form used as a noun, adjective, or adverb. Infinitives do not have subjects so they are never used as predicates. (Example: *to think, to study, to be, to love, to jump, to fall*)

We wanted *to swim.*

An infinitive can be used as noun (as the subject, direct object, predicate nominative), an adjective, or an adverb. However, it can never be an indirect object.

SS SP DO
We wanted [*to swim*].

SS SP DO Adj
James wanted time [*to think*].

SS SP PN
[*To live*] is his only goal.

An infinitive *may* have an object (a preposition must have an object). If the infinitive is a state of being verb (in the "to be" family), then it may also have a predicate nominative or predicate adjective. The infinitive with its complement and modifiers is called an *infinitive phrase*.

SS Adj – infinitive phrase SP PN
John's attempt [*to win the difficult race*] was a failure.

SS SP DO adv – infinitive phrase
Susan baked the cake [*to impress her new teacher*].

SS SP pred nom – infinitive phrase
His goal for the school year is [to make the Dean's List].

1. In the first sentence the infinitive phrase is used as an adjective modifying *attempt*. *Race* is the direct object of the infinitive *to win*.
2. In the second sentence the infinitive phrase is used as an adverb modifying *baked*. *Teacher* is the direct object of the infinitive *to impress*.
3. In the third sentence the infinitive phrase is used as a predicate nominative. *Dean's List* is the direct object of the infinitive *to make*.

Exercise
On your paper write the infinitive phrases found in the following sentences. Label the infinitive and its object or complement. (Infinitive=inf; direct object of the infinitive=DOi, indirect object of the infinitive= IOi; Predicate nominative of the infinitive= PNi; Predicate Adjective of the infinitive=PAi). *Then, tell how the infinitive phrase is used in the sentence.*

Is it the subject, direct object, adjective, or adverb? To figure that out, ask yourself what job the phrase does in the sentence.

Example: To earn the money for his trip is the goal of the fundraiser.

Infinitive phrase: to earn the money for his trip
Used as the subject of the sentence

1. His immediate aim is to become mayor of the city.

2. Some people are quick to judge others unfairly.

3. To be cool is the chief goal in his pathetic life.

4. To know her is to love her.

5. George wants to take the midnight flight to Chicago after the meeting.

6. My sister told 50 people to come to the house for a party after the game.

7. To have taken the plane to California would have been too expensive.

8. The boss likes to give his best workers a big bonus for Christmas.

9. There were several things to consider before the vote.

10. To pass the test, you will need to learn the material in the charts and notes.

Day 3

Writing

Look carefully again at the painting on Day 1 and think about your discussion from Day 2. Today you will write the first draft of a story. You may choose one of the following ideas:

1.) Write a story of the man and the boy in the painting. Did the older man participate in a battle that he is recording? Or is it a story told to him by an ancestor? What is the boy's reaction? Is he an apprentice? Or is the boy telling the story and the historian recording it?

2.) Write a story of your own and then draw a "history picture" to go with it. It can be a fictitious story of some event in history (Boston Tea Party, Midnight Ride of Paul Revere, etc.) or something that happened to you personally.

Don't forget that a story has three parts: *Introduction* in which you set the stage for the story, introduce the characters and the problem; *Body* in which you narrate the action of the story and show how the characters work to resolve the problem; and *Conclusion*, in which the problem is resolved and the characters return to equilibrium.

Write a first draft of your story and save it for review on Day 4.

Even though you are in an advanced study of English composition and grammar, creative writing is still very important. Be sure to take some time each week to write creatively, which exercises your brain in a very different way than structured essay writing. Also, the more creatively you allow yourself to think, the better your more structured essays will be. So, get a spiral bound notebook and commit some time to it!

Grammar Study

Quite often you will find prepositional phrases inside other kinds of phrases. Students often confuse the object of the preposition with the object of a verbal when a preposition is in the verbal phrase.

Inf phrasse   prep phrase   prep phrase
(To earn the money [for his trip]) is the goal [of the fundraiser].

To earn the money for his trip is the entire infinitive phrase. Money is the object of the infinitive "to earn." *For his trip* is a prepositional phrase that is part of the phrase because it modifies *money*.

Exercise

The following sentences have prepositional phrases inside infinitive phrases. Identify the entire infinitive phrase and then identify the prepositional phrase within it. Label the infinitive (inf), the preposition (P), the object of the infinitive if any (DOi or IOi) and the object of the preposition (OP). Say what the preposition is modifying. Say how the infinitive is used in the sentence (subject, direct object, predicate nominative).

NOTE: Some sentences may have more than one prepositional phrases within the infinitive phrase. Prepositions act as adjectives or adverbs.

Example: His immediate aim is to become mayor of the city.

              inf   DOi   P   OP

Infinitive phrase: (to become mayor of the city)   used as the predicate nominative
Prepositional phrase: *of the city* modifies *mayor*

1. George wants to take the midnight flight to Chicago after the meeting.

2. My sister told 50 people to come to the house for a party after the game.

3. There were several things to consider before the vote.

4. To pass the test, you will need to learn the material in the charts and notes.

5. Last weekend, we organized a square dance to raise money for the family who had lost their home.

6. We were immediately ordered by the respective commanders to board the ships all at the same time.

Day 4

Writing

Exercise A

Reread the personal narrative "The Whistle" by Ben Franklin from Week 2. Notice the use of verbs in Franklin's narrative—most are action verbs. Action verbs bring life to your writing. Read the story you wrote this week, checking to see if you have used plenty of action verbs. If you have used "there" at the beginning of any sentences, revise them so that the verb shows action. Not *every* verb in your story must be an action word, but if you use them for the most part, your writing will have more power.

After you have revised for action verbs, ask someone to read your story. Ask your reader the following questions:

1. Is the narrative clear and are the descriptions vivid? What would make it more clear or vivid?
2. Are any questions left in your mind after reading it? These questions show places where your narrative may have gaps.
3. What changes would improve the paper?

After this discussion, make changes in your paper to improve it and then file it in your drafts folder.

Exercise B

Showing versus telling: When writing a narrative, you want your writing to bring the scene to life for your readers. To do this you *show* the reader what happened as opposed to just *telling* him. Here is an example:

> Telling: Tim played the piano well.
> Showing: Striking the keys with precision and sensitivity, Tim astounded his
> listeners with a delightful piano concerto.

Take each of the following "telling" sentences and make them *show* the reader something more about the topic. You may write more than one sentence to complete the scene.

1. Matthew is happy he won the race.
2. All the children ran for the ice-cream.
3. The family enjoyed the lake.
4. The campers sat by the campfire.

Grammar Study

Review prepositional and infinitive phrases. Explain each one and use it in a sentence.

Exercise A
Explain how you can tell if the word "to" in a sentence is introducing an infinitive phrase or if it is a preposition.

Exercise B
Find all the infinitive phrases in the story on Day 1. Write each one on your paper. Label the infinitive (inf), the object of the infinitive if any (DOi). Then label any prepositional phrases that appear within the infinitive. Label the preposition (P) and the object of the preposition (OP).

Buffalo Hunt by George Catlin

Week 4
Participles

Day 1
Read the following poem and reflect upon it.

The Indian Burying Ground

In spite of all the learned have said,
I still my old opinion keep;
The posture that we give the dead,
Points out the soul's eternal sleep.

Not so the ancients of these lands—
The Indian, when from life released,
Again is seated with his friends,
And shares again the joyous feast.

His imaged birds, and painted bowl,
And venison, for a journey dressed,
Bespeak the nature of the soul,
Activity, that knows no rest.

His bow, for action ready bent,
And arrows, with a head of bone,
Can only mean that life is spent,
And not the finer essence gone.

Thou, stranger, that shalt come this way,
No fraud upon the dead commit,
Yet, marking the swelling turf, and say,
They do not lie, but here they sit.

Here, still a lofty rock remains,
On which the curious eye may trace
(Now wasted half by wearing rains)
The fancies of a ruder race.

Here, still an aged elm aspires,
Beneath whose far-projecting shade
(And which the shepherd still admires)
The children of the forest played.

There oft a restless Indian queen,
(Pale Marian, with her braided hair)
And many a barbarous form is seen
To chide the man that lingers there.

By midnight moons, o'er moistening dews,
In habit for the chase arrayed,
The hunter still the deer pursues,
The hunter and the deer—a shade.

And long shall timorous fancy see
The painted chief, and pointed spear,
And reason's self shall bow the knee
To shadows and delusions here.

—Philip Freneau, 1787

Write your first impression of this poem. What scenes are particularly vivid? What thought came to you mind as your read it? What is the main idea of the author?

Cornplanter (Seneca Indians) by F. Bartoli

Grammar Study

Participles

A participle is a verbal (a verb form) that is used as an **adjective**. The present participle is formed by adding *ing* to the verb. The past participle uses the past tense form of the verb (adding *ed* to the end of regular verbs and using the past tense of irregular verbs).

Present participle: Kerry watches the *twirling* leaf cascade to the ground.
Past participle: The *lost* sock was eventually found.
The *frightened* girl jumped at the sound.
Perfect participle: *Having waited* in line for hours, the students were sent home

How can you tell if a word is a adjectival participle or a verb?
1. In sentence one above, the verb *watches* has a subject: *Kerry*. The word *twirling* has no subject.
2. *Watches* is in the third person, singular to agree with its subject *Kerry*. If we changed the subject to *boys*, the verb has to change to *watch* to agree with the subject *boys*. However, twirling, having no subject has neither person nor number.

Exercise
Pick out the participles, and tell whether it is present, past, or perfect. Name the noun or pronoun each participle modifies.

Example: The blackest desperation now gathers over him, broken only by red lightnings of remorse.
Broken is the past participle modifying *desperation*

1. The trees are laden with ripening fruit.
2. In the churchyard here were cattle tranquilly reposing upon the verdant graves.
3. The roaring mob came out and thronged the place.
4. The girls sat weeping in silence.
5. Asked for a dollar, he gives a thousand.
6. Edward marched through Scotland at the head of a powerful army, compelling all ranks of people to submit to him.
7. Arrived at Athens, he soon came to court.
8. I went home that night greatly oppressed in my mind, irresolute, and not knowing what to do.
9. A mountain stood
   Threatening from high, and overlooked the wood.
10. He half rose, with great pain slowly, reclining on his arm and looking wistfully with wide blue eyes.

Day 2

Guided Response

Reread the poem from Day 1, *Indian Burying Ground*. Discuss the following questions with your teacher.

1. What is the author's main idea in this poem?

2. How is the Indian buried? Cite information from the poem in your answer.

3. Does the author think this is a good thing?

4. What is the meaning of stanza 4? What is his finer essence?

5. What is the meaning of stanza 9? (A "shade" is an old-fashioned word for ghost or shadow of reality. In ancient literature, when someone dies, what is left of him—his spirit—in the underworld in called a "shade.")

6. Do you think that the author had first-hand knowledge of the burial practices of the Indians? Give reasons for your answer.

7. Write out in prose (not poetic verse) the author's narration.

Grammar Study

Participle Phrases

Participle phrases include the participle and its objects, complements, or modifiers. It may include prepositional and infinitive phrases.

> *Awakened by the thunder*, Mary tossed in her sleep.
> Jimmie ran clumsily through the dorm room, *awakening the other boys*.
> We could see a woman *pulling a small boat*.
> *Having resolved to be a better student*, Harry sat down to his studies.

Exercise A
Identify the participle phrase and write it on your paper. Tell what noun or pronoun each one modifies.

1. He occupied a pretty farm on seventy acres, situated on the skirts of that pretty little village.
2. Mine was a small chamber near the top of the house, fronting on the sea.
3. The listening crowd admires the lofty sound.
4. This life which seems so fair,
   Is like a bubble blown up in the air.
5. The horses, neighing wildly in panic, stampeded through the barn doors.
6. His bridge was only loose planks laid upon large trestles.
7. She had a little room in the garret, where the maids heard her walking and sobbing at night.
8. The kind creature retreated into the garden, wringing her hands in worry.
9. The colonel, strengthened with some troops of horse from Yorkshire, comes up to the bridge.
10. Having settled herself in the coach, she tapped the roof to tell the driver to proceed.

Day 3

Writing

Persuasive Writing: Opinion papers

An opinion paper falls under the category of persuasive writing because the writer is trying to convince the reader of his opinion. Here is the format for an opinion paper:

Introduction: Explain the reason for giving an opinion. (Describe a situation, a problem, or a reason for a controversy.) And then state your opinion clearly in one sentence. State it as a fact without saying "I think."

> Instead of: *I think that motor boats should not be allowed on the lake.*
> Say: *Motor boats should not be allowed on the lake.*

Body: Support your opinion by explaining your reasons, using examples and anecdotes. Each reason you give and explain should be a separate paragraph.

Conclusion: Remind the reader of your opinion and why it is important.

> *Today you will write the first draft of an opinion paper.*

Think of the story of the country mouse and the city mouse in which each one thought that his home was the best place to live. Consider which you think is best: growing up in a big city or growing up in a small town in the country. Before you begin to write, map or chart the progression of your thoughts. Copy the chart below onto your paper (enlarging it to fit your whole page) and *take notes* on it before you start to write your draft. Each box in your chart becomes one paragraph in your essay.

Note-taking Chart – Opinion Paper

Introduction: Opinion:
Reason #1 Explain!
Reason #2 Explain!
Reason #3 Explain!
Conclusion:

Your introduction should be begin with general statements or descriptions of the two ways of life (city or country). Then state your opinion. The following paragraphs must convince the reader of your opinion, so give reasons, using specific examples and descriptive language. Close with an important thought about your opinion that reminds your reader what you think.

Set your draft aside until Day 4.

Note to the teacher: If the student does not like this topic, please let him or her write on a topic that he or she has a strong opinion about.

Grammar Study

More Practice with Participle Phrases

Rules for punctuating participles

When a participial phrase begins a sentence, a comma should be placed after the phrase.

- *Arriving at the store*, I found that it was closed.
- *Washing and polishing the car*, Frank developed sore muscles.

If the participle or participial phrase comes in the middle of a sentence, it should be set off with commas only if the information is not essential to the meaning of the sentence.

- Sid, *watching an old movie*, drifted in and out of sleep.
- The church, *destroyed by a fire*, was never rebuilt.

Note that if the participial phrase is essential to the meaning of the sentence, no commas should be used:

- The student *earning the highest grade point average* will receive a special award.
- The guy *wearing the chicken costume* is my cousin.

If a participial phrase comes at the end of a sentence, a comma usually precedes the phrase if it modifies an earlier word in the sentence but not if the phrase directly follows the word it modifies.

- The local residents often saw Ken wandering through the streets.
  (The phrase modifies *Ken*, not *residents*.)
- Tom nervously watched the woman, alarmed by her silence.
  (The phrase modifies *Tom*, not *woman*.)

—(Samples from OWL)

Exercise

On your paper write the participle phrases found in the following sentences. Label the participle as past or present and then label the object and any prepositional phrases that appear in the participle phrase (direct object of the participle=DOp; predicate adjective of the participle= PAp; preposition=P, object of the preposition=OP) Not all participles have objects. Then write the noun that the participle modifies. Notice the punctuation of the participle phrases.

Example: At the factory we saw many workers wasting time during work hours.

Participle phrase: Wasting time during work hours   It modifies "workers"
Prepositional phrase: during working hours

44

1. Equipment must be packed neatly in the waiting van before leaving.
2. From the window we saw children playing games in the classroom.
3. Has the modern recording equipment improved the sound of the music?
4. The attendants searched visitors walking through the gate.
5. The fancy new store, erected in January, will not open until the summer.
6. Having changed the tire, the driver jumped in the car and sped off.
7. Respected throughout the world, the statesman was cheered at the bustling airport.
8. Windows decorated with tropical scenes attracted the shoppers' attention.

Day 4

Writing

Revising

In the "revising" stage of the writing process, the writer must attempt to see his piece anew, to look at it with fresh eyes, so to speak. It is a critical stage in the writing process and writers need to allow plenty of time for it. The goal is to make the paper you wrote better.

Read the paper you wrote yesterday about your opinion of the better place to live. Act as if you are an objective reader. Ask yourself how well this writer got his ideas across. Do any questions pop into your mind as you read?

Then choose some things to work on for this revising session. For example, check your transitions. Do you use words at the beginning and end of each paragraph to show the movement from one idea to the next? In the examples you chose, did you write vividly and with power using strong action words. Does every paragraph in the body support the opinion you stated at the beginning?

Make changes to your paper based on your reading and careful scrutiny. You want to find the best way to get your idea across. Take your time—professional writers spend a *long* time on revision.

Save your paper in the drafts folder.

Grammar Study

Review participles and participle phrases. Be able to define a participle and use the three different forms (past, present, and perfect) in a sentence.

Exercise A
Find any participles in the poem *The Indian Burying Ground.*
Write them on your paper and label them as past, present, or perfect.

Exercise B
Think of a participle or participle phrase to enhance each of the following sentences. Remember that a participle acts as an adjective modifying a noun. Write the new sentence on your paper using proper punctuation. (See Day 3.)

1. The boys ran frantically down the street.
2. All the children in the library were amazed by the magician.
3. Last weekend, the literature club invited the author of the book to attend a reception.
4. Whenever we try to learn to ski, we fail miserably.
5. The character in the story seems so real to all of us.

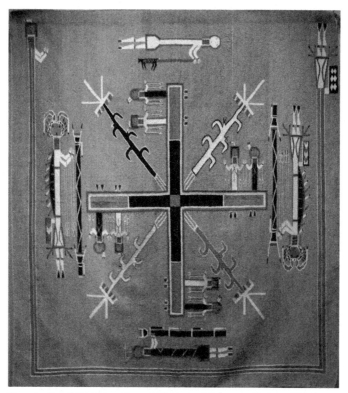

Navajo Sand Painting Rug, Gilcrease Museum, Tulsa, Oklahoma

Week 5
Gerund Phrases

Read this report of a speech given in New York state in 1657 and think carefully about it.

Finally, the Father assumed a louder tone, and with impassioned words he exclaimed: "It is not for purposes of trade that you see us appear in your country. We aim much higher. Your furs are of too little value in our eyes to induce us to undertake so long, so difficult, and so dangerous a journey. Keep your beaver-skins, if you choose, for the Dutch; even those which may come into our hands will be used for your own good. We seek not perishable things. For the Faith, we have left our country; for the Faith, we have abandoned our relatives and our friends; for the Faith, we have crossed the Ocean; for the Faith, we have quitted the great Ships of the French, to embark in your small canoes; for the Faith, we have given up fine houses, to lodge in your bark cabins; for the Faith, we deprive ourselves of our natural nourishment, and the delicate viands that we might have enjoyed in France, to eat your boiled meal and other food, which the animals of our country would hardly touch."

Then, taking up a very fine collar of porcelain beads, artistically made, he continued: " For the sake of the Faith, I hold this rich present in my hand, and I open my mouth to remind you of the word that you pledged us when you came down to Québec to conduct us to your country. You solemnly promised to lend ear to the words of the great God. They are in my mouth; listen to them; I am but his spokesman. He informs you by His Messengers that His Son made Himself man for love of you; that that Man, the Son of God, is the Prince and the Master of Mankind; that He has prepared in Heaven eternal pleasures and joys for those who obey His commandments; and that He kindles horrible fires in Hell for those who refuse to receive His word.

His law is easy; it forbids doing injury either to the property, or the life, or the wife, or the reputation of one's neighbor. Can anything be more reasonable? It commands that respect, love, and reverence be given to Him who has made all and who preserves the universe. Are your minds offended by so natural a truth? *Jesus Christ*, who is the Son of Him who has made all, became our brother and yours by clothing Himself with our flesh; He preached those beautiful truths; He caused them to be painted and written in a book; He ordered that they be carried throughout the world. That is what brings us to your country; that is what opens our mouths; and we are so certain of all those truths, that we are prepared to lose our lives in maintaining them. If thou reject them in thy heart be thou Onnontagheronnon, Sonnontoueronnon, Annieronnon, Oneiogouenronnon, or Onneioutehronnon, know that Jesus Christ, who animates my heart and my voice, will one day cast thee into Hell. But avoid that misfortune by thy conversion; be not the cause of thine own ruin; listen to the voice of the Almighty. "

These and many other words, full of fire and uttered with most Christian vehemence, caused those poor Barbarians such astonishment, that they seemed quite beside themselves; their minds wavered between joy and fear. The approval was so general and universal, that one would have said that all wanted to place the Father in their hearts. No endearment, in their opinion, was sufficiently great to bestow upon him. Tears fell from the eyes of our French, when they saw our Lord so grandly announced in this extremity of the world. For my part, I must admit that what I saw and heard on that occasion surpasses anything that can be said or written of it. If, after that, the devil should turn the heads of these poor people and lead them to kill us, *Justificabitur in sermonibus suis*. We shall, at least, have justified our God in His words.

Jesuit Relations and Allied Documents, Volume 43, page 173-177

Write your first response to this report. Read it again if you need to understand it better. What is the most striking thing about it? What did you find interesting? What thoughts came to your mind as you read it? What are the best parts of it?

Grammar Study

Gerund Phrases

A *gerund* is a verbal form that is used as a noun. A *gerund phrase* is the gerund plus any objects and modifiers, such as prepositional phrases, that go with it.

Walking is a great form of exercise.
Walking to the school everyday helped the boys get enough exercise.

Exercise A

Identify the gerunds and gerund phrases in the following sentences. Say how the gerund is used. (Is it the subject, the predicate nominative, or the direct object of the sentence, or is it the object of a preposition?)

1. His favorite sport is skating.
2. Brushing his teeth was hard work once he had broken his arm.
3. We loved fishing in the creek below our hill.
4. All the children loved eating the fresh hot cookies.
5. Running in the morning made her feel energized all day.
6. She won sainthood by praying.
7. Seeing is believing.

Exercise B

A gerund can have an object.

Walking the crowded streets in the morning improved his heart rate.

In the gerund phrase *walking the crowded streets in the morning*, the word "streets" is the object of the gerund "walking." The prepositional phrase *in the morning* is used as an adverb modifying "walking." (NOTE: *Crowded* is a participle modifying *streets*.) Write the gerund phrases from the following sentences and label any modifiers (prepositional phrases) or objects. Say how the gerund is used (subject, predicate nominative, object of the preposition, or direct object).

Example using the sentence above:
Gerund phrase: Walking the crowded streets in the morning
- used as the subject of the sentence
- "streets" is the object of the gerund
- "in the morning" prepositional phrase modifying walking

1. Eating apples can be a healthy habit.
2. Annie enjoyed doing her best in her schoolwork.
3. Her only consolation during this time was praying with all her might.
4. He had a bad habit of exaggerating his accomplishments.
5. He contemplated leaving home to find a job in the city.

Exercise C

Name the sentences in Exercise A in which the gerund has an object, and those in which the gerund has a modifying prepositional phrase.

Day 2

Guided Response

Reread the report of the speech on Day 1 and discuss the following questions with your teacher.

1. Explain the purpose for the speech. Do you think the priest accomplishes his purpose? How can you tell?

2. Read each paragraph in the speech carefully and on your paper write the main idea of each paragraph. Then, summarize the priest's speech—not the whole selection, just the part where the priest is speaking.

3. What arguments does the priest use to try to convince the Indians to adopt Christianity?

4. Remember that writers and speech makers persuade in three different ways:

    (1) by establishing their credibility as an authority on the topic;
    (2) by using emotional appeals;
    (3) by using logical reasoning.

    Usually persuasive writing includes a combination of these three rhetorical tools. Which of the three kinds of persuasive arguments does the priest employ? Give an example of each one you claim he uses.

5. Why does the writer feel good about the speech by the priest? Give several reasons.

6. What does the writer mean at the end when he says that we will have justified God in His words?

Grammar Study

Practice with Gerunds

Gerunds are used as objects of certain verbs. The following verbs usually have a gerund as its object:

enjoy	quit	avoid	mention	appreciate
finish	keep	suggest	discuss	consider
delay	postpone	stop	mind	put off

Example: Don't put off *working* on your music.

Exercise A
Complete the following sentences by writing a gerund or gerund phrase that would be appropriate.

1. During the movie, we couldn't stop _____.

2. When she first learned to ride a bike, she barely avoided _____.

3. Would you mind _____?

4. Our teacher asked us to consider _____.

5. Even though we'll have to postpone _____, we will meet again next week.

6. Don't delay _____ or you will be sorry later.

7. After I finish _____, I will be able to go for a bike ride.

8. All the children enjoyed _____ so much that they asked to stay longer.

Exercise B
Listed below are a few more verbs that can take a gerund as an object. Use each one in a sentence, including a *gerund phrase* as the object. In your sentence, label the gerund, its object, and any modifying prepositional phrases).

Example: prefer

                        gerund   DOg   mod
    The girls prefer baking their bread (on Saturday).

begin	like	hate	start	continue	love

Day 3

Writing

In an opinion paper, the writer wants to convince the reader of his opinion; in a persuasive paper the writer wants the reader to *do* something. He intends to move the reader to *action*. This week you will write a persuasive paper in which you try to convince someone to take a particular action.

Here is the form of a persuasive paper:

Introduction: Describe a situation and the specific response you want the reader to make to it. ("Call to action.")

Body: Give a first reason and support it
Give a second reason and support it
Acknowledge any opposing views and answer them
Give the third and strongest reason and support it

Conclusion: Wrap up and call to action.

In order to be effectively persuasive, you must understand your audience and find the best way to convince them.

You will write a persuasive paper this week. Choose one of the following topics for your paper:

1. Convince your reader to give up watching television.
2. Convince your reader to support a particular political candidate.
3. Convince your reader that video games are good or bad for users and should be either encouraged or banned.
4. Convince your reader to volunteer at the local homeless shelter.
5. Convince the library to purchase a particular book that you like.

(You may select your own topic with the permission of your teacher, but remember that that the purpose of your paper is to get someone to **do** something.

Prewriting: Think carefully about your chosen topic and decide exactly what action you want to persuade people to take. Your paper will be focused around this action. It becomes the thesis statement of your paper.

Do not use the words *I think* in your "call to action" statement.

Example:

Instead of: I think that the state legislature should enact a law to require trash cans at every street corner.

Say: The state legislature should immediately enact a law to require trash cans at every street corner.

Once you have a strong thesis statement, think of reasons or arguments that will convince people to take the action you want. List your reasons. Put them in order from least to most convincing. You will save the most convincing argument for last. Then, use the chart on the next page to chart your paper. Jot *notes* (not complete sentences, necessarily) about the information that supports each of your reasons. Use examples from your own experience, information you have researched, or anecdotes as your support.

When you are done with your chart, set it aside until Day 4.

Note-taking Chart for Persuasive Paper

Introduction **(describe problem)**   **Suggested course of action:** **(thesis statement/call to action)**
Reason #1 **Explain, use examples**
Reason #2
Acknowledge possible objections to your idea:
Reason #3 (The strongest, most convincing reason)
Conclusion   **Call to Action:**

Note: You may include more than 3 reasons if you like. If you do, make another box for the chart.

Grammar Study

Review Gerunds

A gerund is a verbal noun that can be used as the subject, direct object, or predicate nominative of a sentence. They may also be used as the object of a preposition.

A gerund may also take an object and have prepositional phrase modifiers.

Exercise A

Write 4 sentences using a gerund in each one. In the first use the gerund as the subject of the sentence; in the second, use the gerund as the direct object of the sentence; in the third, use the gerund as the predicate nominative of a sentence (be sure there is a linking verb as the predicate); and in the last sentence, use the gerund as the object of a preposition.

Exercise B

Identify the gerund phrases in the following sentences and write them on your paper. Tell how the gerund is used in the sentence. Label the gerund, its object, and any modifiers (prepositional phrases).

Example: Her first mistake was not trusting her own intuition in the matter.

Ger   DOg   prep phrase-adj

Gerund phrase: trusting her own intuition (in the matter)

Used as the predicate nominative

1. Traveling from one city to the next is difficult in this small car.
2. Worried about the clumsiness of the workers, Mrs. Clonert began moving her furniture to the deck.
3. She was rewarded for giving her life in service to the poor.
4. They found out that the little boy liked playing the clown around his friends.
5. Preparing for the trip was taking most of the week.
6. After trying every other option, they thought of writing to the governor.

Day 4

Writing

Today you will write a first draft of your persuasive paper. Review the notes you made yesterday. Add to them as needed. To write your paper, begin by explaining the problem and then giving your "call to action" or thesis statement. Then the body of your paper is spent convincing your reader that your course of action is the best.

Use your chart to help you keep your paper in order as your write. Each box in the chart becomes one paragraph in your paper. Use transition words as you begin each paragraph. For example,

> Another reason . . .
> Besides . . .
> Above all . . .
> Moreover . . .
> Finally . . .

Transitions helps papers read more smoothly. They help your reader make connections between thoughts. Appropriate use of them will make your paper more organized and understandable because they improve the connections and transitions between thoughts.

Write a strong conclusion so that the reader has no doubt what action you want him to take.

After you write your draft, ask someone to read it for you. Ask your reader if your arguments are convincing and if the progression of your thought is logical. Then make any changes in your paper based on the feedback you receive. You might consider having several different people read it to get several different opinions on it.

Save this paper in your drafts folder.

Grammar Study

Review – Phrases: Prepositional and Verbal

Review the four kinds of phrases discussed in the last 3 weeks. Be able to explain the construction of each one and say how each on is used. Copy the chart below onto your

56

paper and use it to explain each kind of phrase to your teacher. Use each kind of phrase in a sentence to demonstrate your understanding of it.

Name	Prepositional	Infinitive	Gerund	Participle
How is it formed	**Preposition + object**	**To (verb)**	**_____ing**	**_____ing** **_____ed** **Have _____**
Function	**Modifier**	**Noun or modifier**	**Noun**	**modifier**

Verbals – can be used alone (don't have to have a phrase)

Exercise

Identify the prepositional, gerund, infinitive, and participle phrases in the following sentences and write them on your paper. Label them (gerund=G, infinitive=Inf, participle=PPpast or present, and preposition=PS) and their objects/complements.

Example: (Lost[in the raging storm]), the frightened campers tried (to console each other [with uplifting stories]).

1. Listening to music is his favorite way to relax after a busy day.
2. During the exciting climax of the movie, the loud talking of the people behind us was unbearable.
3. In the middle of the raging battle, the frightened civilians heard the wailing of the air-raid sirens.
4. Are those crying children going to the school nurse to put splints on their broken arms and legs?

If you need more practice with phrases, see Appendix B Extra Practice.

Week 6
Clauses

Day 1

Read the following essay on beavers.

The American Beaver

When hiking or walking near a stream, have you ever found a smooth limb of wood with perhaps some narrow depressions in it? This is a sign that beavers have been active in the area; such limbs are the leftovers from a beaver meal, complete with tooth marks. A pond held back by a dam of small logs is an even clearer indication of beavers. Such signs were avidly sought by trappers for whom the beaver's pelt formed a mainstay of their trade. At a time before the existence of synthetic fabrics, such pelts might make the difference between survival and death. Thus beavers were actively trapped for more than a century. Nevertheless, they continue to flourish in the temperate forests of North America.

The favored food of the beaver is the inner bark of deciduous trees and their tender shoots, although it will eat leaves and other green matter during the growing season. Beavers fell trees both for food and for construction: they especially enjoy the tender growth at the treetops but cannot climb to get it. They bring down a tree by chewing around its trunk, enabled by their sharp teeth and strong jaws. Fifteen minutes suffices for a pair of adults to cut down a tree four inches thick. This is, of course, rather hard on the teeth. Therefore, the outer surface of their teeth is covered with orange-yellow enamel that is especially durable. Also, like other rodents, beavers have teeth which grow continuously to replace what has been worn.

Although the beaver gets its food on land, it is primarily an aquatic mammal. The American variety dwells in a "lodge" built in the still water of a pond or shallow lake. If a suitable pond is not available, the beaver will dam a stream or small river using logs, sticks, stones, and mud. The dam causes the water to back up behind it, producing a beaver pond with a typical depth of about a yard (see photograph). The beavers then build a lodge within the pond, and store food for the winter underwater and within easy swimming distance of the lodge. This is done by trimming the desired branches from trees and dragging them to the pond, and then towing them to the underwater storage area.

The lodge, also constructed within the pond, is made of materials similar to the dam. However, the lodge has different features, enabling it to be used as a home by the beavers. A typical lodge will have within it a single chamber, constructed above water level so that it remains dry. The one or more entrances are, however, underwater. This provides protection to the beavers from predators who are poorer swimmers than they. The outside of the lodge is plastered with mud for weather-proofing, except for a "ventilation shaft" in which air is free to pass between the logs and sticks. One family of beavers, that is, the parents and their young up to the age of about 2 years, live in one lodge. However, a large pond or lake may contain many beaver lodges. Dams are often used by many generations of beavers, who repair and maintain them as needed. Such dams may eventually contain tens or even hundreds of tons of wood.

As noted, the beaver is an aquatic mammal; it lives its life in or near water. It is indeed well designed for such a life. Except for its scaly tail, it is covered with a double-layered fur. The inner fur is thick and soft and acts like a sweater to help the beaver maintain its body temperature in the cold water. The outer fur (or guard hairs) is longer and behaves much like a slicker to keep the inner fur and skin dry. The fur's dark brown color also blends in with its surroundings. The beaver's back legs have feet shaped like flippers to help propel it in the water; however, the front legs do not, so that it can grasp its food. The tail acts as a prop on land and a rudder when swimming, and is also used to give other beavers warning of danger when slapped against the water surface. The beaver has a pair of clear eyelids that function rather like swimmers' goggles to help it see underwater. Its streamlined shape (for example its small ears) enables the beaver to swim more swiftly, and valves in its nose and ears close when underwater. The beaver usually dives for about 5 minutes at a time, but in danger can stay submerged for up to about 15 minutes.

The beaver is a fascinating animal. The habits of the American variety, in particular, have earned it the nickname of the "engineer of the animal world." It is an animal that is admirably well suited to its habitat. It continues to thrive in spite of more than a century of vigorous trapping, and can be found in a wide range over much of the temperate forest of the United States and Canada.

—Suchi Myjak

Write your first impression of this essay. What was most interesting? What new things did you learn about the beaver? What questions, if any, came to your mind as you read?

Grammar Study

Clauses

A part of a sentence that contains a subject and a predicate is called a *clause*.

Example: The sun rose and the mist cleared away.

This statement consists of two independent sentences. They could each stand alone as a complete sentence; but when statements are closely connected in thought they are often written together to form one sentence. Such statements are then connected by a conjunction (as in the example above) or they separated by a comma or a semicolon:

Example: Beauty is good, courage is better, but kindness is best of all.

Exercise A

Name the clauses in the following sentences. Give the subject and predicate of each clause.

1. The north wind doth blow, and we shall have snow.
2. The lightning flashed, the thunder roared, and the rain fell.
3. Knowledge is the greatest good; ignorance is the greatest evil.
4. The silver birch is a dainty lady,
   She wears a satin gown.
5. Spring is dancing o'er the lea;
    Birds are nesting in the tree.
6. Darkness broods o'er the earth and sky, and silence covers all.

Exercise B

Read the narratives you have written so far in this course. Find at least two places where you can combine sentences that are related. Use conjunctions and/or commas to combine the thoughts into one sentence. To avoid making a run-on sentence, place a comma after the conjunction when you combine independent clauses. (See sentence #1 and #6 above.)

Day 2

Guided Response

Reread the essay on the beaver. This style of writing is called *expository*. Expository writing informs, explains, describes, defines, or instructs. Examples of this type of writing are descriptions, reports, research papers. The paper is controlled by one main idea that the author is trying to say about the topic. What do you think is the main idea of the beaver essay?

It's important to have a well-laid plan before beginning to write this kind of paper, so many people use outlines. Using the outline frame on the following page, create an outline for the beaver essay.

I. Introduction
    A. Signs of beaver
        1.

        2.

    B.

II. Body
    A. Food
        1.

        2.

    B. Dwelling
        1. Dam
            a.

            b.

        2. Lodge
            a.

            b.

    C. Fur
        1.

        2.

D. Habits
    1.

    2.

III. Conclusion
    A.

    B.

Grammar Study

Subordinate or Dependent Clauses

> A part of the sentence that contains a subject and predicate but is not the main thought of the sentence is called a *subordinate* or *dependent* clause. It depends on the main clause to give it meaning.

A **subordinate clause** is usually introduced by a conjunction or relative pronoun. It does not express a complete thought, so it does not stand alone. It must always be attached to a main clause *that completes the meaning*.

Exercise A
Name the principal, or main clause, of each sentences and the subordinate or dependent clause of each sentence. Label the subject and predicate of *every* clause.

Example: If you feed the bears, they will come back for more.

Main clause: they will come back for more

Subordinate clause: if you feed the bears

Remember that in a command, the noun "you" is understood. Also remember that many clauses begin with a pronoun which is the subject of the clause.

1.   God rules the world which He created.
2.   Make hay while the sun shines.

3. The man who finds wisdom is happy.
4. He who has found his work is indeed blessed.
5. They who despise good counsel can never be wise.
6. Strike while the iron is hot.
7. He that does good to another does good to himself.

Challenge:
8. If we unite in this great bond, the Great Spirit will smile upon us, and we shall be free, prosperous, and happy; but if we remain as we are, we shall receive his frown.

Exercise B

Rewrite the following sentences, changing the phrases enclosed in parentheses to clauses.

Example: A man (of wealth) can do much good.

A man *who has wealth* can do much good.

1. Children rejoice (at the first snowfall).
2. The mountains (in the distance) look blue.
3. A watch (without hands) is useless.
4. The leaves (of the early spring) are a beautiful green.
5. The flowers are refreshed (by the gentle rain).
6. The tree (on the mountain top) is a pine.
7. (During the storm) the cattle huddled under the trees.
8. The brook (in the meadow) sings a drowsy song.

Day 3

Writing

Today you decide on a topic for your own expository essay and do the prewriting for it.

Choose a topic that you know well. (This is not a paper that you need to research.) You will be speaking from your own experience and knowledge. Remember that an expository paper informs, explains, describes, defines, or instructs. Think of something that you are good at, a sport or hobby, perhaps, that you can explain. Think of an animal—like a pet or animal that your family raises—that you observe often and can describe. Think of a person that you know well.

Prewriting

When you have decided upon a topic, do a 5-10 free-write on the topic. Set a timer, or ask someone to watch the clock for you and write all the thoughts that come to your mind about the topic. Write continuously without stopping. Don't worry about spelling or punctuation; no one else but you will read this paper. It's a time for you to get your thoughts out, question them, and elaborate upon them. Take longer if you're on a roll!

After the free-write time is done, read over your writing and decide upon a focus for your paper. If you are writing about your brother, perhaps you'd focus on one personality trait. If you are writing about a hobby or craft you know well, perhaps you'd focus on how to get started with it.

Outline your paper using the chart provided on the following page.

Introduction
Think of a clever way to grab your reader's attention. Maybe you'd describe a funny incident involving your topic, or introduce your topic using a figurative comparison. For example:

> I have a Tasmanian Devil in my house, and I have been observing him for 4 years. You'd think I would have figured him out by now, but he is full of surprises. Even if he is dressed in his pajamas ready for bed, he'll find a way to amaze us with his energy.

Body
Decide what few things you will say about your topic. Each box on the chart should contain notes on only *one* thing about the topic. You may add additional boxes as needed. (The beaver essay had 4 main sub-topics.)

Conclusion
Leave your reader with some last interesting thought about your topic.

Note-taking Chart

Introduction: Attention grabber
One aspect
Another aspect
Another aspect
Conclusion

Set aside your prewriting for Day 4.

Grammar Study

Subordinate clauses normally act as *single part of speech*. If the clause acts as an adjective, it is called an **adjective clause**; if the clause acts as an adverb, it is called an **adverbial clause**; and if the clause acts as a noun, it is called a **noun clause.**

Examples:

> Adjective Clause: Eeyore was a donkey *who was always grumpy.*
> Adverb Clause: *When winter comes,* the pond freezes over.
> Noun Clause: *What he wanted to say* came slowly to his lips.

Exercise A

Analyze each of the following sentences and determine what part of speech the clause is acting as. To do this you must ask yourself what role the clause plays in the sentence. Is it modifying a noun? (adjective) Is it modifying a verb? (adverb) Is it the subject of the sentence, a direct object, or the object of a preposition? (noun)

1. The boy Tarcisius carefully guarded the Sacrament *which had been entrusted to him.*
2. Passing trains that stop traffic at crossings annoy drivers *who are impatient.*
3. *Whatever books the school board selects for this course* will probably be acceptable to the parents.
4. Our grandparents lived in the same house *until they died.*
5. The lost camper waited nervously *while the park ranger searched through his pack for the right map.*
6. During the summer our boss hired an office manager *who is also a computer specialist.*
7. Not everyone realizes *that the road to disaster is paved with good intentions.*
8. *Because the used couch was so ugly,* we decided not to keep it in the den.
9. The judge gives a long sentence to *whoever is convicted of a serious crime.*
10. The book *which he chose for his report* was Tolkein's *The Hobbit.*

Exercise B

Write three sentences of your own. Make the first include an adjective clause, the second an adverb clause, and the third a noun clause. Underline your clause after you write the sentence.

Day 4

Writing

Reread the free-write and the notes you wrote yesterday. Add anything to your notes that comes to your mind as your read them over. Then write a rough (first) draft of your expository paper. Follow the chart you made using one paragraph for each box of the chart. Consider your paragraphs as links in a chain, and the chain as a whole supports your main idea. The links must be attached to each other somehow. They do not exist as separate entities, but flow from one to another. So, you must use transitions to tie them together.

Reread paragraph 2 and 3 of the beaver essay. Notice that the second paragraph is about how beavers harvest and eat trees on land. The third paragraph then begins:

> Although the beaver gets its food on land, it is primarily an aquatic mammal.

The author has used the *idea* from the second paragraph and combined with her topic for the third paragraph. This kind of transition is called a "hook." It hooks onto something from the previous paragraph to introduce something in the next. After you have finished writing your first draft, go back through your paragraphs and find at least one place to use a hook transition.

Show your paper to your teacher and explain where you have used transitions. Then file your paper in your drafts folder.

Grammar Study

A *simple sentence* is a sentence that contains only a single statement, question, or command.

A *compound sentence* is a sentence that contains two or more independent clauses (simple sentences) connected by a conjunction.

A *complex sentence* is a sentence that contains a principal clause and one or more subordinate clauses.

Exercise A

Decide whether each sentence is simple, complex, or compound and give your reason. You may do this orally with your teacher or write out your answers.

(HINT: the subordinate clause in a sentence starts with a connecting word or a pronoun, such as which, who, that, unless, until, when, because, or if.)

1. We never miss the water until the well runs dry.
2. We will fight for our country in time of war, and we will work for it in time of peace.
3. The robin and the bluebird are the harbingers of spring.
4. They talk most who think least.
5. The night is dark and I am far from home.
6. Man shall not eat unless he works.
7. The days are cold; the nights are long.
8. The swallows are flying low and we shall have rain.

Exercise B

Rewrite the following selections, combining some of the simple sentences into compound or complex sentences so as to make the whole read more smoothly. Be ready to explain whether your new sentences are complex or compound.

1. The sun arose. The noises of the day began. The cocks crowed. The hens cackled. The dogs barked. The cattle lowed. Each in his own way welcomed the coming day.

2. Summertime had arrived. The sun warmed the earth. Sunflowers stretched toward the sky. Bees came and went among the orchards and flower beds.

Exercise C

Write a paragraph about your favorite sport in which you use *at least* one compound sentence and two complex sentences. Highlight them or label them in the margin. Say whether your dependent (or subordinate) clauses are noun clauses, adjective clauses, or adverb clauses.

Week 7
Clauses

Day 1

Read the following poem and reflect upon it.

Concord Hymn

By the rude bridge that arched the flood,
Their flag to April's breeze unfurled,
Here once the embattled farmers stood,
And fired the shot heard round the world.

The foe long since in silence slept;
Alike the conqueror silent sleeps;
And Time the ruined bridge has swept
Down the dark stream which seaward creeps.

On this green bank, by this soft stream,
We set to-day a votive stone;
That memory may their deed redeem,
When, like our sires, our sons are gone.

Spirit, that made those heroes dare
To die, and leave their children free,
Bid Time and Nature gently spare
The shaft we raise to them and thee.

—Ralph Waldo Emerson, 1837

Write your first reaction to this poem. You may include in your response discussion of
any of the following questions: What parts to do you like or dislike? What parts, if any, are
confusing? What event does it commemorate? Why do you think it is called a *hymn*? What is
the main idea of the poem?

Grammar Study

Adjective Clauses

Exercise A

Identify the adjective clauses in the following sentences and tell which noun each one modifies.

Example: The cake that stood on the windowsill drew a great crowd of admirers.

> Clause: that stood on the windowsill
> Modifies: cake

1. Children who do not know their responses will be held after class.
2. The book that her mother read aloud was enjoyed by all.
3. Look for the girl whose father won the grand prize.
4. The test, which was harder than the students expected, ended promptly at noon.
5. We waited for hours to see the musicians who had played the concert last night.
6. The peach pie that his sister had made cooled on the rack.
7. Cynthia bought a hat that perfectly matched her dress and shoes.
8. We were unsure what to make of the little monkey who took the money from our hands.
9. Every afternoon the train that comes from Chicago passes through our town.
10. Despite his best efforts, the dog that he had found on the bridge could not be trained.

What conclusion can you draw about adjective clauses from this exercise?

Exercise B

Insert an adjective clause into the following sentences. Make the clause modify the underlined noun.
1. The <u>coach</u> stood near the finish line.
2. After the show the <u>actors</u> rushed to get ready for the next performance.
3. Therese endured many little <u>crosses</u> for love Her Savior.
4. The <u>natives</u> were open to the words of the missionary.
5. <u>Ben Franklin</u> never gave up working on his inventions.
6. All last winter the boys worked to build a snow <u>fort</u>.
7. All the <u>money</u> was donated to third-world relief efforts.
8. We suspected that the <u>cat</u> had been living in the neighbor's barn.

Day 2

Guided Response

Reread the poem Concord Hymn. In case you didn't know, this poem is posted on a monument at the bridge where the colonial minutemen faced the British regulars and engaged in the first skirmish of the Revolutionary War. It was placed there at a special ceremony to mark the completion of the monument 100 years after the battle.

1. Explain the main idea of each stanza.

2. Why do you think the author choose the word "rude" to describe the bridge?

3. What other vivid images does the author use?

4. The phrase "The shot heard round the world" has become quite famous. Why do you think it has? What do you think is its figurative meaning?

5. The author of a poem is almost like a writer of persuasive prose. He wants to move you to something. What do you think this author wants you to feel about this event in history?

Grammar Study

Adverb Clauses

Adverb clauses are introduced by *subordinating conjunctions*, such as

after, before, until, while, because, since, as, so that, in order that,
if, unless, whether, though, although, even though, and *where.*

Like a regular adverb, adverb clauses can modify verbs, adjectives, and other adverbs. Most often, however, they modify verbs. Here are the most common kinds of adverb clauses:

> Place – answers the question where
> Time – answers the question when
> Cause – answers the question why, what caused it
> Purpose – answers the question why, for what reason
> Concession – answers the question why is this unexpected
> Condition – answers the question under what conditions (uses "if")

When an adverb clause is at the beginning of the sentence, it is always set off with a comma.

Exercise A

Read each sentence below and tell what kind of adverb clause is italicized (place, time, cause, purpose, concession, condition).

1. *Wherever the boy went*, the dog followed him.
2. *If you remember to brush your teeth regularly*, you will not have tooth decay.
3. John jumped up and down *because he had finally finished his work*.
4. Cassandra brushed the mare's coat *so that it would shine for the horse show*.
5. *Although she studied for hours*, she did not pass the entrance exam.
6. The children put their sleds away *after the snow melted*.
7. *Since we cannot go to fair*, let's watch a movie instead.
8. Rinse the dishes *before the food sticks to them*.

Exercise B

Identify the adverb clauses in the sentences below. (There may be more than one in a sentence.) Then say what the adverb clause modifies.

1. After they finished washing all the cars, they rested on the porch with a glass of lemonade.
2. Andrew was confident that he could finish on time.
3. He always breaks something when he tries to work on the car.
4. Susan kept her room tidy so that she could find things when she needed them.
5. Although the weather man had predicted a warm sunny day, the picnic was rained out.
6. Unless the price of materials goes down, the building industry will continue to decline.
7. Because he did not watch where he was going, his stepped into the wet cement.
8. I was happy that I hadn't locked my keys in the car.

Exercise C

Write 3 sentences that each contain an adverb clause. Then say which kind of adverb clause you wrote.

Day 3

Writing

Literary Analysis of a Poem

An analysis of a poem explains what the poem means (interpretation) and how the author brings about this meaning. It includes a defense of this interpretation. As a work of art, the poet created his poem with an end in view, with the knowledge that someone would read it and seek to understand it. Begin your analysis with the assurance that the author has something he is trying to say with his poem.

By analyzing a poem, we accomplish several important intellectual ends: a deeper understanding and appreciation for poetry in general and the poem studied in particular; exposure to language and images used to create meaning that will improve your own efforts at writing; an appreciation for the historical and cultural contexts of poetry; and participation in the "great conversation" of universal ideas that man has considered since the beginning of the written word.

Today you will begin to analyze the poem *Concord Hymn* in order to write a literary analysis of it. The beginning of your analysis is at the literal level of the poem. You must first understand what the poem is saying before you can interpret it. So, reread your answers to question 1 on the Guided Response section of Day 2. This is the literal comprehension of the poem. Then use an analysis chart to jot notes about *Concord Hymn*. Here is a sample done using *The Indian Burial Ground*.

Main Idea of the Poem: The Indians bury their dead in preparation for an active after life.
Structure: How are stanzas related – the first stanza introduces the main idea. The next three talk about what the Indian has with him as he is buried and what he will use them for. The fifth stanza addresses the reader again and marks a shift in the poem. The rest talk about still seeing the Indian in his native haunts.
Tone: reverenced awe in awe of the Indian, reverencing his lifestyle, mysterious: shades behind rocks and trees, the Indian lurking in his old hunting grounds.
Imagery: trace fancies on rock, aged elm provides shade, midnight moons, moistening dews in habit for the chase arrayed. Both hunter and deer a shade
Sound: every other line rhymes, not metered, not all the lines have the same rhythm
What basic ideas about the world are expressed: sees the Indian as the noble savage. Good and innocent in life, still hunting, keeping traditions when dead. Spirit of the Indian not extinguished.

Poem Analysis Chart – *Concord Hymn*

Main Idea of the Poem:
Structure: How are stanzas related
Tone
Imagery
Sound
What basic ideas about the world are expressed

Save your chart for Day 4.

Grammar Study

Noun Clauses

Noun clauses are introduced by a *subordinating conjunction* such as *how, why, what, where, when, who, that, which, whose, whether, if, whoever, whenever, whatever* and *wherever.*

A noun clause does the work of a noun in a sentence. So it can be used as the subject, a direct object, a predicate nominative, the object of a preposition, gerund, infinitive, or participle, and as an adjective complement. Here is an example of each kind:

Subject: *That he should show such ingratitude* cuts to the heart.
Direct Object: My father wished *that this tree be cut down.*
Predicate Nominative: My hope was *that some ship might be sighted.*
Object of the Preposition: With *what he needed to perform the rescue,* he descended into the mine.
Object of a gerund: Finding out *that they had left their food behind,* filled them with despair.
Object of a participle: Realizing *that we were late,* we ran as fast as we could.
Object of an infinitive: She needs to learn *that lying is wrong.*
Adjective Complement: I was sorry *that she had to go back to England.*

NOTE: How can you tell if the verbal used is a gerund or a participle? Ask yourself if the verbal is being used as a noun, such as the subject of the sentence. If it is, then the verbal is a gerund. Try removing the noun clause in the examples above and that help you to see how the verbal is used.

Exercise A
Analyze the italicized noun clause in the following sentences. Tell how the noun clause is used in the sentence. (See the list above.)

1. *Whether we go to park or not* should not affect your plans at all.
2. I am glad *that you want to work on your handwriting.*
3. One reason is *that he doesn't want to wait so long at the grocery store.*
4. Hearing *that she had arrived in town,* Henry ran to the train station.
5. I wonder *whether father needs help chopping wood.*
6. The book was about *why he stole the money from the railroad company.*
7. *Whose trash it is* does not matter.
8. Her employers wanted to know *what she would do under pressure.*
9. Please tell me *how I can get to the amusement park.*
10. Her spending *whatever she wanted* cost the family plenty.

Exercise B
Write 3 sentences of your own in which you use a noun clause. Make your noun clause fulfill a different function in each sentence. (No repeats!) Tell how the noun clause in used in the sentence. (See the list above.)

Day 4

Writing

Literary Analysis of a Poem

Today you will use the notes you made yesterday to write a literary analysis of the poem *Concord Hymn*. Reread your notes and reflect about the poem. Think of one idea about the poem that you want to expand upon in your paper. This one idea becomes the thesis statement that controls the rest of the essay.

Here are some sample thesis statements based on the poem *Indian Burying Ground*:

1. *The poem evokes a feeling of awe and mystery about the Indian that is hard to resist.*

2. *Through the use of vivid images, the author paints a picture of the Indian that is at once attractive and mysterious.*

3. *By romanticizing the life the Indians, the poet shows that he thinks the life of the Indian is better than the Europeans who found them.*

If the writer chooses thesis #1, his paper would focus on describing and explaining the feeling of mystery that the poem evokes. He would quote specific examples (lines) from the poem that show the mystery and explain *how* the line or section evokes mystery or awe. (Focus of this paper is on the tone of the poem.)

If the writer chooses thesis #2, his paper would focus on describing and explaining vivid images and effect they have on the reader. He would quote specific lines from the poem and explain how the vivid images contribute to making the Indian attractive.
(Focus of this paper is the on the vivid images in the poem.)

If the writer chooses thesis #3, his paper would focus on the idea that the author believes all the pieces together show that the Indian had a better life. He would use the structure of the poem to make his point, and find key lines that express this opinion. These lines would be quoted and explained. (Focus of this paper is on the structure of the poem and between-the-lines meaning it conveys.)

Once you have your thesis statement, do a 10-15 free-write with the thesis statement in mind. Write freely without worry of grammar or spelling. This is what is called a "thinking piece." Explore your ideas fully.

Then use the chart on the next page to map out your essay.

Chart to Map Literary Analysis of a Poem

Use this chart to take notes and order your thoughts about your topic.

Introduction
Thesis statement:
First argument/example to show your thesis
Second argument/example to show your thesis
Third argument/example to show your thesis
Conclusion Tie the arguments together

Note: Each box in the chart corresponds to one paragraph in your paper. Although there are 5 boxes on this chart, do not feel trapped into writing "five paragraph essay." Use as many paragraphs as it takes to adequately cover your topic.

Remember that this is the framework for an expository essay:

Introduction: Begins with general statements about your topic. When analyzing a piece of literature, name it and the author. Then narrow to your thesis statement.

Body: Use paragraphs to defend and explain your thesis statement. Keep the thesis in mind at all times, and only include that which supports it. Refer back to it so that the reader remembers your main idea.

Conclusion: Leave the reader with an interesting/profound thought about your thesis, or pose another question. Remind the reader of the thesis *without* saying "In conclusion," or "Therefore," or "To sum up."

You may choose to do the thinking piece and the chart today and write the first draft tomorrow. Or do it all in one day. After you have a first draft, get some feedback from a reader and then file it in your drafts folder.

Grammar Study

Review – Clauses

Review the three kinds of clauses discussed in this chapter. Be able to explain the construction of each one and say how each one is used. Use each kind of phrase in a sentence to demonstrate your understanding of it.

Exercise A

Find the clauses in the following sentences and copy them on your paper. Then label them as adjective, adverb, or noun clauses. There may be more than one kind in a sentence.

1. When my brother was younger, he wanted to become a policeman who would save the world from criminals.
2. If you want to give someone who has a lot of money a nice gift, consider making something yourself.
3. Keep your beaver-skins, if you choose, for the Dutch; even those which may come into our hands will be used for your own good.
4. He informs you by his Messengers that his Son made Himself man for love of you.
5. It commands that respect, love, and reverence be given to Him who has made all and who preserves the universe.
6. He ordered that they be carried throughout the world.
7. If thou reject them in thy heart, know that Jesus Christ, who animates my heart and my voice, will one day cast thee into Hell.

8. You, the Mohawks, who are sitting under the shadow of the great tree, whose branches spread wide around, and whose roots sink deep into the earth, shall be the first nation, because you are warlike and mighty.
9. I went directly to a shop where they sold toys for children; and being charmed with the sound of a *whistle,* that I met by the way in the hands of another boy, I voluntarily offered and gave all my money for one.
10. As I grew up, came into the world, and observed the actions of men, I thought I met with many, very many, who gave too much for the whistle.

Exercise B

Write one sentence that contains a noun clause, another that contains an adjective clause and another that contains an adverb clause.

Check the literary analysis paper you wrote today and see if you find any clauses in it. What kinds of clauses did you use?

Minuteman National Historic Park at Concord Bridge

Week 8

Day 1

Read the following selection about the Boston Tea party written by someone who participated in it.

A Recollection of the Boston Tea Party

In the evening, I dressed myself in the costume of an Indian, equipped with a small hatchet, which I and my associates denominated the tomahawk, with which, and a club after having painted my face and hands with coal dust in the shop of a blacksmith, I repaired to Griffin's wharf, where the ships lay that contained the tea. When I first appeared in the street after being thus disguised, I fell in with many who were dressed, equipped and painted as I was, and who fell in with me and marched in order to the place of our destination.

When we arrived at the wharf, there were three of our number who assumed an authority to direct our operations, to which we readily submitted. They divided us into three parties, for the purpose of boarding the three ships which contained the tea, at the same time. The name of him who commanded the division to which I was assigned was Leonard Pitt. The names of the other commanders I never knew. We were immediately ordered by the respective commanders to board all the ships at the same time, which we promptly

obeyed. The commander of the division to which I belonged, as soon as we were on board the ship, appointed me boatswain, and ordered me to go to the captain and demand of him the keys to the hatches and a dozen candles. I made the demand accordingly, and the captain promptly replied and delivered the articles; but requested meat the same time to do no damage to the ship or rigging. We then were ordered by our commander to open the hatches and take out all the chests of tea and throw them overboard, and we immediately proceeded to execute his orders, first cutting and splitting the chests with our tomahawks, so as thoroughly to expose them to the effects of the water.

During the time we were throwing the tea overboard, there were several attempts made by some of the citizens of Boston and its vicinity to carry off small quantities of it for their family use. To effect that object, they would watch their opportunity to snatch up a handful from the deck, where it became plentifully scattered, and put it into their pockets.

One Captain O'Conner, whom I well knew, came on board for that purpose, and when he supposed he was not noticed, filled his pockets, and also the lining of his coat. But I had detected him, and gave information to the captain of what he was doing. We were ordered to take him into custody, and just as he was stepping from the vessel, I seized him by the skirt of his coat, and in attempting to pull him back, I tore it off; but springing forward, by a rapid effort, he made his escape. He had however to run a gauntlet through the crowd upon the wharf; each one, as he passed, giving him a kick or a stroke.

The next day we nailed the skirt of his coat, which I had pulled off, to the whipping post in Charlestown, the place of his residence, with a label upon it, commemorative of the occasion which had thus subjected the proprietor to the popular indignation.

Another attempt was made to save a little tea from the ruins of the cargo, by a tall aged man, who wore a large cocked hat and white wig, which was fashionable at that time. He had slightly slipped a little into his pocket, but being detected, they seized him, and taking his hat and wig from his head, threw them, together with the tea, of which they had emptied his pockets, into the water. In consideration of his advanced age, he was permitted to escape, with now and then a slight kick.

In about three hours from the time we went on board, we had thus broken and thrown overboard every tea chest to be found in the ship, while those in the other ships were disposing of the tea in the same way, at the same time. We were surrounded by British armed ships, but no attempt was made to resist us.

We then quietly retired to our several places of residence, without having any conversation with each other, or taking any measures to discover who were our associates; nor of I recollect of our having had the knowledge of the name of a single individual concerned in that affair. Except that of Leonard Pitt, the commander of my division, whom I have mentioned. There appeared to be an understanding that each individual should volunteer his services, keep is own secret, and risk the consequence for himself. No disorder took place during that transaction, and it was observed at that time, that the stillest night ensued that Boston had enjoyed for many months.

—George R.T. Hewes, 1823

Write your first reaction to this recollection. What did you find interesting? What more did you learn about the Boston Tea Party from the recollection?

Grammar Study

Punctuating Clauses

Punctuation rules for clauses:

Comma

1. When an adverb clause begins a sentence, place a comma after the clause.

   If you want to get ahead in life, you had better study your lessons.

2. When a clause is nonessential to the understanding of the sentence (nonrestrictive clause), place a comma before and after the clause. If the clause is essential to the understanding, no comma is necessary (restrictive clause).

   Non-restrictive, non-essential: Mr. Knightly, *who knew her father,* left the party early.
   Restrictive, essential: The man *who sat to the left of her* was her father.

3. When an adjective clause describes a proper noun, it is set off by commas.

4. When joining two or more independent clauses, place the comma after the first clause before the coordinating conjunction.

   They lifted the heavy box up, *and* then they set it down immediately.

Semi-colon

Use a semi-colon to connect two independent clauses when you don't use a coordinating conjunction.

   They had not realized the box was *there; it* was camouflaged.

Exercise A

Identify the subordinate clauses in the following sentences and write them on your paper. Label the clause adjective, adverb, or noun and then punctuate the sentence correctly. If it is already correct, write "correct" on your paper. Check the rules listed on the previous page as you work.

1. We enjoyed Paris where we spent our vacation.
2. At the zoo you can see an African elephant which has large ears.
3. Nancy left the concert early because she didn't feel well.
4. That she took the wrong bus was obvious to all of us.
5. When all was said and done they were the better sportsmen.
6. She wondered what she would say to her class about her trip to Rome.
7. The meteorologist who gave a presentation to our group predicted another hurricane.
8. Goats which were first tamed more than 9000 years ago in Asia have provided people with milk, meat, and wool since prehistoric times.
9. After they left the park they realized they had forgotten their jackets.
10. Whether or not you like the results is beside the point.

Exercise B

Combine the following sentences by making one of them a subordinate clause to the other. Say what kind of clause you created. Be sure to punctuate it correctly.

1. They own an original Monet painting. The value of the painting is over a million dollars.
2. He dropped his friend off at the bus station. He dropped him there when the concert was over.
3. Their group ordered a lot of pasta. The restaurant ran out of pasta.
4. This river is polluted. It is not safe for swimming.
5. The genocide in Africa should be stopped. That is my belief.

Day 2

Guided Response

Reread the recollection on Day 1 and discuss the following questions.

1. Since this was written a long time ago, the language and sentence structure are a little different than what you may be used to. Look at the first sentence of the recollection and try to identify the main clause and how the subordinate clauses fit in to the sentence.

2. What is the tone of the piece? What gives the piece a sense of authenticity? Find specific passages where the author's own experience makes the piece seem real. This is called "voice," and we will be discussing it more in Unit 2.

3. Why do you think the Army ships did nothing to stop the "Indians"?

4. According to this piece, what factors do you think made the "party" successful?

5. What do you think are the most well written parts of the recollection? Give your reasons.

6. Make a brief outline of the order of events as described in the piece.

Grammar Study

A Note About Noun Clauses

Sometimes, when "that" is used as the introductory word of a noun clause, it is omitted.

> Example: He decided *that it was best to go.*
> He decided *it was best to go.*

The second sentence still contains a noun clause. You must be able to recognize it even if the introductory word is left out. The word "that" may *not* be omitted if the noun clause is the subject of the sentence.

Exercise A

Identify the noun clause in each of the following sentences and say how it is used in the sentence (subject, direct object, object of the preposition, complement of the adjective).

1. I wonder whose book that is.
2. Stephen always listens to what his mother says.
3. She saw it was the best way to travel.
4. I was happy she could come with us to the fair.
5. Whether she would come was not clear to the rest of us.
6. Lisa can't decide what she will do about new litter of kittens.
7. I didn't know she was going to leave so soon.
8. Louis was afraid the dog would run away.

Exercise B

Write 3 sentences with the word "that" omitted from the beginning of a noun clause.
Write one sentence with an adjective clause.
Write one sentence with an adverb clause.

Exercise C

Find an example of each of the following in the essay on beavers in Week 6.

1. Two independent clauses joined by a semi-colon.
2. Two independent clauses joined by a conjunction.
3. Adjective clause
4. Adverb clause

Day 3

Writing

Today you will write a first hand account of an event that you have witnessed. It is different from a personal or autobiographical narrative because you are not necessarily reflecting on your experience of the event. You report on the event objectively and draw conclusions based on the whole event, not particularly your personal experience of it. In the *Recollection of the Boston Tea Party*, the author tells what he and the others did, but his observations did not include a reflection on the significance of the event to him *personally*.

Please read this excerpt from a newspaper account of the Chicago Fire of 1871. Notice the inclusion of descriptive details in the account.

The firemen labored like heroes. Grimy, dusty, hoarse, soaked with water, time after time they charged up to the blazing foe only to be driven back to another position by its increasing fierceness, or to abandon as hopeless their task. Or, while hard at work, suddenly the wind would shift, a puff of smoke would come from a building behind them, followed by belching flames, and then they would see that they were far outflanked. There was nothing to be done but to gather up their hose, pull helmets down on their heads, and with voice and lash to urge the snorting horses through the flames to a place of safety beyond.

The people were mad. Despite the police—indeed, the police were powerless—they crowded upon frail coigns[1] of vantage, as fences and high sidewalks propped on rotten piles, which fell beneath their weight, and hurled them, bruised and bleeding, into the dust. They stumbled over broken furniture and fell, and were trampled under foot. Seized with wild and causeless panics, they surged together, backwards and forwards, in the narrow streets, cursing, threatening, imploring, fighting to get free. Liquor flowed like water—for the saloons were broken open and despoiled, and men on all sides were seen to be frenzied with drink. Fourth Avenue and Griswold Street had emptied their denizens into the throng. They smashed windows reckless of the severe wounds inflicted on their naked hands, and with bloody fingers impartially rifled till, shelf and cellar, fighting viciously for the spoils of their forays. Women, hollow-eyed and brazen-faced, with foul drapery tied over their heads, their dresses half torn from their skinny bosoms, and their feet thrust into trodden down slippers, moved here and there, —scolding, stealing, scolding shrilly, and laughing with one another at some particularly "splendid" gush of flame or "beautiful" falling-in of a roof.

One woman on Adams Street was drawn out of a burning house three times, and rushed back wildly into the blazing ruin each time, insane for the moment. Everywhere, dust, smoke, flame, heat, thunder of falling walls, crackle of fire, hissing of water, panting of engines, shouts, braying of trumpets, roar of wind, tumult, and uproar.

[1] – a projecting corner for observation

For *your* paper, begin by selecting an event to report. You may choose something from your own life that you have witnessed. It could be the building of a building, or the cutting down of a tree, or a baby's first steps, or an accident, or a play or concert, etc. You might also choose something from history that you have read about and tell about it as if you were there.

Prewriting: List the events in the order they happened. What conclusion can you draw about the event and its effect on the participants? What consequences, good or bad, did this event have?

Do a free-write on the event (writing continuously for a short period of time, perhaps 10-15 minutes), thinking of anything and everything you can about it. Be sure to think about the consequences of this event or its larger significance. Try to think of vivid details about the event.

Writing:
Once you have done your free-write, begin your first draft. Your opening is a critical part of this paper. You want to set the stage for the story and draw your reader in. Do not begin, "One day, I . . . " or "A few years ago . . ." *Begin with action.*

Write your draft and save it for Day 4.

Grammar

Exercise A

1. Participle Phrase
2. Adjective Clause
3. Infinitive phrase
4. Adverb Clause
5. Prepositional Phrase

Exercise B

Imitate the structure in each of the following sentences to write an original sentence of your own.

> **Example:**
> Model: Although the beaver gets its food on land, it is primarily an aquatic mammal.
>
> New sentence: Although the movie is rated for general audiences, it is too scary for young children.

(Note that the model sentence begins with an adverb clause, so the new sentence must also.)

1. Dams are often used by many generations of beavers, who repair and maintain them as needed.
2. Its streamlined shape enables the beaver to swim more swiftly, and valves in its nose and ears close when underwater.
3. The favored food of the beaver is the inner bark of deciduous trees and their tender shoots, although it will eat leaves and other green matter during the growing season.
4. During the time we were throwing the tea overboard, there were several attempts made by some of the citizens of Boston and its vicinity to carry off small quantities of it for their family use.
5. They smashed windows reckless of the severe wounds inflicted on their naked hands, and with bloody fingers impartially rifled till, shelf and cellar, fighting viciously for the spoils of their forays.

Day 4

Writing

Revising

After writing your first draft, the next step in the writing process is to get feedback and then revise. Read the recollection you read yesterday. Ask someone to read the paper for you and comment on the following questions specifically. Take notes on the comments of your reader.

Is the event explained clearly with vivid describing words? Where does it need better description or more clarification?

Does the writing seem to be done by someone who actually witnessed the event? (Does it seem to be authentic?)

Do the paragraph divisions make sense; is each paragraph cohesive, focusing on one part of the event?

What suggestions do you have to make the paper better?

After discussing your paper with someone, make improvements to your paper based on your discussion. Then consider the following things that may need revising in your paper.

1. Have I limited the use of "to be" verbs (is, are, was, were)?
   Notice in the Chicago Fire example, how the writer makes effective use of a "to be" verb. To begin his second paragraph, he simply writes "The people were mad." The previous paragraph talks about the scene of the fire; then in the beginning of the next paragraph he lets you know that the focus is shifting. This simple statement has power because he redirects your attention and then goes on to give a vivid account of the crazy things that people were doing to show that they were mad.

   If you have a lot of sentences with *is, are, was, were* in them, however, your writing will be weaker. So only use them on purpose!! Revise any sentences that can be made stronger, or an image made clearer, by changing the sentence to include an action verb and other modifiers.

   Example: Susan was unsure what to do.
   Undecided, Susan turned over all the options in her mind.

89

2. Where can I use participles as modifiers to make the writing more sophisticated? Look at the sample sentence above. Simply adding the adjectival participle undecided to the sentence, both makes it more complex and gives more information to the reader. Notice the use of participles in these examples from the Chicago Fire piecw.

> Grimy, dusty, hoarse, *soaked with water*, time after time they charged up to the *blazing* foe only to be driven back to another position by its *increasing* fierceness, or to abandon as hopeless their task.

> Or, while hard at work, suddenly the wind would shift, a puff of smoke would come from a building behind them, *followed by belching flames*, and then they would see that they were far outflanked.

Find places in your piece where you can increase the sophistication of your sentences by inserting adjectival participles. Improve as many sentences as you can without overdoing it!

Grammar Study

Reveiw

Review the 3 kinds of clauses and the 4 kinds of phrases.

Exercise

Identify and label the clauses and phrases in the following sentences.

Example: The boy (at the gate), (who was anxiously waiting), left (to buy tickets)
[Prep phrase] [adj clause] [inf phrase]
(from the box office).
[Prep phrase]

1. When we left to visit the shrine, we made sure that we took our lunches because we planned to stay all day.

2. If the stuffed animal does not fit into the wrapping paper that you bought at the bargain store, you might try wrapping it in the expensive box that I gave you, because expensive boxes are usually stronger.

3. A letter written in haste may create problems that the writer doesn't foresee as he is writing.

Week 9
Review and Assessment

Day 1

Washington Crossing the Delaware by Emanuel Leutze

Study the picture carefully and try to remember as many details as you can. Then close the book and write a description of the scene. You may write it as an eye witness or one of the participants. Or you may take the voice of the painter describing his painting and why he chose to include what he did. Do not use the words "there is" or "there are" at the beginning of your sentences. For example, instead of saying: *There is a man standing on the thwart wearing a cloak,* say *A man stands defiantly on the middle thwart, his hand clutching his cloak about him to ward off the chill.*

Grammar Study

Review

Review

1. The Parts of Speech: Name them and say the function of each.

2. 4 kinds of phrases: Name and describe them. Use each one in a sentence.

3. 3 kinds of clauses: Name and describe them. Use each one in a sentence.

Exercise A
Identify the part of speech of each of the words in the following sentences. Then label the simple subject and simple predicate, and the direct object, predicate nominative, or predicate adjective, if any, in each sentence.

Example:

```
               Sub        pred         DO
      adj  adj   N    adv  V-t  adj adj  N
      The hungry dog hungrily bites the meaty bone.
```

Parts of speech: adjective=adj, adverb=adv, pronoun=PN, noun=N, transitive verb=V-t, linking verb=LV, conjunction=C
Parts of a sentence: subject=sub, predicate=pred, direct object= DO, predicate nominative=pr nom, predicate adjective=pr adj

1. The happy girl skipped down the street.

2. Seven sons left their books carelessly on the shelf.

3. With little practice, the team still won the game.

4. The evergreen trees in our yard do not lose their leaves in winter.

5. He is not very happy today.

Exercise B
Identify the main simple subject, simple predicate, and complement of the following sentence. Then identify the clauses and say what role they play in the sentence (what they modify if it is a adjective or adverb clause, and how it is used in the sentence if a noun clause.(HINT: There is one of each kind of clause in this sentence.)

One Captain O'Conner, whom I well knew, came on board for that purpose, and when he supposed he was not noticed, filled his pockets, and also the lining of his coat.

Day 2

Writing

This week you will review all the pieces you have written in the unit and choose one to revise. You will then make a final copy and file it in your writing portfolio. You have written something in each of the 3 modes of writing: narrative, expository, and persuasive.

Week 2 Personal narrative
Week 3 Story narrative
Week 4 Opinion paper
Week 5 Persuasive paper
Week 6 Expository
Week 7 Literary Analysis
Week 8 Eye-witness account (expository)

Once you have selected your paper to revise, read it slowly and carefully. You may see right away changes that need to be made. Then revise for the following items:

1. **Active verbs**: Remove any place in your paper where you begin "There is," "There was," "There are," or "There were." Doing this will force you to use an action verb instead. This will make your writing more powerful and interesting.

2. **Participle phrases**: Add participle phrases where you can to add depth to your descriptions.

3. **Sentence combining**: Combine some of your shorter, simple sentences to make complex or compound sentences. Vary your sentence structure so that every sentence you write is not simply subject-verb-object construction. Add at least one new adjective clause and one new adverb clause. Try putting a clause at the beginning of a sentence.

4. **Transitions**: Make sure that you have used transitions purposefully and that they move the reader through your train of thought. See if you can make a hook transition by mentioning something from a previous paragraph in the first sentence of your next paragraph.

Once you have inputted your changes, ask someone to read your paper and give you suggestions for making it better. See if he or she has any questions after reading it since the questions a reader has gives you a clue as to where your writing was not clear enough.

Then set your paper aside until Day 3.

Grammar Study

Review Phrases

Exercise

Copy the sentences onto your paper. Identify the part of speech of each of the words in the sentences. Then label the simple subject, simple predicate, and complement, if any, in each sentence. Then highlight or underline any phrases in the sentence. Label them. Remember that one phrase can be inside another.

Here is an example of each kind of verbal phrase to study before you begin.

> **(Gerund phrase)**
> ------Sub-------   pred   DO
>
> **V (ger)   N   V   adj   N**
>
> Gerund: (Drinking water) quenches my thirst.

> **(Participle phrase)**
> **Sub Pred DO**
> **PN   V   N   V(part)   N   adv**
>
> Participle: We saw children (playing games outside).

> **(Inf phrase [prep phrase])**
> **Sub   pred   Direct object**
> **Adj   N   V   V(inf)   P   adj   N**
>
> Infinitive: The children wanted (to jump [across the creek]).
>   (In this sentence, the entire infinitive phrase is the direct object.)

Parts of speech: adjective=adj, adverb=adv, pronoun=PN, noun=N, verb=V, conjunction=C
Parts of a sentence: subject=sub, predicate=pred, direct object= DO, predicate nominative=pred nom

Phrases: prepositional phrase=prep phrase, infinitive phrase=inf phrase, gerund phrase=ger phrase, participle phrase=part phrase

1. Our favorite sport is skating in the winter.

2. The men began to load the boxes.

3. Frightened by the lightning, the children huddled under the bed.

4. Living without food or water fatigued the soldiers.

5. To write well is the goal of the program.

Day 3

Writing

Reread the paper you are revising this week and make any changes that seem necessary as you read.

Today you will move to the next step in the writing process: editing. In the editing stage you check your grammar, spelling, and punctuation and make corrections in your paper. You may have to have someone else read it for you to help you find your errors, or places where you left out needed punctuation. Review the punctuation rules for phrases given in Week 4, and the rules for clauses in Week 8.

Once you have proofread your paper and made corrections, set it aside for Day 4. The longer you take to do the last step, the better. That way you can read and possibly revise your paper one more time.

Grammar Study

Review Clauses

Exercise A

Identify the clauses in the following sentences and say how they are used. Remember that one clause can be inside of another.

Example: When they had finished reading the book, the children who attended story hour completed a craft.

> *When they had finished reading the book* – adverb clause modifying completed
> *Who attended story hour* – adjective clause modifying children

1. Sir Walter had made a voyage with his older brother, Sir Humphrey Gilbert, who had tried again and again to find the Northwest Passage of which the Cabots so long before had talked and written.

2. They named their territory Georgia in honor of the King, and when the laws for this new colony were drawn up, wise General Oglethorpe firmly declared that there should be no rum allowed there, and that any sale of it to the Indians should be punished as one of the greatest crimes.

3. He often wrote letters to her and to her husband, who was also a warm friend of Governor Winthrop, begging them to leave the old country and come with their children to the new colony where there was more than enough of all the good things of life.

4. When the French and Indian War broke out, George Washington was a young man, only about as old as those big boys that you see coming now and then from their colleges to spend their vacations at home.

5. One bright morning the English officers came into the village and demanded that the people be gathered in the churches to hear a message which the English brought to them.

6. Meantime, the followers of Captain Church went to the other Indians lying about before their camp-fires, and told them that their chief was taken, that there were hundreds of white men just outside the camp, and that their lives should be spared, if they would surrender at once.

—From *American History Stories*, Volume I
by Mara Pratt

Day 4

Writing

Today you will make a final copy of the paper you have been revising and editing. Type it or write it in your best handwriting. Save it in your portfolio folder.

Grammar Study

The whole point of learning about grammar is to improve your writing and give you the tools and vocabulary to talk about sentence structure. Sometimes, however, what you do in grammar exercises seems removed from the creative process that your mind undertakes when you write. But, the more you learn about complex grammatical forms, the more you can improve your writing.

If you were to write down your speech for a day, you would find that you use clauses and phrases quite a bit without even thinking about it. In the writing process, we want to be purposeful about it. In the prewriting and writing stages, we write our ideas and form words from our thoughts. In the revising stage we find ways to make our ideas more appealing and understandable to our readers and that is really where the *craft* of writing comes into play.

Exercise

Revise the following sentences, inserting clauses (adjective, adverb, noun) or phrases (prepositional, gerund, infinitive, participle) to improve them. Write the new sentence on your paper and say what you added. (Keep in mind that sometime phrases and clauses are found within one another.) You may change the wording of the sentence as needed.

Example: The wet dogs splashed water on the kitchen floor.

<small>Adv clause</small>   <small>participle phrase</small>
After we bathed them, the wet dogs, shaking their bodies vigorously, splashed

<small>Adjective clause</small>
water on the kitchen floor that mother had just mopped.

1. Last night the children enjoyed a rousing campfire.
2. The boys hoisted the sail and set out across the lake.
3. Every time we play this team, we lose.
4. Cassandra never understood why.

Unit 2

Week 10

Day 1

Read the poem below and write your first impressions of it.

When the Frost is on the Punkin

When the frost is on the punkin and the fodder's in the shock,
And you hear the kyouck and gobble of the struttin' turkey-cock,
And the clackin' of the guineys, and the cluckin' of the hens,
And the rooster's hallylooyer as he tiptoes on the fence;
O, it's then the time a feller is a-feelin' at his best,
With the risin' sun to greet him from a night of peaceful rest,
As he leaves the house, bareheaded, and goes out to feed the stock,
When the frost is on the punkin and the fodder's in the shock.

They's something kindo' harty-like about the atmusfere
When the heat of summer's over and the coolin' fall is here—
Of course we miss the flowers, and the blossoms on the trees,
And the mumble of the hummin'-birds and buzzin' of the bees;
But the air's so appetizing'; and the landscape through the haze
Of a crisp and sunny morning of the airly autumn days
Is a pictur' that no painter has the colorin' to mock—
When the frost is on the punkin and the fodder's in the shock.

The husky, rusty russel of the tossels of the corn,
And the raspin' of the tangled leaves as golden as the morn;
The stubble in the furries—kindo' lonesome-like, but still
A-preachin' sermuns to us of the barns they growed to fill;
The strawstack in the medder, and the reaper in the shed;
The hosses in theyr stalls below—the clover overhead!—
O, it sets my hart a-clickin' like the tickin' of a clock,
When the frost is on the punkin and the fodder's in the shock.

Then your apples all is gethered, and the ones a feller keeps
Is poured around the cellar-floor in red and yaller heaps;
And your cider-makin's over, and your wimmern-folks is through
With theyr mince and apple-butter, and theyr souse and sausage too!...
I don't know how to tell it—but ef such a thing could be
As the angels wantin' boardin', and they'd call around on *me*—
I'd want to 'commodate 'em—all the whole-indurin' flock—
When the frost is on the punkin and the fodder's in the shock.
— James Whitcomb Riley. 1853–1916

Grammar Study

Concrete and Abstract Nouns

Concrete nouns can be touched or seen. *Abstract nouns* (like love, bitterness, happiness, or joking) cannot be touched or seen but, despite this, are still nouns because they name entities.

Abstract nouns are generally more difficult to identify. They signify ideas or qualities. An example of an abstract noun is a kindness, which is considered to be a quality. Another example of an abstract noun is courage, which is considered to be an idea.

Often, an abstract noun will have one of the following suffixes:

-tion   -ity   -ism   -ment   -ness   -age   -ance/-ence   -ship   -ability   -acy

Exercise A
Identify the abstract nouns in the following sentences and write them on your paper.

7. People were terrified by the force of their own imagination.
8. You misuse the reverence of your place.
9. There is hardly any place or any company where you may not gain knowledge if you please.
10. Their mastiffs are of unmatchable courage.
11. Society has been called the happiness of life.
12. There is a great difference between knowledge and wisdom.
13. The men found themselves in a predicament trying to choose the better leader.
14. All the country in a general voice cried hate upon him.

Exercise B
An abstract noun is often made by taking an adjective or a verb and turning it into a noun.
   Name the abstract noun that might be made from each of the following words.

Example: true—truth

1. false   7. cautious
2. careless   8. evil
3. grieving   9. amiable
4. free   10. valiant
5. beautiful   11. natural
6. sorry   12. angry

Day 2

Guided Response

Reread the poem "When the Frost is on the Punkin" by James Whitcomb Riley and discuss the following questions with your teacher.

1. What is the overall tone of the poem? What in the poem contributes to the tone?

2. What is the effect of the creative spelling in the poem? (atmusfere, punkin, hosses)

3. Does the author think that the time of year he is describing is a good time of year? How can you tell?

4. Describe the kind of person who would write this poem.

5. Use a highlighter to mark your favorite lines from the poem. Underline the lines that create a vivid image in your mind.

6. Make a list of the things *you* like about the harvest time. Be as descriptive as you can.

Grammar Study

The use of abstract nouns can make your writing too generalized and vague. It's hard to get your specific meaning across because these words (love, beauty, freedom, justice) may mean different things to different people. Their use also quite often requires the use of awkward phrases and passive verb constructions. Sometimes the true subject of the sentence in lost in a subordinate part of the sentence. As a result, the writing is weakened. So while abstract nouns fill an important function in communication, a writer should limit their use. If you find that you must use one, supply concrete nouns to support it.

Exercise A
For each of the abstract nouns listed below, think of a concrete example that would support it. Use an action verb in your concrete example.

Example: truth—boy admits that he broke a window
love—a mother cuddles her baby

1. freedom
2. peace
3. faith
4. knowledge
5. hospitality

6. education
7. friendship
8. trust
9. pride
10. misery

Exercise B

Find the abstract nouns in these quotes by Ben Franklin. It is common to see moral admonitions using abstract nouns. Why do you think that is the case?

1. The absent are never without fault. Nor the present without excuse.
2. If passion drives you, let reason hold the reins.
3. Let thy discontents be thy secrets.
4. Admiration is the daughter of ignorance.
5. Educate your children to self-control, to the habit of holding passion and prejudice and evil tendencies subject to an upright and reasoning will, and you have done much to abolish misery from their future and crimes from society.

Exercise C

Choose one of the following abstractions and write a short paragraph that supports it with concrete examples.

1. Courage is the greatest virtue.
2. The girls were the picture of good health.
3. The acquisition of knowledge is useless without common sense.
4. Her pride was as large as the sky.
5. His maturity was evident to all.

Day 3

Writing

This week you will write a "color" poem taking an abstract idea and creating concrete images to explain. To do this you choose a color to represent one of the abstract nouns and make your title or first line " (color) is (abstract noun) "

Example: White is Peace, Gold is Glory, Yellow is Light, Black is Sadness

The rest of your poem provides images that portray things *in the chosen color* that represent and make concrete the abstract noun.

Here is a sample poem:

> White is Peace
>
> White flags waved in battle
> Surrender to a common ground
> Surrender to forgiveness.
> Open to stains and colors new
> But pure as light, no color's hue.
> Like bandages on a wounded heart
> Mending bleeding victims there,
> Peace flies on the wings of prayer
> Doves on the wings of prayer.

The concrete images in this poem are the white flags of surrender, bandages, doves. There are figurative images in this poem as well: A wounded heart needing a bandage, and that bandage being the peace that comes from prayer; that peace needs forgiveness.

Prewriting: Begin by brainstorming a list of colors and a list of abstract nouns. See the list of abstract nouns in the Appendix if you need help thinking of some. Then choose an abstract noun to write about and a color that you think represents that noun.

Write your chosen combination on your paper. Do an extended *thinking piece* using the noun and the color. Write continuously for 10 minutes on the topic, writing everything that comes into your head. Here is a student sample:

Yellow is Light
sunshine, daisies, flowers across the meadow, friends laughing, music playing,
frisbees on the beach, sunlight glistening on the lake, rays of sun streaming

through the clouds touching the ground, gold ring on a finger, gold, Pharoah's tomb, darkness brought to light, Easter morning bringing victory over death, light is victory over darkness—understanding the truth, believing, wishing on a star, first light in the night sky, stars and planets light up ancient world

Set your thinking piece aside for a day and just think more about your chosen abstract noun and things with the color you chose that might represent the noun.

Grammar Study

Collective Nouns

A collective noun is the name of a group, class, or multitude, and not of a single person, place, thing, or idea. (class, fleet, army, host, company, family, nation, herd, flock)

Usually they are common nouns, unless they name a particular group of people. (Congress, Wildcat Soccer Club)

Collective nouns take a singular verb.

Exercise A
Pick out the collective nouns in the sentences below and write them on your paper.

1. He leads toward Rome with a band of warlike Goths.
2. By ten o'clock the whole party was assembled at the Park.
3. The Senate has letters from the general.
4. Here comes another troop to seek for you.
5. Our family dined in the field, and we sat, or rather reclined around a temperate repast.
6. Our society will not break up, but we shall settle in some other place.
7. He is banished, as enemy to the people and his country.
8. The king hath called his Parliament.

Exercise B
Give some collective noun which stands for a number or group of each of the following words.

1. cows   6. sailors
2. musicians   7. birds
3. soldiers   8. ants
4. ships   9. bees
5. flowers   10. stars

Exercise C

Sometime the use of collective nouns is figurative, such as *a sea of faces*. The "faces" refers to a group of people as vast as the sea. Use each of the following figurative collective noun phrases in a sentence. Can you think of any figurative use of collective nouns other than these examples?

1. a swarm of suitors
2. an army of caterpillars
3. a bevy of beauties
4. a fistful of dollars

Day 4

Writing

Today you will write your "color" poem. Reread the thinking piece you made yesterday on your chosen color and abstract noun. Add any ideas that come to your mind as you read it. Add any ideas that you have been mulling over since you set it aside yesterday.

Now you will write your poem by taking phrases from your thinking piece and organizing them in a poetic way. Your poem does not have to rhyme; it merely must have a poetic flow to it. Here is another student example:

Blue is Eternity

Miles and miles of sky
Stretching on forever,
Contemplation
As far as the eye can see.

A soft and rippling sea
The sky dances in her waves
Reflection
As far as the eye can see.

The depth of your eye
As I gaze at you intently
Meditation
As far as the soul can see.

This student used the repetition of another abstract noun on the third line of each stanza and similar words on the fourth line of each stanza. The concrete images he included are the blue sky, the blue ocean reflecting a blue sky, a person's blue eye. The sample poem on Day 3 only used one stanza, whereas this author created 3 stanzas. Your poem should be at least 8-10 lines long, but organize it any way you like.

Some students really like writing this kind of poem and ask to write more. Write as many poems as you like using different colors and abstract ideas.

Save your drafts in your writing folder.

Grammar Study

Review

Review abstract and collective nouns. Explain each one and then give an example of each one in a sentence.

Parsing

This week you will be learning how to parse a sentence. You will begin with simple sentences so that you can learn the method and then the sentences will get progressively more difficult as the weeks go on.

What is parsing?
Parsing is breaking a sentence into its component parts of speech with an explanation of the form, function, and relationship of each part.

Here is a basic example:

> **Sub**   **pred**   **complement (direct object)**
> **Adj**   **adj**   **N**   **adv**   **V-t** **adj** **adj**   **N**
> The hungry dog hungrily bites the meaty bone.
>
> Explanation: *Dog* is the simple subject; *bites* is the present tense transitive predicate; and *bone* is the direct object of the verb *bites*. *Hungry* modifies *dog* and *meaty* modifies *bone*.

When you parse a sentence, the first level tells what part of speech the word is. The second level tells how the word, phrase, or clause is used in the sentence. The explanation lays out the relationships between the parts of the sentence. If you parse orally, just name each word, its part of speech, and how it is used in the sentence.

Exercise

Copy the following sentences onto your paper and parse them using the following abbreviations:

Parts of speech: adjective=adj, adverb=adv, pronoun=PN, noun=N, verb=V, conjunction=C, preposition=P

Parts of a sentence: subject=sub, predicate=pred, predicate nominative=pred nom; predicate adjective=pred nom, or direct object=DO)

You may give your explanation orally.

1. The happy girl skipped down the street.
2. Seven sons left their books carelessly on the shelf.
3. With little practice, the team still won the game.
4. The evergreen trees in our yard do not lose their leaves in winter.
5. He is not very happy today.

Pumpkin Patch by Winslow Homer

Week 11
Appositives

Day 1

Read the following selection and think about it.

Apple-Seed John

There was once a farmer who had worked in the fields all his life. Every year he had ploughed and planted and harvested, and no one else had raised such fine crops as he. It seemed as if he needed to only touch the corn to have it yellow and ripen upon the ear, or lay his hand upon the rough bark of a tree to be sure that the blossoms would show and the branches hang low with fruit.

But, after years and years, the farmer grew to be an old man. His hair and beard became as white as the blossoms on the pear trees, and his back was bent and crooked, because he had worked so hard. He could only sit in the sunshine and watch some one else ploughing and planting where he wanted so much to plough and plant. And he felt very unhappy, because he wished to do something great for other people, and he was not able, for he was poor.

But one morning he got down his stout cane from the chimney corner, and he slung an empty bag over his crooked old shoulders, and he started out into the world, because he had thought of a good deed that even an old man could do.

Over the meadows and through the lanes he traveled, stopping to speak to the little wild mice, or the crickets, or the chipmunks, who knew him—all of them—and were never afraid when he went by. At every farmhouse he rested and rapped at the door and asked for— what do you think?—just a few apples! And the farmers had so many apples that they were glad to give some of them away, and the old man's bag was soon full to the very brim.

On and on he went, until he left the houses far behind, and took his way through the deep woods. At night he slept upon a bed of moss out under the stars, with the prairie dogs barking in his ears, and the owls hooting in the tops of the trees; and in the morning he started on his way again.

When he was hungry he ate of the berries that grew in the woods, but not one of his apples—oh, no! Sometimes an Indian met him, and they walked along together; and so, at last, the old man came to a place where there were wide fields, but no one to plant them, for there were no farms.

Then he sat down and took out his jack-knife, and began carefully cutting the core from every apple in his bag. With his stout cane he bored deep holes in the earth, and in every hole he dropped an apple core, to sleep there in the rain and the sun. And when his bag was emptied he hurried on to a town where he could ask for more apples.

Soon the farmers came to know him, and they called him old Apple-seed John. They gave him their very best apples for seed—the Pound Sweets, and the Sheep's Noses, and the Pippins, and the Seek-no-Farthers. They saved clippings from the pear trees, and the plum trees, and the peach trees for him; and they gave him the corner of the settle which was nearest the fire when he stopped with them for a night.

Such wonderful stories as he told the children of the things he had seen in his travels—the Indians with their gay blankets and feathers, the wolves who came out of the wood at night to look at him with their glaring eyes, the deer who ran across his path, and the shy little hares. And no one wished Apple-seed John to travel on the next morning, but he would never stay. With his bag over his shoulder, his clippings under his arm, and his trusty cane in his hand, he hurried on to plant young orchards by every river and in every lonely pasture. And soon the apple seeds that had been asleep when Apple-seed John had dropped them into the earth awoke and arose, and sent out green shoots, and began to be trees. Higher and higher they grew, until, in the wind and the sun, they covered the ground with blossoms, and then with ripe fruit, so that all the empty places in the country were full of orchards.

After a while old Apple-seed John went to live with the angels, but no one ever forgot him; and the children who knew him, when they had grown to be grandfathers themselves, would sit out under the trees, and say to each other: "This orchard was planted by Apple-seed John."

—From *For the Children's Hour* by Caroline S. Bailey

Write your first impression of this story. Does it fit with stories you have heard about Johnny Apple-Seed? How is it the same of different? What are the best parts of this telling of the story?

1972 Postcard of Commemorative Stamp

111

Grammar Study

Appositives and Appositive Phrases

An appositive is a noun or pronoun that usually follows and describes another noun.

Pontiac, the Indian *chief*, died in 1769.
The *tree*, a great *elm*, fell last night.

In such sentences, the second noun of the pair is said be in apposition with the first.

A phrase containing an appositive is called an *appositive phrase*. It may include the appositive and any other modifying words, phrases, or clauses.

John, *the miller who lived on the outskirts of the village*, took care of the widows.
His sword, *the shining Excalibur*, rested on his knees.

Exercise A
Fill in the blanks with appositives.

1. Mr. Jones, the _____, is building a home for me.
2. Have you seen Charlie, my _____, anywhere?
3. Chapman, the _____ of the team, broke his collar bone.
4. Washington, the _____ of the United States, is on the Potomac.
5. Who has met my young friend _____ today?
6. Charles I, _____ of England, was beheaded in 1649.
7. The sultan was fond of tiger-hunting, a dangerous _____.
8. Millie, a pretty good _____, won first prize at the state fair.

Exercise B
Identity the appositive phrases in the following sentences and write them on your paper. Label the appositive in the phrase.

1. An Englishwoman, the wife of one of the officers, was sitting on the battlements with her child in her arms.
2. I went to visit Mr. Degas, the famous artist.
3. We hoped to capture the flag of the opposing team, our sworn enemies in the game.
4. Spring, the sweet Spring, is the year's pleasant king.
5. Then forth they all out of their baskets drew
   Great store of flowers, the honor of the field.
6. He was speedily summoned to the apartment of his captain, Lord Crawford.

7. No rude sound shall reach thine ear,
   Armor's clang and war-steed champing.
8. And thus spake on that ancient man,
   The bright-eyed mariner.
9. There lived at no great distance from this stronghold a farmer, a bold and stout man, whose name was Binnock.
10. The next day we nailed the skirt of his coat, which I had pulled off, to the whipping post in Charlestown, the place of his residence, with a label upon it.

Exercise C

Write 3 sentences using an appositive phrase. Vary the structure of the phrase in each sentence.

Day 2

Guided Response

Reread the tale of John Apple-Seed from Day 1 and discuss these questions with your teacher.

1. In what ways is this story like the legends you have heard about this character?

2. Find places in the story where the author uses vivid language. Choose at least 3 and copy the phrases or sentences onto your paper. What is it about each one that makes it bring a picture to your mind? What kinds of word does the author use?

3. Why do you think the author portrays John as an old man? How does that add to the story? How old did you think he was in the other legends you have heard?

4. Why do you think the people wanted John to come? Why did want him to stay and not move on?

5. A tall tale is a uniquely American story form that includes some of the following characteristics:

   - a larger-than-life, or superhuman, main character with a specific task,
   - a problem that is solved in a humorous or outrageous way,
   - exaggerated details that describe things larger than they really are, and
   - characters who use everyday language.

Many tall tales are based on actual people or on a composite of actual people. Exaggeration is the major element in tall tales. Like most "tall tales," this story had some basis in truth. There really was a man named John Chapman who was nicknamed Johnny Appleseed. Name as many other tall tales or American folklore legends as you can think of.

6. Why do you think people like "tall tales?" Why do you think this kind of story became an American phenomenon? (Why are they so popular in American folklore?)

Grammar Study

Punctuation of appositives

Sometimes, the noun being described or renamed by an appositive is too general. The information the appositive provides is essential to the meaning of the sentence. When this is the case, do *not* place commas around the appositive; just leave it alone (restrictive appositive). If the sentence would be clear and complete without the appositive, then commas are necessary to set the appositive off from the rest of the sentence (non-restrictive appositive).

Examples

Restrictive, no commas needed:
> *The popular magician Houdini was known for his daring escapes.*

Here we do not put commas around the appositive, because it is essential information. Without the appositive, the sentence would be, "The popular magician was known for his daring escapes." We wouldn't know which magician was being referred to.

Nonrestrictive, comma needed:
> *Houdini, the popular magician, was known for his daring escapes.*

Here we put commas around the appositive because it is not essential information. Without the appositive, the sentence would be, Houdini was known for his daring escapes." We still know who the subject of the sentence is without the appositive.

Exercise A
Read the following sentences and decide if they are punctuated correctly. If they are, mark the sentence as correct. If not add in punctuation that is needed, or take out punctuation that is not needed.

1. Pecos Bill, legendary cowboy hero of the American Southwest, personified the frontier virtues of strength, courage, ingenuity, audacity, and humor.

2. Johnny Inkslinger the camp's head clerk invented bookkeeping about the same time that Paul Bunyan invented logging.

3. One among a legion of blacks just freed from the war John Henry went to work rebuilding the Southern states whose territory had been ravaged by the Civil War.

4. The story of Mike Fink has been beautifully told by the late Morgan Neville, of Cincinnati, a gentleman of the highest literary taste.

5. David Crockett United States Representative from Tennessee already a folk hero in his home state, became one of the most famous men in the nation.

6. In 1767 John Finley a courageous Indian trader pushed far into Kentucky's depths, and returned with thrilling stories of his adventures and tempting descriptions of the beauty and fertility of the land.

7. These he told to Daniel Boone, an adventure-loving Pennsylvanian, who had made his way to North Carolina, and built himself a home in the virgin forest at the headwaters of the Yadkin.

8. Right after that Babe would eat a ton of grain for lunch and then come pestering around the cook, Sourdough Sam, begging for another snack.

9. His friend Slue-foot Sue had plenty of tales of her own.

Exercise B

Another kind of phrase will often serve in apposition. A noun phrase, a gerund phrase, or an infinitive phrase may also be used as an appositive phrase.

Examples:

Noun phrase: My favorite pie, a smooth, flavorful peach and blueberry medley, sat cooling on the counter.
Gerund phrase: The best cure, sleeping for 8 hours, was not possible for the riders.
Infinitive phrase: Sally's recipe for success, to be as cheerful as possible, was a great inspiration to the youth group.

Write 3 sentences using an appositive phrase in each sentence. Make one a noun phrase, another a gerund phrase, and the third an infinitive phrase. Be sure that your appositive actually renames the noun with which it is in apposition.

Day 3

Writing

Over the next few weeks, you will be writing a tall tale or folklore legend. To begin, take a look at the following tall tale and use the worksheet on the next page to analyze it.

John Henry

Now John Henry was a mighty man, yes sir. He was born a slave in the 1840's but was freed after the war. He went to work as a steel-driver for the Chesapeake & Ohio Railroad, don't ya know. And John Henry was the strongest, the most powerful man working the rails.

John Henry, he would spend his day's drilling holes by hitting thick steel spikes into rocks with his faithful shaker crouching close to the hole, turning the drill after each mighty blow. There was no one who could match him, though many tried.

Well, the new railroad was moving along right quick, thanks in no little part to the mighty John Henry. But looming right smack in its path was a mighty enemy—the Big Bend Mountain. Now the big bosses at the C&O Railroad decided that they couldn't go around the mile and a quarter thick mountain. No sir, the men of the C&O were going to go through it - drilling right into the heart of the mountain.

A thousand men would lose their lives before the great enemy was conquered. It took three long years, and before it was done the ground outside the mountain was filled with makeshift, sandy graves. The new tunnels were filled with smoke and dust. Ya couldn't see no-how and could hardly breathe. But John Henry, he worked tirelessly, drilling with a 14-pound hammer, and going 10 to 12 feet in one workday. No one else could match him.

Then one day a salesman came along to the camp. He had a steam-powered drill and claimed it could out-drill any man. Well, they set up a contest then and there between John Henry and that there drill. The foreman ran that newfangled steam-drill. John Henry, he just pulled out two 20-pound hammers, one in each hand. They drilled and drilled, dust rising everywhere. The men were howling and cheering. At the end of 35 minutes, John Henry had drilled two seven foot holes—a total of fourteen feet, while the steam drill had only drilled one nine-foot hole.

John Henry held up his hammers in triumph! The men shouted and cheered. The noise was so loud, it took a moment for the men to realize that John Henry was tottering. Exhausted, the mighty man crashed to the ground, the hammer's rolling from his grasp. The crowd went silent as the foreman rushed to his side. But it was too late. A blood vessel had burst in his brain. The greatest driller in the C&O Railroad was dead.

Some folks say that John Henry's likeness is carved right into the rock inside the Big Bend Tunnel. And if you walk to the edge of the blackness of the tunnel, sometimes you can hear the sound of two 20-pound hammers drilling their way to victory over the machine.

—Retold by S.E. Schlosser

Review the characteristics of a tall tale on Day 2.

Tall Tale Analysis Worksheet

Title _____

Setting:
    Who Tells the Tale:

    Characters:

    Place:

Truthful Events:

    First Exaggeration:

    Second Exaggeration:

    Other Exaggerations:

Foolish Conclusions:

(You may choose another tall tale that you have read or heard if you prefer.)

Grammar Study

Adjective Clauses and Adjective Phrases

Often times an adjective clause and an appositive adjective phrase can be used interchangeably. You have to decide which one is the most concise and effective way to get your point across.

Adjective clause
Susan Stanley, who wrote the book *St. Monica, Mother and Saint*, spoke at the conference.

Adjective phrase
Susan Stanley, author of *St. Monica, Mother and Saint*, spoke at the conference.

Exercise A
Change the appositive adjective phrases in the following sentences to adjective clauses.

1. She read *Johnny Tremain*, a novel written by Esther Forbes.
2. The experiment, conducted at the agricultural test farm, was hugely successful.
3. Sister Thomas Aquinas, president of the university, invited parents to an orientation.
4. I was born in Dos Palos, a tiny town in central California.
5. The Circus Maximus, an ancient Roman theater, was a venue created for chariot racing.

Exercise B
Combine the following sentences. Use the second sentence as an adjective phrase.

Example: Scranton was founded in 1813. It is known as the Electric City.
    Scranton, known as the Electric City, was founded in 1813.

1. John Quincy Adams was born on July 11, 1767. He was the sixth president of the United States.
2. The Jefferson Memorial is famous landmark in the nation's capital. It is a round building with intricate pillars.
3. American beavers were hunted by fur companies in North America. They were highly prized by Europeans.
4. The sloth is found in the tropical forests of Central and South America. It is a slow moving animal.
5. Mercury is the nearest planet to the sun. It is the smallest of the nine planets orbiting the sun.

Day 4

Writing

Over the next few weeks you will be writing a tall tale or a legend in stages. Today you will think of a story idea and make a preliminary planning chart.

You will have first have to think of a story to tell. Remember that tall tales include the following characteristics:

- a larger-than-life, or superhuman, main character with a specific task,
- a problem that is solved in a humorous or outrageous way,
- exaggerated details that describe things larger than they really are, and
- characters who use everyday language.

If you choose to write a tall tale, you will have to think of a character who solves a problem in a superhuman way. (Example: Paul Bunyan, Pecos Bill) Events in your tale will be exaggerated.

A legend is a traditional historical tale generally regarded as true but usually containing a mixture of fact and fiction. (Example: Davy Crockett, Annie Oakley) If you choose to write a legend, your character can be a real person (such as someone in your family or some historical figure) portrayed in truth but with some exaggerated parts. Use the charts reprinted below to plan your story. You may have to try a few different ideas, filling out several different charts until you decide on the best story to tell. You may also want to do a free write on your chosen character to get your ideas flowing.

Most tall tales and American legends are set in the frontier or Wild West eras. You can make your setting in the past, in the future, or in current times. Be creative!!!

Legend Planning Worksheet

Characters: Setting: Problem:
True event or information
True event or information
Exaggerated or fictionalized event
Exaggerated or fictionalized event
Conclusion (resolution of the problem and where the character goes/does after)

Tall Tale Planning Worksheet

Characters: Setting: Problem:
True event or information
Exaggerated event
Exaggerated event
Other Exaggerations
Foolish ending

Go over your planning charts with your teacher and discuss the story plan. Is your idea something that could be developed into an interesting story within the genre of tall tales and legends? Can the sequence of events and conclusion be accomplished in a reasonably-sized paper (not a 30 page saga, but a 2 or 3 page short story)? Make changes in your plan based on your conversation with your teacher.

Set your chart aside until next week.

Grammar Study

Review

Review the appositive: Explain an appositive and an appositive phrase and use each one in a sentence.

Find the appositives in the following passage.

> Roger, aged seven, and no longer the youngest of the family, ran in wide zigzags, to and fro, across the steep field that loped up from the lake up to Holly Howe, the farm where they were staying for part of the summer holidays. He ran until he nearly reached the hedge by the footpath, then he turned and ran until he nearly reached the hedge on the other side of the field. Then he turned and crossed the field again. Each crossing of the field, brought him nearer to the farm. The wind was against him, so he was tacking up to the farm where at the gate his patient mother was awaiting him. He could not run straight against the wind because he was a sailing vessel, a tea-clipper, the Cutty Sark.

> —From *Swallows and Amazons* by Arthur Ransome

Parsing

Remember parsing is identifying the grammatical purpose of each word in a sentence and its relationship to other words. This week we will add phrases to our parsing exercise.

Please study each of the following examples for parsing verbal phrases and prepositional phrases.

<pre>
             (Gerund phrase)
              Sub   pred   comp-DO

             N (gerund) N   V   adj   N
Gerund: (Drinking water) quenches my thirst.
</pre>

> Explanation: *drinking water* is the subject; *quenches* is the predicate, *thirst* is direct object of the verb *quenches*.
> *Water* is the object of the gerund *drinking*.
> Adjective *my* modifies *thirst*

<pre>
                           Adj
                    (Participle phrase)
           Sub Pred Comp adj
            PN   V   N   adj   N   adv
Participle: We saw children (playing games outside).
</pre>

122

Explanation: *We* is the subject; *saw* is the predicate; *children* is the direct object of the verb *saw*.

Playing games is the participle phrase modifying children. *Games* is the object of the participle *playing*.

The adverb *outside* modifies the participle, telling where.


```
                              DO          adv
                    (Inf phrase [prep phrase])
             Sub      pred  (DO                    )
     Adj    N         V     V(inf)  P    adj  N
```
Infinitive: The children wanted (to jump [across the creek]).

Explanation: *Children* is the subject, *wanted* is the predicate; the infinitive phrase is the direct object of the verb *wanted*.

To jump across the creek is the infinitive phrase. The prepositional phrase *across the creek* is used as an adverb modifying the infinitive *to jump*. *Creek* is the object of the preposition *across*.


```
                         Adj        adj                      adv
                (App phrase [prep phrase] [prep phrase])      [prep phrase]
          Sub                                     pred  comp-DO
          N      adj   N    P  adj  N    P   PN    V    N    P  adj  N    C
```
Appositive: Mr. Howe, (the farmer   [up the hill]   [from us]), plants corn [in the spring and
N
fall].

Explanation: *Mr. Howe* is the subject; *plants* is the predicate; *corn* is the direct object of the verb *plants*.

The farmer up the hill from us is the appositive phrase modifying *Mr. Howe*. The prepositional phrase *up the hill* is used as a adjective modifying *farmer*. *Hill* is the object of the preposition *up*. *From us* is used as an adjective phrase modifying *hill*; *us* is the object of the preposition *from*. *In the spring and fall* is a prepositional phrase used as an adverb modifying *plants*; *spring* and *fall* are compound objects of the preposition *in*.

Exercise

Parse the following sentences using the abbreviations provided.

Parts of speech: adjective=adj, adverb=adv, pronoun=PN, noun=N, verb=V, conjunction=C

Parts of a sentence: subject=sub, predicate=pred, complement=comp (direct object =DO, predicate nominative=PrNom; Predicate adjective=PrAdj)

Phrases: prepositional phrase=prep phrase; infinitive phrase=inf phrase; gerund phrase=ger phrase; participle phrase=part phrase; appositive phrase=app phrase.

You have seen some of these sentences in a previous Week's lessons. Try not to look back at your answers. Be sure to account for every word in your explanation. Remember that a prepositional phrase is often within another phrase. Copy the sentence onto your paper and label as directed above. Always begin by first identifying the subject and predicate of the sentence. You may do the "explanation" orally with your teacher.

1. Our favorite sport is skating in the winter.
2. The men began to load the boxes.
3. Frightened by the lightning, the children huddled under the bed.
4. Sally, my older sister, told the frightened children a story to calm them.
5. To write well is the goal of the program.

John Chapman, a.k.a. Johnny Appleseed

Week 12

Day 1

Read the story printed below and consider it as an example of the tall tale genre.

A Tale of Pecos Bill and his Lasso

Yes sir, that ole Pecos Bill was sure enough a great cow puncher. He invented lots of tricks that made the cowboy's work more efficient and kept the boys hoppin'. One of the things he invented was branding the cattle with an emblem of the ranch, so that even if the cattle wandered off, no one could mistake who owned which cattle. Believe it or not, he also invented the rodeo. After every roundup he held a big party and every hand in the outfit had a chance to show off their roping and riding expertise. There's nothing a cowboy likes better than showing off. One of his best inventions, though, was the lasso, and Bill became so clever at it that he could lasso an owl out of the top of a tree while his bronco was galloping at full speed.

Well, sometimes Bill had a bit of trouble and his lasso came in quite handy. One summer it was the weather that was plaguing him. First came a drought. The range grass dried up, and the cattle had nothing to eat. All the springs and rivers dried up. Bill dug a canal, hoping that it would solve his problem. It was a lovely canal, you can be sure, but no water flowed into it. So Bill took his lasso and roped a ten-mile piece of the Rio Grande River. This was enough to last the ranch a day. Every morning before breakfast Bill had to rope himself another length.

As though this were not bad enough, the sky grew green. From the mountains came the wild roar of a tornado. The boys divided the cattle to keep them from stampeding and they did their best to keep them of the cyclone's path. It wasn't any use: the tornado headed for them whichever way they went.

To save his ranch, Bill risked his own life. He slung his lasso around his head and let fly. The noose caught the tornado and Bill was yanked up, up, up on into the middle of the ugly green cloud.

The thought that a human had roped it was unbearable to the cyclone. It whipped around and around, bucked up and down, tried side-kicking and sky-walking, all the tricks of a bucking steer. Bill held on for dear life. Over plains and mountains they raced. The cyclone tried to brush him off against the Rockies. It slapped him against the walls of the Grand Canyon. It bumped his head against the sky. Still Pecos Bill held his seat.

At last seeing that there was no other means of shaking off its rider, the tornado headed for the Pacific Ocean and tried to rain out from under him. Bill decided he had had enough. He picked out a pleasant spot in California and jumped. The force with which he landed dug a big hole. Today this is known as Death Valley.

—Adapted from a story by Anne Malcolmson

Write your first impression of this tale of Pecos Bill. It is one of many written about this character. Can you think of any other stories about him?

Grammar Study

Verb Phrases

When the verb consists of several words, the last one is the principal verb, and the others are helping or auxiliary verbs. Several words used as a verb make a verb phrase, but we generally call the whole verb phrase the verb. Auxiliary verbs used in a verb phrase indicate the mood, tense, and voice of the verb, which we will discuss later this week.

The following words may be used as auxiliary verbs:

is, was, had, had been, will, will be, has been, have been, may, might, may be,
might have been, can, should, should have, could have been, do, must, would

Exercise A
In each of the following sentences, identify the auxiliary verb. Tell whether it is transitive or intransitive. Identify the objects, predicate nominatives, and predicate adjectives.

1. The south wind is warm.
2. April showers bring May flowers.
3. A darker day may never dawn.
4. An honest man never breaks his promise.
5. Laziness will cloth a man in rags.
6. The September sun will have ripened the grapes.
7. Pride must have a fall.
8. A rolling stone will gather no moss.
9. Elias Howe was the inventor of the sewing machine.
10. The driver could have prevented the accident.
11. Another blue day has been dawning.
12. Somewhere the sun is always shining.

Exercise B
Write a sentence for each of the following auxiliary verbs in combination with a main verb. Tell whether the verb phrase you formed in each sentence is a transitive or intransitive verb.
1. have been
2. will be
3. must have been
4. should have
5. could
6. had been
7. might have been
8. may be

Day 2

Guided Response

American tall tales gained popularity in the 1800s with the pioneer expansion into wilderness lands. They were a way to combat in story all the difficulties facing the pioneers: the extreme weather, unusual and dangerous animals, the difficulty of travel, homesteading and tilling new land. "Tall" characters conquered the new, untamed land with superhuman feats. All tall tales have in common certain elements, such as one person battling a force of nature much bigger than himself, yet beating it.

1. In what ways does the tale of Pecos Bill reprinted on Day 1 fit this description of tall tales? Review the characteristics of tall tales in Week 10. Which of those characteristics does this retelling have?

2. Which event is the most outrageous? Explain.

3. What real things did the author include in his tale? What things in nature did the story explain?

4. Make an outline of the story.

5. How does the use of everyday language give the story a tone? Give examples.

6. Rewrite the introductory paragraph the story *Apple-Seed John* from Week 11, making it more interesting and inviting to a reader.

Grammar Study

Verbs: Mood

Verbs have four moods: indicative, imperative, conditional, and subjunctive. A verb's mood shows whether the sentence is conveying a fact, a wish, a command, or a possibility.

The *indicative* mood is used in most sentences we write. It simply indicates something.

Susan likes oranges.

The *imperative* mood expresses a command or a request. It only occurs in the present tense. The subject of an imperative mood verb is often not written in the sentence. It is "you" that is *understood.*

Put those oranges on the table.

The *conditional* mood expresses the possibility that something might occur.

I could read the letter.

The *subjunctive* mood represents something contrary to fact.

If I were taller, I could reach the shelf.

Exercise A
Identify the verb (verb phrase) in the each sentence. Tell the mood of each of the verbs in the following sentences. Tell whether the verb is transitive or intransitive.

1. You must always work diligently on your chores.
2. If I were the president, I would lower taxes for all citizens.
3. Please keep your feet off the coffee table.
4. The children swam all day at the pond behind the barn.
5. I would never ride a hurricane like a bucking bronco.
6. You could reach the highest level if you were to try harder.
7. Gather the apples into this basket and leave it on the porch.
8. Bishop Timothy officiated at the school's graduation.

Exercise B
Write 4 sentences and in each one use a different mood for the verb.

Day 3

Writing

The Introduction

Read the introductions printed below and complete the exercises below.

1. Believe it! It would seem that the last little cat was born in the last place a
cat should be born—even a last little cat. The little black kitten was born in a
kennel! And it was the last kitten of a whole litter of kittens—six kittens had
been born, after that the last little cat still was born. Born in a nest—mind you—
in a chicken nest in a barn that was now a dog kennel.

   —From *The Last Little Cat* by Meindert DeJong

2. Roger, aged seven and no longer the youngest of the family, ran in wide
zigzags, to and fro, across the steep field that loped up from the lake up to
Holly Howe, the farm where they were staying for part of the summer holidays.
He ran until he nearly reached the hedge by the footpath, then he turned and ran
until he nearly reached the hedge on the other side of the field. Then he turned
and crossed the field again. Each crossing of the field, brought him nearer to the
farm. The wind was against him, so he was tacking up to the farm where at the
gate his patient mother was awaiting him. He could not run straight against the
wind because he was a sailing vessel, a tea-clipper, the Cutty Sark.

   —From *Swallows and Amazons* by Arthur Ransome

3. It was winter at Valley Forge. Indeed, it was that famous and dreadful winter when
Washington and his little army of patriots were encamped there. Half-clad, half-fed,
chilled by the raw, cold winds, is it not a wonder that these brave men did not lose all
hope and disperse to their homes? Every one of them performed a golden deed when
he kept up his courage and stuck to his post and thus did his part towards keeping the
American army together. But the hero of whom I shall tell you was not a soldier; he
did not even believe it right to fight.

   —From "A Hero of Valley Forge" in *An American
   Book of Golden Deeds* by James Baldwin

4. Two men appeared simultaneously at the two ends of a sort of passage running along
the side of the Apollo Theatre in the Adelphi. The evening daylight in the streets was
large and luminous, opalescent and empty. The passage was comparatively long and
dark, so each man could see the other as a mere black silhouette at the other end.

Nevertheless, each man knew the other, even in that inky outline; for they were both men of striking appearance and they hated each other.

—From "The Man in the Passage" in *The Wisdom of Father Brown* by G. K. Chesterton

5. The great pullman was whirling onward with such dignity of motion that a glance from the window seemed simply to prove that the plains of Texas were pouring eastward. Vast flats of green grass, dull-hued spaces of mesquite and cactus, little groups of frame houses, woods of light and tender trees, all were sweeping into the east, sweeping over the horizon, a precipice.

—From *The Bride Comes to Yellow Sky* by Stephen Crane

Exercise A

After reading them carefully, write what you think are the strengths of each of these introductions.

Exercise B

Consider the characteristics of "showing" (as opposed to "telling") writing. Review Week 3 Day 4. "Showing" writing has three characteristics:

- concrete nouns
- action verbs
- vivid modifiers.

Evaluate each of the introductions to see which of the 3 characteristics they employ. Choose 2 introductions that you like the best from the selections above and list the action verbs and concrete nouns in them. Then list at least 2 modifiers (these can be phrases).

Exercise C

You will now write the introduction for your tall tale. The introduction should introduce your character and the setting using "showing" writing so that your reader is drawn into your tale. Don't forget that tall tales use everyday language to give "flavor" and set the tone of the story. Here is a sample written by a student:

Now a hundred years ago in the territory of Tennessee, lived a girl named Hudja-luv (who-ja-love) who was 6 feet tall. She and her dog Hudja-paw romped rambled all over them hills, hunting and exploring, cavorting and gallivanting. One day Huja-luv spied a young man and his father hunting on the other side of the hill and, oh my, she had never seen such a fine young feller. She fixed in her mind that this was the feller that had been plopped on this earth for her. She simply knew she should marry him. Little did she know what an uphill battle she had ahead of her to make that man her own.

Grammar Study

Verbs: Tense

The tense of a verb refers to the *time* of the action or state of being. In English, only two tenses are marked in the verb alone: present (as in "he jumps" or "he runs") and past (as in "he jumped" or "he ran"). All other tenses are marked by the auxiliary verbs. Understanding the six basic tenses will give you enough information, for now, to choose the correct word to express time in your sentences.

Present tenses: Simple Present: They walk
Present Perfect: They have walked

Past tenses: Simple Past: They walked
Past Perfect: They had walked

Future tenses: Future: They will walk
Future Perfect: They will have walked

What does "perfect" mean?
A perfect tense indicates that an action has been completed.

Simple:
Sam walks over the bridge (present)
Sam walked over the bridge (past)
Sam will walk over the bridge (future)

Perfect:
Sam has walked over the bridge (present perfect)
Sam had walked over the bridge (past perfect)
Sam will have walked over the bridge (future perfect)

Exercise A
For each of the simple present verbs below, change the sentence to show all 6 tenses as in the examples above.

1. The children break the bubbles.
2. Monsters hide under the bed.
3. The opera singer sings the aria.

Exercise B
Identify the verb phrases in the following sentences. Tell the tense of each verb in the sentence.

1. Each crossing of the field, brought him nearer to the farm.
2. Sandy will think of all the ways he had wasted his time.
3. Lost in the city, we had walked past the same fountain 3 times.
4. Davy Crockett has become a legendary figure.
5. When she has finished, she will have worked on the painting for 3 months.

Day 4

Writing

Today you will write the first draft of your tall tale. Continue on from the introduction you wrote yesterday. Review the chart you made in Week. As you write, divide events into paragraphs. Each box in your chart should be the start of a new paragraph. However it may take several paragraphs to cover what it is in one box.

Use "showing" writing to bring the story to life. Avoid the use of "There is," "There are," "There was," and "There were" in your story. This will force you to use an action verb. For example, *There are many buffalo on the prairie* can be changed to *Buffalo cover the prairie for as far as the eye can see.*

Save your draft for next week.

Davy Crockett

Grammar Study

A Little More about Tense

For continuing action, use the progressive tense, as in

Present	I am running. He is/They are running.
Past	I was running. He was/They were running.
Future	I will be running. He will be/They will be running.

Perfect Progressive combines ongoing action with completed or future action, as in

Present	I have been running. He has been/They have been running.
Past	I had been running. He/They had been running.
Future	I will have been running. He/They will have been running.

You may also use the emphatic tense, as in

> I do run.
> I did run.

For a complete list of the tenses studied in this book and an explanation of each one, please see the Appendix.

Exercise A

Use the simple past, past progressive, or emphatic tense as appropriate in the following sentences.

1. I am eating at a restaurant right now. I (eat) _____ at this same restaurant yesterday.

2. I don't want to play soccer today because it is raining. The same thing happened last weekend. I _____ (want) to play because it (rain) _____.

3. It was beautiful yesterday when we made the pilgrimage. The sun (shine) _____ and a cool breeze (blow) _____.

4. While Mrs. Jones (read) _____ the children a story, they (fall) _____, so she (close) _____ the book and (turn) _____ off the light.

5. Stephen (climb) _____ the monkey bars when his hands (slip) _____ and he (fall) _____.

133

Exercise B

Create a sentence using each of the following irregular verbs in a verb phrase with the indicated tense.

Example: sleep in a tent (past perfect)

   Bob had slept in a tent only one other time in his life.

1. build a house (present progressive)
2. catch a butterfly (future perfect)
3. break a window (past)
4. play a violin (future)
5. hold a snake (present perfect progressive)
6. make cookies (emphatic)

Annie Oakley, sharpshooter (circa 1880)

Week 13
Voice

Day 1

Read the following story and think about it.

The Capture of Father Time

Jim was the son of a cowboy, and lived on the broad plains of Arizona. His father had trained him to lasso a bronco or a young bull with perfect accuracy, and had Jim possessed the strength to back up his skill he would have been as good a cowboy as any in all Arizona.

When he was twelve years old he made his first visit to the east, where Uncle Charles, his father's brother, lived. Of course Jim took his lasso with him, for he was proud of his skill in casting it, and wanted to show his cousins what a cowboy could do.

At first the city boys and girls were much interested in watching Jim lasso posts and fence pickets, but they soon tired of it, and even Jim decided it was not the right sort of sport for cities.

But one day the butcher asked Jim to ride one of his horses into the country, to a pasture that had been engaged, and Jim eagerly consented. He had been longing for a horseback ride, and to make it seem like old times he took his lasso with him.

He rode through the streets demurely enough, but on reaching the open country roads his spirits broke forth into wild jubilation, and, urging the butcher's horse to full gallop, he dashed away in true cowboy fashion.

Then he wanted still more liberty, and letting down the bars that led into a big field he began riding over the meadow and throwing his lasso at imaginary cattle, while he yelled and whooped to his heart's content.

Suddenly, on making a long cast with his lasso, the loop caught upon something and rested about three feet from the ground, while the rope drew taut and nearly pulled Jim from his horse.

This was unexpected. More than that, it was wonderful; for the field seemed bare of even a stump. Jim's eyes grew big with amazement, but he knew he had caught something when a voice cried out:

"Here, let go! Let go, I say! Can't you see what you've done?"

No, Jim couldn't see, nor did he intend to let go until he found out what was holding the loop of the lasso. So he resorted to an old trick his father had taught him and, putting the butcher's horse to a run, began riding in a circle around the spot where his lasso had caught. As he thus drew nearer and nearer his quarry he saw the rope coil up, yet it looked to be coiling over nothing but air. One end of the lasso was made fast to a ring in the saddle, and when the rope was almost wound up and the horse began to pull away and snort with fear, Jim dismounted. Holding the reins of the bridle in one hand, he followed the rope, and an instant later saw an old man caught fast in the coils of the lasso.

His head was bald and uncovered, but long white whiskers grew down to his waist. About his body was thrown a loose robe of fine white linen. In one hand he bore a great scythe, and beneath the other arm he carried an hourglass.

While Jim gazed wonderingly upon him, this venerable old man spoke in an angry voice:

"Now, then—get that rope off as fast as you can! You've brought everything on earth to a standstill by your foolishness! Well—what are you staring at? Don't you know who I am?"

"No," said Jim, stupidly.

"Well, I'm Time—Father Time! Now, make haste and set me free—if you want the world to run properly."

"How did I happen to catch you?" asked Jim, without making a move to release his captive.

"I don't know. I've never been caught before," growled Father Time. "But I suppose it was because you were foolishly throwing your lasso at nothing."

"I didn't see you," said Jim.

"Of course you didn't. I'm invisible to the eyes of human beings unless they get within three feet of me, and I take care to keep more than that distance away from them. That's why I was crossing this field, where I supposed no one would be. And I should have been perfectly safe had it not been for your beastly lasso. Now, then," he added, crossly, "are you going to get that rope off?"

"Why should I?" asked Jim.

"Because everything in the world stopped moving the moment you caught me. I don't suppose you want to make an end of all business and pleasure, and war and love, and misery and ambition and everything else, do you? Not a watch has ticked since you tied me up here like a mummy!"

Jim laughed. It really was funny to see the old man wound round and round with coils of rope from his knees up to his chin.

"It'll do you good to rest," said the boy. "From all I've heard you lead a rather busy life."

"Indeed I do," replied Father Time, with a sigh. "I'm due in Kamchatka this very minute. And to think one small boy is upsetting all my regular habits!"

"Too bad!" said Jim, with a grin. "But since the world has stopped anyhow, it won't matter if it takes a little longer recess. As soon as I let you go Time will fly again. Where are your wings?"

"I haven't any," answered the old man. "That is a story cooked up by some one who never saw me. As a matter of fact, I move rather slowly."

"I see, you take your time," remarked the boy. "What do you use that scythe for?"

"To mow down the people," said the ancient one. "Every time I swing my scythe some one dies."

"Then I ought to win a life-saving medal by keeping you tied up," said Jim. "Some folks will live this much longer."

"But they won't know it," said Father Time, with a sad smile; "so it will do them no good. You may as well untie me at once."

"No," said Jim, with a determined air. "I may never capture you again; so I'll hold you for awhile and see how the world wags without you."

136

Then he swung the old man, bound as he was, upon the back of the butcher's horse, and, getting into the saddle himself, started back toward town, one hand holding his prisoner and the other guiding the reins.

When he reached the road his eye fell on a strange tableau. A horse and buggy stood in the middle of the road, the horse in the act of trotting, with his head held high and two legs in the air, but perfectly motionless. In the buggy a man and a woman were seated; but had they been turned into stone they could not have been more still and stiff.

"There's no Time for them!" sighed the old man. "Won't you let me go now?"

"Not yet," replied the boy.

He rode on until he reached the city, where all the people stood in exactly the same positions they were in when Jim lassoed Father Time. Stopping in front of a big dry goods store, the boy hitched his horse and went in. The clerks were measuring out goods and showing patterns to the rows of customers in front of them, but everyone seemed suddenly to have become a statue.

There was something very unpleasant in this scene, and a cold shiver began to run up and down Jim's back; so he hurried out again.

On the edge of the sidewalk sat a poor, crippled beggar, holding out his hat, and beside him stood a prosperous-looking gentleman who was about to drop a penny into the beggar's hat. Jim knew this gentleman to be very rich but rather stingy, so he ventured to run his hand into the man's pocket and take out his purse, in which was a $20 gold piece. This glittering coin he put in the gentleman's fingers instead of the penny and then restored the purse to the rich man's pocket.

"That donation will surprise him when he comes to life," thought the boy.

He mounted the horse again and rode up the street. As he passed the shop of his friend, the butcher, he noticed several pieces of meat hanging outside.

"I'm afraid that meat'll spoil," he remarked.

"It takes Time to spoil meat," answered the old man.

This struck Jim as being queer, but true.

"It seems Time meddles with everything," said he.

"Yes; you've made a prisoner of the most important personage in the world," groaned the old man; "and you haven't enough sense to let him go again."

Jim did not reply, and soon they came to his uncle's house, where he again dismounted. The street was filled with teams and people, but all were motionless. His two little cousins were just coming out the gate on their way to school, with their books and slates underneath their arms; so Jim had to jump over the fence to avoid knocking them down.

In the front room sat his aunt, reading her Bible. She was just turning a page when Time stopped. In the dining-room was his uncle, finishing his luncheon. His mouth was open and his fork poised just before it, while his eyes were fixed upon the newspaper folded beside him. Jim helped himself to his uncle's pie, and while he ate it he walked out to his prisoner.

"There's one thing I don't understand," said he.

"What's that?" asked Father Time.

"Why is it that I'm able to move around while everyone else is—is—froze up?"

"That is because I'm your prisoner," answered the other. "You can do anything you wish with Time now. But unless you are careful you'll do something you will be sorry for."

Jim threw the crust of his pie at a bird that was suspended in the air, where it had been flying when Time stopped.

"Anyway," he laughed, "I'm living longer than anyone else. No one will ever be able to catch up with me again."

"Each life has its allotted span," said the old man. "When you have lived your proper time my scythe will mow you down."

"I forgot your scythe," said Jim, thoughtfully.

Then a spirit of mischief came into the boy's head, for he happened to think that the present opportunity to have fun would never occur again. He tied Father Time to his uncle's hitching post, that he might not escape, and then crossed the road to the corner grocery. The grocer had scolded Jim that very morning for stepping into a basket of turnips by accident. So the boy went to the back end of the grocery and turned on the faucet of the molasses barrel.

"That'll make a nice mess when Time starts the molasses running all over the floor," said Jim, with a laugh.

A little further down the street was a barber shop, and sitting in the barber's chair Jim saw the man that all the boys declared was the "meanest man in town." He certainly did not like the boys and the boys knew it. The barber was in the act of shampooing this person when Time was captured. Jim ran to the drug store, and, getting a bottle of mucilage, he returned and poured it over the ruffled hair of the unpopular citizen.

"That'll probably surprise him when he wakes up," thought Jim.

Near by was the schoolhouse. Jim entered it and found that only a few of the pupils were assembled. But the teacher sat at his desk, stern and frowning as usual.

Taking a piece of chalk, Jim marked upon the blackboard in big letters the following words: "Every scholar is requested to yell the minute he enters the room. He will also please throw his books at the teacher's head. Signed, Prof. Sharpe."

"That ought to raise a nice rumpus," murmured the mischiefmaker, as he walked away.

On the corner stood Policeman Mulligan, talking with old Miss Scrapple, the worst gossip in town, who always delighted in saying something disagreeable about her neighbors. Jim thought this opportunity was too good to lose. So he took off the policeman's cap and brass-buttoned coat and put them on Miss Scrapple, while the lady's feathered and ribboned hat he placed jauntily upon the policeman's head.

The effect was so comical that the boy laughed aloud, and as a good many people were standing near the corner Jim decided that Miss Scrapple and Officer Mulligan would create a sensation when Time started upon his travels.

Then the young cowboy remembered his prisoner, and, walking back to the hitching post, he came within three feet of it and saw Father Time still standing patiently within the toils of the lasso. He looked angry and annoyed, however, and growled out:

"Well, when do you intend to release me?"

"I've been thinking about that ugly scythe of yours," said Jim.

"What about it?" asked Father Time.

"Perhaps if I let you go you'll swing it at me the first thing, to be revenged," replied the boy.

Father Time gave him a severe look, but said:

"I've known boys for thousands of years, and of course I know they're mischievous and reckless. But I like boys, because they grow up to be men and people my world. Now, if a man had caught me by accident, as you did, I could have scared him into letting me go instantly; but boys are harder to scare. I don't know as I blame you. I was a boy myself, long ago, when the world was new. But surely you've had enough fun with me by this time, and now I hope you'll show the respect that is due to old age. Let me go, and in return I will promise to forget all about my capture. The incident won't do much harm, anyway, for no one will ever know that Time has halted the last three hours or so."

"All right," said Jim, cheerfully, "since you've promised not to mow me down, I'll let you go." But he had a notion some people in the town would suspect Time had stopped when they returned to life.

He carefully unwound the rope from the old man, who, when he was free, at once shouldered his scythe, rearranged his white robe and nodded farewell.

The next moment he had disappeared, and with a rustle and rumble and roar of activity the world came to life again and jogged along as it always had before.

Jim wound up his lasso, mounted the butcher's horse and rode slowly down the street. Loud screams came from the corner, where a great crowd of people quickly assembled. From his seat on the horse Jim saw Miss Scrapple, attired in the policeman's uniform, angrily shaking her fists in Mulligan's face, while the officer was furiously stamping upon the lady's hat, which he had torn from his own head amidst the jeers of the crowd.

As he rode past the schoolhouse he heard a tremendous chorus of yells, and knew Prof. Sharpe was having a hard time to quell the riot caused by the sign on the blackboard.

Through the window of the barber shop he saw the "mean man" frantically belaboring the barber with a hair brush, while his hair stood up stiff as bayonets in all directions. And the grocer ran out of his door and yelled "Fire!" while his shoes left a track of molasses wherever he stepped.

Jim's heart was filled with joy. He was fairly reveling in the excitement he had caused when some one caught his leg and pulled him from the horse.

"What're ye doin' here, ye rascal?" cried the butcher, angrily; "didn't ye promise to put that beast inter Plympton's pasture? An' now I find ye ridin' the poor nag around like a gentleman o' leisure!"

"That's a fact," said Jim, with surprise; "I clean forgot about the horse!"

* * * *

This story should teach us the supreme importance of Time and the folly of trying to stop it. For should you succeed, as Jim did, in bringing Time to a standstill, the world would soon become a dreary place and life decidedly unpleasant.

—Frank L. Baum

Write your first impression of this story? Say whether you liked it or not and give your reasons. Do you agree with the moral at the end? Say why or why not. Does it fit with the story?

Grammar Study

Voice

There are two voices: active and passive. Voice is that property of verbs which indicates whether the subject acts (active) or is acted upon (passive). In English there is no separate verb form to show voice, so just as in mood and tense, it is shown by the use of a verb phrase with auxiliary verbs.

Example:

> Active: John struck Thomas.
> Passive: Thomas was struck by John.

In a passive sentence, the agent performing the action may appear in a "by the . . ." phrase or may be omitted, as in

> Your car has been towed.

There is no "by" phrase to indicate who towed the car.

Exercise A
Find the passive verbs in the sentences below and write them on your paper.

1. My command was promptly obeyed.
2. One of the men who robbed me was taken.
3. Now were the gates of the city broken down by General Monk.
4. Suddenly while I gazed, the loud crash of a thousand cymbals was heard.
5. Judgment is forced upon us by experience.
6. Nature is often hidden, sometimes overcome, and seldom extinguished.
7. Youth is always delighted with applause.
8. The hall was immediately cleared by the soldiers.
9. Just before midnight the castle was blown up.
10. My spirits were raised by the rapid motion of the journey.
11. A great council of war was held in the king's quarters.
12. Many consciences were awakened; many hard hearts were melted into tears; many a penitent confession was heard.

Exercise B
Change each of the sentences from Exercise A into active verb construction. If there is no "by" phrase in the sentence, you will have to supply a subject. Then say whether you think the sentence sounds better, or gives clearer meaning in the active or the passive voice.

Example: Your car has been towed
> The policeman towed your car.

Day 2

Guided Response

Reread the story "The Capture of Father Time" by Frank L. Baum and discuss the following questions.

1. Describe the boy in the story. Do you think his pranks were harmless? Explain, giving your reasons.

2. What would you have done if you had captured Time?

3. Make an outline of the story, charting the events in the order they happened.

4. Do you agree with the moral at the end of the story? Explain your answer. Do you think that it is an appropriate moral for the story? Explain your answer: If yes, say how the story matches it. If not, say why it does not match it. Write your own moral for this story.

5. Think of another abstract idea and imagine how it might be personified. For example courage might be personified as a soldier with a huge sword. What would happen if someone captured courage? Think of each of the following abstract nouns and think of a way to personify each one. Then imagine what would happen to the world if someone captured it.

Happiness	Mercy
Trust	Sorrow
Humor	Idea

NOTE: Frank L. Baum is the author of the much beloved "Oz" books which began with his first book *The Wizard of Oz*.

Grammar Study

A verb may have a passive form in each of the tenses of the indicative mood.

Present tense

Person	Singular	Plural
1st	I am struck	We are struck.
2nd	You are struck.	You are struck.
3rd	He/She/It is struck	They are struck

(Simple) Past Tense

Person	Singular	Plural
1st	I was struck.	We were struck
2nd	You were struck.	You were struck.
3rd	He/She/It was struck.	They were struck.

Future

Person	Singular	Plural
1st	I will be struck.	We will be struck
2nd	You will be struck.	You will be struck
3rd	He/She/It will be struck.	They will be struck.

Exercise A

Identify the verb in each of the following sentences and write it on your paper. Then write the tense, number, and person of each one.

1. The spears are uplifted; the matches are lit.
2. Burton was staggered by the news.
3. Thus was Corinth lost and won.
4. Old Simon is carried to his cottage door.
5. You will be surprised at her good spirits.
6. They are bred in the principles of honor and justice.
7. The prisoner was surrounded, pinioned with strong fetters, and hurried away to the prison of the great tower.
7. Nothing will be gained by hurry.
8. For my own part, I swam as Fortune directed me, and was pushed forward by wind and tide.
9. Some of the cargo was damaged by the sea water.
10. Our blows were dealt at random.

Exercise B

Choose 5 of the sentences above and change them from passive to active voice. Remember that if the sentence does no contain a "by" phrase, you will have to make up a subject for the sentence.

Example: George was ushered into the little drawing room.
Changed to:
Mother ushered George into the little drawing room.

Day 3

Writing

Today you will revise the story you wrote last week. Before you begin, please take a look at this student sample and answer the questions on the next page. (See the introduction for this story on Day 3 Week 12.)

Hudja-luv was shy about talking to Hudja-no because he was the son of a rich, fine, slick townsman who was mighty proud of his son. He didn't want Hudja-no to marry 'cepting to the right girl. So Hudja-luv stayed right on hankering after Hudja-no and Hudja-no went right on not knowing she was hankering after him, until one day Hudja-no was out for a ride with his father. A mountain lion, biggest you ever seen, name of Thunderin' Coyote, saw them and he says to himself he says,"I'm gonna make a meal of a six-foot-tall boy and his father." So he starts to stalk them, quiet like. Hudja-no and his father saw the lion but they kept on riding because they didn't know what to do. Then Hudja-luv came by. When she saw the mountain lion, she a gave a "Yaaaaahoo" so loud it turned the desert pink and purple and to this day it's called the painted desert. She got her lasso and lassoed the mountain lion and whirled it around a might, then let loose. It soared way up to the top of a mountain peak a mile away? And then Hudja-luv got her courage up and asked Hudja-no's father if she could marry him. But Hudja-no's father wasn't convinced she was the right girl. As he thought, a storm came on. He said to Hudja-luv, "If you can lasso me one of them lightning' bolts, you're the gal for me." So Hudja-luv took her rope and lassoed one of the lightning bolts, but just then it took off across the sky and pulled Hudja-luv up. For a minute, she dodged the thunder and clouds and big a big clap sent both the lightning bolt and Hudja-luv tumbling to the earth. They landed in a pool and the lightning bolt gouged out a new water channel. Today they call it the Mississippi River. So Hudja-luv and Hudja-no were married. On their wedding day, Hudja-no's father had got some new-fangled fireworks and one went off right under Hudja-no's father. He went a-shooting up into the air and Hudja-luv got to laughing. She laughed so hard she just couldn't stop, she just laughed and laughed and laughed, and some say she is laughing still.

1. Does this sample fit the description of a tall tale? (a larger-than-life, or superhuman, main character with a specific task, a problem that is solved in a humorous or outrageous way, exaggerated details that describe things larger than they really are, and characters who use everyday language)

2. Does this sample use "showing" as opposed to "telling" language (concrete nouns, vivid modifiers, action verbs)? Find places in the piece to explain your answer.

3. What revisions do see that need to be made to this piece? List them and or mark them on the text.

4. If you were the teacher of this student, what would say to him/her about her piece?

Now, try to look at your paper as if you are seeing it anew, or as if it is the paper of another student. Check for these things in your paper and make changes based on what you find.

A. **Paragraphing**: Do you have paragraphs that divide up the story into cohesive chunks? (one kernel of the story covered in one paragraph)
Have you made a new paragraph when the speaker changes?
Do the paragraphs move smoothly from one to another?

B. **Showing language**: Highlight every verb in your paper. How often are you using action verbs? Is there any place where you can change the verb to a stronger or more specific one? Is there any place where you have used the word "there" so that you were forced to use a state-of-being word in stead of an action word?

   Check for concrete nouns. Remove any abstract nouns until their use is central to your paper.

   Have you included enough modifiers to bring the action to life? In additional to simple adjectives and adverbs, a modifier can be an adjective phrase or clause, an adverb phrase, or an appositive phrase.

C. **Sentence Structure**: Go through your paper and for *each* sentence tell whether it is simple, compound, or complex. If you find you have a lot of simple sentences, combine them to make more elegant sentences.

   Simple sentences *can* be used for an effect, as in

   The ball came nearer and nearer, spinning on the wind. Bob's heart pumped. His hands sweat on the bat. He sighed. He could hardly catch his breath. Suddenly he swung his bat and heard the wondrous crack as . . .

   When possible, combine simple sentences to add variety, as in

George had always wanted to win the town bicycle race. He had practiced for months. His practice course was the town parade route.

Combined:

George had always wanted to win the town bicycle race, so he trained for months using the town parade route as his practice course.

D. Conclusion: Does your story come to a conclusion that solves the problem in the story? (Don't leave the reader hanging!) Your ending can be a foolish resolution to the problem since this is a tall tale.

E. Voice: Look at every sentences and check for any passive voice constructions. Change them to active and see if it is better way to say what you want to say. (Not all passive constructions are bad.)

For example, if you said: *The huge dragonfly was captured by Professor Magnum*, change it to *Professor Magnum captured the huge dragonfly*.

If the passive sentence does not have a "by" phrase, it is sometimes hard to tell whether a sentence is passive.

If you said: *The monster's eye was punctured*, change it to *Odysseus punctured the monster's eye*.

When you have completed your revision, ask someone to read your paper. Ask him/her to tell you if the story is entertaining and if they have any questions about it or suggestions to improve the paper.

When you are satisfied with it, file it in your drafts folder.

Day 4

Grammar Study

Voice

Review the distinction between active and passive voice. Write a sentence using each one.

Although most writers and teachers of writing encourage students to avoid the passive voice so that writing is more forceful, there are times when the passive voice is appropriate.

Reasons to use the passive voice:
The agent (doer) of the action is unimportant.
   The trench was dug by engineers.
The agent is unknown.
   Several papers were left on the table.
The agent is common knowledge, and mentioning it would be redundant.
   Eve was tempted with an apple.
The writer desires to control focus of sentence to either emphasize the person or thing receiving the action (1), or de-emphasize the "doers" role in the action (2).
   (1) Sam was picked up.
   (2) The fire alarm was pulled by the principal's son. (The passive shifts focus away from the son's responsibility.)

Reasons to use the active voice:
The active voice is shorter and more direct.
   Example:
   Active: The girl picked flowers all afternoon.
   Passive: The flowers were picked by the girl all afternoon.
The active voice is less awkward and clearly states relationship between subject and action.
   Example:
   Passive: The thief was kept from escaping by the dog.
   Active: The dog kept the thief from escaping.

Exercise A
Examine the passive voice constructions in the following sentences. Try to change them to the active voice and then decide if it's more appropriate to leave them in the passive voice.

1. Forty percent of the earth's oxygen is produced in the Amazon River valley.
2. My friend was interviewed by the police.
3. Andrew was treated at the hospital for a bad burn.
4. Today the museum is supported by gifts from private donors.
5. Certain prices are controlled by the government.

Exercise B

Parsing: Now that you have learned about mood, tense, and voice, you can include that information when you parse a sentence. Parse the following sentences including an explanation of the mood, tense, and voice of the verb in your explanation. Some sentences have more than one verb.

Example: The fox was waiting at the brown stump.

						adv	
						Prep phrase	
	Sub	**predicate**					
Adj	**N**	**V**	**V**	**P**	**adj**	**adj**	**N**
The	fox	was	waiting	(at	the	brown	stump).

Explanation: Fox is the subject; was waiting is the predicate (past progressive, indicative mood, active voice). At the brown stump is a prepositional phrase used as an adverb modifying waiting. Stump is the object of the preposition at.

1. If you were smiling, the camera did not notice.
2. The fox slipped quietly through the fence while the chickens were sleeping.
3. Release the prisoner into my custody.

Week 14

Day 1

Study the painting below and write your initial response to it.

Daniel Boone at Cabin on Osage Lake by Thomas Cole

Write your first impression of the painting. What tone is conveyed by the painting?

Writing

Figurative Language

Figurative language is used to create a special effect or feeling by going beyond the immediate meaning of the words used. A word or phrase is used to heighten the meaning by using comparative or exaggerated language; it means something other than what it first appears to mean. Figurative language always makes use of a comparison between different things. By appealing to the imagination, figurative language provides new ways of looking at the world. For example, "All the world's a stage."

Metaphor: A figure of speech in which a *comparison* is made between two things essentially unalike. *The shoppers were barracudas grabbing sale items from each other's arms.*

Simile: A figure of speech in which a comparison is expressed by the specific use of a word or phrase such as: *like, as, than, seems* or *as if. The devil is like a roaring lion.*

Symbol: A thing (could be an object, person, situation or action) which stands for something else more abstract. For example our flag is the symbol of our country.

Personification: A type of metaphor in which distinct human qualities, e.g., honesty, emotion, volition, etc., are attributed to an animal, object or idea.

Apostrophe: A figure of speech in which someone absent or dead OR something nonhuman is addressed as if it were alive and present.

Synecdoche: A figure of speech which mentions a part of something to suggest the whole. As in, "All hands on deck," meaning all sailors to report for duty. Hands = sailors.

Allegory or Parable: A poem in the form of a narrative or story that has a second meaning beneath the surface one.

Paradox: A statement or situation containing apparently contradictory or incompatible elements, but on closer inspection may be true.

Hyperbole: A bold, deliberate overstatement not intended to be taken literally, it is used as a means of emphasizing the truth of a statement.

Understatement: A situation is deliberately made to seem less important or serious than it is.

Idiom: Idioms are groups of words whose meaning is different from the ordinary meaning of the words. The context can help you understand what an idiom means. For example: "Put a lid on it." Our teacher tells us to put a lid on it. She's not really telling us to put a lid on something but to be quiet and pay attention.

Exercise A

Identify the figurative language in the following passages and say what kind of figures are used (see the list on the previous page).

1. Bowed by the weight of centuries he leans
   Upon his hoe and gazes on the ground,
   The emptiness of ages in his face,
   And on his back the burden of the world.

   > From the poem "The Man with the Hoe" by Edwin Markham.

2. When Spring, with dewy fingers cold,
   Returns to deck their hallow'd mould,

   > From the poem How Sleep the Brave" by William Collins

3. How is the valiant man fallen that delivered Israel.
   In his acts he was like a lion, and like a lion's whelp roaring for his prey.

   > From *The Hammer* by Alfred Church

4. a. To Bendeguz the words she spoke were like her elusive reflection in the water, the same words he knew but subtly different.

   b. Their happiness seemed to have touched a gentle chord in the wild hearts of the Hun warriors.

   > From *The White Stag* by Kate Seredy

5. The energy, the faith, the devotion which we bring to this endeavor will light our country and all who serve it—and the glow from that fire can truly light the world.

   > From the Inaugural Address of John F Kennedy, 1961

Exercise B

Write a sentence (or more if you like) including figurative language for each of the following subjects. Tell which figures you use.

1. desert
2. battleground
3. horse
4. light

Day 2

Guided Response

Study the painting by Thomas Cole reproduced on Day 1 and discuss these questions with your teacher.

1. What time of year is it in the painting? How can you tell?

2. Describe the kind of life Boone might have there near the lake.

3. What do you think Cole thinks about Boone by his portrayal of him?

4. What tone or mood is conveyed by the painting? What in the painting helps to give it the tone?

5. Examine the two following paintings and decide on the mood or tone they portray. Explain your answer using things from the painting (color, light, subject, setting, etc). Are either of them the same tone or mood as Cole's Daniel Boone at Lake Osage? Explain.

6. Write something (2 or 3 sentences) about each of the paintings that includes figurative language. (Think of the title of the paintings and see if something in the title can be understood figuratively.)

1. On the Fence by Winslow Homer

2. Twilight at Leeds New York by Winslow Homer

Writing

"Showing" Language: Copy Change Imitation

At various places in this course so far, we have reviewed "showing" writing, that is, the use of words and phrases that brings the scene to life for the reader: "showing" him the action instead of telling him about it. "Showing" writing includes the following characteristics: concrete nouns, action verbs, and strong modifiers.

Today you will examine a few professional pieces of "showing" writing and imitate the piece with your own topic by practicing *copy change*. *Copy change* is a writing exercise in which you take the structure and rhythm of the original author but insert a new topic. Here is a sample

Original: With the first dips in August's temperature, before the hardwoods' colors soften, mallards, canvasbacks, and other species of ducks gather in "families" and rehearse for their migration to the sloughs and waterways in the south.

Copy change: With the first notes suspended on the air, before the rapt crowd breathes, the violinist, cellists, and other members of the orchestra pause and release the crescendo with prefect timing and emotion in the final stroke.

Exercise

Carefully read the following passages and the notes that follow them. Then choose one to use for a copy change. To prepare for the copy change, notice what the author does (what is described first, second, and then how it ends).

1. I sat down in the middle of the garden, where snakes could scarcely approach unseen, and leaned my back against a warm yellow pumpkin. There were some ground-cherry bushes growing along the furrows, full of fruit. I turned back the papery triangular sheaths that protected the berries and ate a few. All about me giant grasshoppers, twice as big as any I had ever seen, were doing acrobatic feats among the dried vines. The gophers scurried up and down the ploughed ground. There in the sheltered draw-bottom the wind did not blow very hard, but I could hear it singing its humming tune up on the level, and I could see the tall grasses wave. The earth was warm under me, and warm as I crumbled it through my fingers. Queer little red bugs came out and moved in slow squadrons around me. Their backs were polished vermilion, with black spots. I kept as still as I could. Nothing happened. I did not expect anything to happen. I was something that lay under the sun and felt it, like the pumpkins, and I did not want to be anything more. I was entirely happy. Perhaps we feel like that when we die and become a part of something entire, whether it is sun and air, or goodness and knowledge. At any rate, that is happiness; to be dissolved into something complete and great. When it comes to one, it comes as naturally as sleep.

   From *My Antonia* by Willa Cather

Cather uses a variety of sentence structure patterns to beautifully illustrate the sense of contented happiness. She uses a mix of action and state of being verbs to create a vivid picture in the reader's mind. Highlight the action verbs. Underline the vivid concrete nouns and circle any particularly effective modifiers (these can be phrases or clauses, not just single words). If you choose this passage as your copy change model, you may stop after the words *I was entirely happy*.

2. Suddenly the last porter slipped. In what seemed to be the same instant I heard the ominous scraping of boot nails and, turning, saw a wildly gesticulating figure plunge sideways into the abyss. There was a scream as the next porter followed him. I remember frantically trying to dig into the ridge with my axe, realizing at the same time it would no more hold against the weight of the falling men than a pin stuck in a wall. Then I heard Nace shout, "Jump!" As he said it, the rope went tight about my waist and I went hurtling after him into space on the opposite side of the ridge. After me came the nearest porter.

   From *Island of the Blue Macaws* by
   James Ramsay Ullman

Ullman creates a feeling of fear and suspense as he recounts his climbing experience. He also uses a variety of sentence structure patterns and action and state of being verbs. Highlight the action verbs. Underline vivid concrete nouns and circle any effective modifiers.

Day 3

Writing

Creating a Mood—Setting a tone

Just as a painter creates a mood by his painting, so a writer creates a mood by his descriptions. Tone is the attitude of style or expression used to write. Mood is the emotion the writing delivers to the reader.

Today you will write the first draft of a description of a place that evokes a particular mood by the tone of the writing. Use as much showing writing as you can and use figurative language to intensify your images.

Here is the first paragraph of a student sample:

> Hands in my pockets, head thrown back against the wind, I ambled thoughtlessly along the sand. I heard nothing but the constant push and slush of the waves foaming at the tide's edge. A lone seagull, like me, landed near the water and tended thoughtfully to the sand. The sun, slipping now behind the fog was obviously leaving me, too. Forever, as far as I could see, the ocean stretched and then disappeared. My footsteps washed away with the repeating waves. It seemed like all around me, things were leaving, going, washing away.

Prewriting
Before you begin to write, choose a place to describe. Think of the mood that the place evokes in your mind. Is it a place that makes one feel happy, safe, contented, peaceful, joyful, sad? Do a 10-15 minute free-write on the place, writing everything you think of when you think of this place. After your free-write, decide what mood you will focus on for the paper. Perhaps you'll choose a different mood than the one you first thought of.

Writing
Write your first draft without worry about spelling, grammar, or form. Just get your ideas out. You want to describe the place such that the mood of it comes across. Use "showing" language and include some figurative language as you think of it.

After making your first draft, read it out loud to yourself and make any changes that seem necessary. Look for places where you can improve your sentences by changing to action verbs and including figurative images.

Save you draft for Day 4

Day 4

Grammar Study

Review Case of Nouns

Nominative: A noun or pronoun used as the subject of a sentence or subordinate clause or as a predicate nominative is said to be in the nominative case.

Objective: Nouns and pronouns used as direct or indirect objects, objects of verbals, and objects of prepositions are said to be in the objective case.

Exercise A
Identify the case of the underlined nouns in the passage below.

Although it was only four o'clock, the winter <u>day</u> was fading. The road led southwest, toward the streak of pale, watery <u>light</u> that glimmered in the leaden sky. The light fell upon the two sad young faces <u>that</u> were turned mutely toward it: upon the eyes of the girl, who seemed to be looking with such anguished <u>perplexity</u> into the future; upon the sombre eyes of the boy, who seemed already to be looking into the past. The little <u>town</u> behind them had vanished as if <u>it</u> had never been, had fallen behind the <u>swell</u> of the prairie, and the stern frozen <u>country</u> received them into its bosom. The homesteads were few and far apart; here and there a windmill gaunt against the <u>sky</u>, a sod house crouching in a hollow. But the great fact was the <u>land</u> itself, which seemed to overwhelm the little beginnings of human society that struggled in its sombre wastes. It was from facing this vast hardness that the boy's mouth had become so bitter; because he felt that men were too weak to make any <u>mark</u> here, that the land wanted to be let alone, to preserve its own fierce strength, its peculiar, savage kind of beauty, its uninterrupted <u>mournfulness</u>.

—From O Pioneers by Willa Cather

Exercise B
Review the grammatical forms we have discussed so far by parsing the following sentences. In addition to adding the tense, mood, and voice of the verb to your explanation, include the case and number (singular or plural) of each noun. You may do the explanation orally.

Example:

		adv								**adv**		
		(Prep phrase							**[adj clause (prep phrase)]**			

Subj pred

Adj	**N**	**V**	**adv**	**P**	**adj**	**N**	**P**	**adj**	**adj**	**N**	**PN**	**V**	**P**	**adj**	**adj**
The	road	led	southwest,	toward	the	streak	of	pale,	watery	light	that	glimmered	in	the	leaden

									Sub	**pred**

N
sky]).

Explanation: *road* is the subject (singular, nominative case), *led* is the predicate (past tense, indicative mood, active voice); *toward the streak of pale, watery light that glimmered in the leaden sky* is a prepositional phrase used as an adverb modifying *led*. *Streak* (singular, objective case) is the object of the preposition *toward*. *Of Pale watery light* is a prepositional phrase used as an adjective modifying *streak*. *Light* (singular, objective case) is the object of the preposition *of*. *In the leaden sky* is a prepositional phrase used as an adverb modifying *glimmered*. *Sky* (singular, objective case) is the object of the preposition *in*.

That glimmered in the leaden sky is an adjective clause modifying light.
That is the subject (singular, nominative case), *glimmered* is the predicate (past tense, indicative mood, active voice)

1. We were singing rhymes to tease Ántonia while she was beating up one of Charley's favourite cakes in her big mixing-bowl.

2. We had begun to roll popcorn balls with syrup when we heard a knock at the back door.

Writing

Even though we often think of descriptive writing as being more creative, it is mode of expository writing (informs, explains, describes, defines, or instructs). The point of it is to show or reveal something about your subject, and you want to do it in the most expressive way possible so that the reader can see what you see.

There are three characteristics of a purely descriptive essay:

- a descriptive essay has one, clear dominant impression. If, for example you are describing a snowfall, it is important for you to decide and to let your reader know if it is threatening or lovely; in order to have one dominant impression it cannot be both. The dominant impression guides the author's selection of detail and is thereby made clear to the reader in the thesis sentence.

- a descriptive essay can be objective or subjective, giving the author a wide choice of tone, diction and attitude. For instance, an objective description of one's dog would mention such facts as height, weight, coloring and so forth. A subjective description would include the above details, but would also stress the author's feeling toward the dog, as well as its personality and habits.

- the purpose of a purely descriptive essay is to involve the reader enough so he or she can actually visualize the things being described. Therefore, it is important to use specific and concrete details.

—Source: OWL at Purdue University

Reread the descriptive paper you wrote yesterday with these characteristics in mind. To what extent does your paper fit the description? Make any changes that seem needed as you read.

Then ask someone else to read your paper. Ask him/her if they can tell what mood you were trying to create or the dominate impression you were focusing on. Have as many people read it as you can and get feedback on how to improve the paper. Take notes on the comments of your readers.

Use the rubric on the following page to evaluate your draft. Think carefully and evaluate the job you have done. How would you score yourself in each of the categories: purpose, organization, elaboration, and use of language. Note places you would like to improve for a final draft.

File this draft and your self-scored rubric in your drafts folder.

Summertime by Mary Cassatt, 1894

Descriptive Essay Evaluation Rubric

	Audience and Purpose	Organization	Elaboration	Use of Language
Score 6	Creates a memorable main impression, supported with effective use of many sensory details.	Well organized, with strong transitions helping to link the words and ideas.	Vivid, sensory details support main idea; creative use of figurative language provides interesting comparisons	Varied sentence structure; good word choices.
Score 5	Creates a strong main impressions, supported with relevant sensory details.	Clearly organized, although an occasional lapse may occur.	Sensory details strongly support main idea; figurative language beginning to make interesting comparisons.	Some sentence variety and good word choices.
Score of 4	Creates a main impression, supported by sensory details.	Is consistently organized, although perhaps simplistically.	Sensory details support main idea. Figurative language used to create comparisons.	Sentence structures and word choices may be appropriate but are occasionally awkward.
Score of 3	May create a main impression, but does nor adequately support it with sensory details.	May have organization in parts, but lacks organization in other parts.	Details in support of main idea not consistently effective; attempts at figurative language not always successful or interesting.	Inconsistent control of sentence structure, and incorrect word choices
Score of 2	Sensory details may be present, but do not add up to a clear main impression.	Very disorganized, and not easy to follow.	Limited use of sensory details in support of main idea; no figurative language.	Problematic sentence structure and frequent inaccuracies in word choice.
Score of 1	Contains details that are unfocused or do not work in support of a clear main impression.	Lacks organization, and is confused and difficult to follow; may be too brief to assess organization.	No sensory details used in support of main idea; no use of figurative language	Little or no control over sentences and incorrect word choices may cause confusion.

— Adapted from Prentice Hall *Writing and Grammar Scoring Models*

Week 15

Day 1

Read this reflection and think about it.

Buds and Birds-voices

Balmy Spring—weeks later than we expected, and months later than we longed for her—comes at last to revive the moss on the roof and walls of our old mansion. She peeps brightly into my study window, inviting me to throw it open and create a summer atmosphere by the intermixture of her genial breath with the black and cheerless comfort of the stove. As the casement ascends, forth into infinite space fly the innumerable forms of thought or fancy that have kept me company in the retirement of this little chamber during the sluggish lapse of wintry weather—visions gay, grotesque and sad, pictures of real life tinted with nature's homely gray and russet, scenes in dreamland bedizened with rainbow-hues which faded before they were well laid on. All these may vanish now, and leave me to mold a fresh existence out of sunshine. Brooding Meditation may flap her dusky wings and take her owl-like flight, blinking amid the cheerfulness of noontide. Such companions befit the season of frosted window-panes and crackling fires, when the blast howls through the black-ash trees of our avenue, and the drifting snowstorm chokes up the wood paths and fills the highway from stone wall to stone wall. In the spring and summer time all somber thoughts should follow the winter northward with the somber and thoughtful crows. The old paradisiacal economy of life is again in force: we live, not to think nor to labor, but for the simple end of being happy; nothing for the present hour is worthy of man's infinite capacity save to imbibe the warm smile of heaven and sympathize with the reviving earth.

* * *

One of the first things that strikes the attention when the white sheet of winter is withdrawn is the neglect and disarray that lay hidden beneath it. Nature is not cleanly, according to our prejudices. The beauty of preceding years, now transformed to brown and blighted deformity, obstructs the brightening loveliness of the present hour. Our avenue is strewn with the whole crop of autumn's withered leaves. There are quantities of decayed branches which one tempest after another has flung down, black and rotten, and one or two with the ruin of a bird's nest clinging to them. In the garden are the dried bean-vines, the brown stalks of the asparagus-bed, and melancholy old cabbages which were frozen into the soil before their unthrifty cultivator could find time to gather them. How invariable throughout all the forms of life do we find these intermingled memorials of death! On the soil of thought and in the garden of the heart, as well as in the sensual world, lie withered leaves—the ideas and feelings that we have done with. There is no wind strong enough to sweep them away; infinite space will not garner them from our sight. What mean they? Why may we not be permitted to live and enjoy as if this were the first life and our own the primal enjoyment, instead of treading always on these dry bones and mouldering relics from the aged accumulation of which springs all that now appears so young and new? Sweet must have been the spring-time of Eden, when no earlier year had strewn its decay upon the virgin turf, and no former experience had ripened into summer and faded into autumn in the hearts of its inhabitants! That was a world worth living in.—Oh, thou murmurer, it is out of the very wantonness of such a life that thou feignest these idle lamentations. There is no decay. Each human soul is the first created inhabitant of its own Eden.—We dwell in an old moss-covered mansion and tread in the worn footprints of the past and have a gray clergyman's ghost for our daily and nightly inmate, yet all these outward circumstances are made less than visionary by the renewing power of the spirit. Should the spirit ever lose this power—should the withered leaves and the rotten branches and the moss-covered house and the ghost of the gray past ever become its realities, and the verdure and the freshness merely its faint dream— then let it pray to be released from earth. It will need the air of heaven to revive its pristine energies.

* * *

Thank Providence for spring! The earth—and man himself, by sympathy with his birthplace—would be far other than we find them if life toiled wearily onward without this periodical infusion of the primal spirit. Will the world ever be so decayed that spring may not renew its greenness? Can man be so dismally age-stricken that no faintest sunshine of his youth may revisit him once a year? It is impossible. The moss on our time-worn mansion brightens into beauty, the good old pastor who once dwelt here renewed his prime, regained his boyhood, in the genial breezes of his ninetieth spring. Alas for the worn and heavy soul if, whether in youth or age, it have outlived its privilege of springtime sprightliness! From such a soul the world must hope no reformation of its evil—no sympathy with the lofty faith and gallant struggles of those who contend in its behalf. Summer works in the present and thinks not of the future; autumn is a rich conservative; winter has utterly lost its faith, and clings tremulously to the remembrance of what has been; but spring, with its outgushing life, is the true type of the movement.

—Excerpted, Nathaniel Hawthorne in
The Oxford Book of American Essays

Write your first reaction to this excerpt. What images are the strongest? What sections are confusing? What is the tone and/or mood of the essay?

Writing

Voice

Voice has two meanings for writers:

- the author's style, the quality that makes his or her writing unique, and which conveys the author's attitude, personality, and character; or
- the characteristic speech and thought patterns of a first-person narrator; a persona.

Because voice has so much to do with the reader's experience of a work of literature, it is one of the most important elements of a piece of writing.

> "Voice is the sum of all strategies used by the author to create the illusion that the writer is speaking directly to the reader from the page."
>
> (Don Fry, quoted by Roy P. Clark, *Writing Tools*, 2006)

A combination of word choice and "view of the world" creates voice in your writing. When writing personal narrative and reflections, you want your own "voice" to come through. Critics will want to see if your voice is *authentic*, that is, if it *sounds* like the events really happened to you. When writing a story, the character's voice should come through.

Exercise

Think about each of the following pieces that are printed in this course and consider the author's voice. First say whether the piece is written in first person or third person. Then consider the style of the writing and say what mood the author creates. Then say what voice comes across in the piece of writing.

1. Ben Franklin's The Whistle
2. A Recollection of the Boston Tea Party
3. Jesuits Persuading the Indians (Week 5)
4. Capture of Father Time

Exercise B

Choose a well known fairy tale, folktale, or nursery rhyme and write it in a different voice than the original. For example, you can write "Little Red Riding Hood" as a policeman investigating the scene, or "Three Billy Goats Gruff" as an environmentalist studying the effects of animal grazing. You may alternatively, write one of the folktales from the point of view of one of the characters, writing in first person. For example, Cinderella from the perspective of the prince, or one of the step-sisters; or the Pied Piper taking the voice of the Piper or the one of the townspeople; or The Emperor's New Clothes from the perspective of the boy who called out.

Day 2

Reread the reflection essay "Buds and Bird-voices" on Day 1 and complete the following activities.

1. Highlight the parts in the essay that you think are the most descriptive.

2. Mark with an asterisk or a star the places where the authors changes from description to reflection.

3. Write the main idea of each paragraph.

4. What tone or mood comes across in the writing? Give example to show it.

5. Find at least 3 instances of figurative language and say what kind of figurative language it is.

6. What are the author's reflections about the start of spring (what does the start of spring make him think of)?

Writing

Voice

The elements of voice include diction, syntax, detail, imagery, and tone. All of these work together to create the voice of any particular piece.

Diction: Word choice is the most basic and important element.

Details: Facts, individual incidents.

Imagery: Brings the senses to life in words.

Syntax: Syntax is the grammatical structure of a sentence, the way words are arranged. Various sentence structures pace the writing and determine the focus.

Tone: Tone is the attitude of the speaker or writer as revealed in the choice of vocabulary or the intonation of speech.

Exercise A

Reread "Buds and Bird-voices" by Nathaniel Hawthorne. Find an example of each of the elements of voice in the essay and explain how your sample demonstrates the element. (For syntax, find a place where a shortened or lengthened sentence or an interesting grammatical formation changes the pace of the writing.)

> Example:
> **Diction** (word choice): One of the first things that strikes the attention when the white sheet of winter is *withdrawn* is the neglect and disarray that lay hidden beneath it.
>
> The word *withdrawn* here completes the comparison of the snow to a sheet on a bed. It has been pulled back, like a sheet being taken off a bed, to reveal the earth underneath. This sounds better than simply saying the snow has melted.

Exercise B

Choose one other piece from this course and analyze its voice by searching for the 5 elements discussed above. List each element and say how the elements are represented in the piece.

Day 3

Writing

Today you will write the first draft of a reflective essay. In a reflective essay the author reflects on an event or incident giving his own personal perspective on the event. This is not the same as a personal narrative where the author describes something that has happened to him and the significance of the event to his life. The writer takes personal events (including what he/she heard, saw, or read) and tells us how it reflects people or aspects of society. The goal of reflection is not to find "the answer" or to exhaust the subject. Rather, the goal is to explore ideas. Unlike the expository or the persuasive paper, in which you prove a particular point or take a certain side, the reflection essay does not necessarily seek to draw conclusions. The author merely explains his thoughts about something he has seen or experienced. For example, if the author has just seen a hockey game, perhaps he would reflect on the place of violence in the sport, what the fist fights and penalties do to the game.

This type of essay writing is often assigned as an entrance requirement to many colleges. They may ask you to reflect on your idea of education, or on the importance of family in your life. They may ask a rhetorical question, such as, *What is literature?* It is the style of writing used in many "blogs" and newspaper columns.

Reflective writing begins with a specific event and then moves into an abstract reflection about it.

Here is a possible outline of a reflective essay:

I.   Introduction
        A. Attention grabbing opening, perhaps an anecdote
        B. A hint at the significance or reflection

II.   Body
        A. Background information
        B. Details and narrative of the event observed
            1. including description
            2. including figurative language where appropriate
            3. including dialogue where appropriate
        C. A look back from the present
        D. Hint at significance or thoughts about the event
            1. interior monologue about significance

III.   Conclusion
        A. Significance of the event
        B. Statement about life, or what this event makes you think about life

Here is another possible outline, possibly a simplistic way of presenting the same material as in the previous outline:
I.   Involve the reader in the story by including interesting details, personal

experiences. The style must be very vivid and therefore to appeal to the reader as if it was conversation on the meaning of deep life issues.

II. The author expounds on his ideas on the topic.

III. The conclusion summarizes the main ideas and give a reflection on the author perception on the topic.

As a third possible outline, reread the excerpts from "Buds and Bird-Voices" printed on Day 1. Notice how the author weaves small reflections in and out of his description, but his largest, most broad reflection comes in the last paragraph.

There is no one definitive way to write the reflection, except that the reader must be lead through your description to the reflection and the reflection must make sense to the reader.

Prewriting

First you must think of a topic! Think about the things that have been going on in your life recently. Is there some topic that you have been wondering about? Did you observe something in nature that made you think of larger issues? Or perhaps you've made some observation about people in your life, people on your sports teams, people in your parish? Perhaps there is something you have heard on the news that you have ideas about.

If you have trouble finding a topic, consider one of these options:

What is love?
What is the culture of life?
Reflection on musical or theatrical performance you have participated in
The effects of singing on a person
How television the Internet shapes people's perceptions
Someone you look up to
What is friendship, or how do you know someone is a true friend

Once you decide on a topic, do a 10-15 minute free-write, writing anything that comes into your head on the topic. List all the questions that this topic makes you think of. Write details about the event, person, or issue. After your free-write, decide on the reflection that will go at the end of your paper and select the details that will be most important to include in your reflection.

Writing

Using your free-write and one of the outlines above, write your first draft of the reflective essay. Write without worrying about the conventions of grammar and spelling, just get your thoughts out.

Save your draft for Day 4.

Day 4

Writing

Reread the reflection by Nathaniel Hawthorne printed on Day 1. Then reread your reflection. Today you will do some revising of your paper.

Exercise A

As we stated in a previous lesson, the point of learning grammatical forms is to be able to use them purposefully in your writing, to ultimately improve your writing. Go through your paper now and see if you have any of the following constructions in your paper.

Adverb clause beginning a sentence
Adjective clause
Participle phrase beginning a sentence
Gerund
Compound sentence
Appositive phrase
Figurative language (metaphor, simile, personification, etc.)
Vivid, unusual adjectives

Revise your sentences to include the grammatical forms listed above at least once. If you find passive voice construction, try and change it to active voice. Then search and replace any overused, vague language, such as *a lot, great, really, there is, there are, there was, there were.*

Exercise B

Now that your have improved your paper, identify the elements of voice in your paper (diction, tone, syntax, images, details). Find an example of effective use of each of the elements in your paper and explain how your sample demonstrates the element.

Exercise C

Think critically about your paper and score it according to the rubric on the following page.

File your paper and your scoring sheet in your drafts folder.

Rubric for Reflection Essay

	4. Advanced	3. Above Average	2. Average	1. Below Average
Occasion for Reflection (thing experienced)	Meets all level 3. criteria and - memorably presents the experience for the reflection; -uses extended detail; - uses language to be convincing; - is creative and original; -reveals ideas through use of comparison and imagery.	- Presents the experience through use of concrete, sensory language, quotations and narrative accounts; - effectively focuses on a single subject, including related experiences and observations	- Does not go deep enough into the reflection; - talks too much about himself/ herself instead of the experience; - uses concrete details.	Assumes experience that prompted reflection is not explicitly described
Reflection	- Reveals feelings and thoughts through the presentation of the experience (showing as opposed to telling); - makes reader understand the abstract ideas underlying the reflection by using specific details.	-Is thoughtful and convincing; - reveals strong connection between the experience and the reflection; - analyzed the experience by looking at more than one angle; - explores the subject in personal and general reflections.	-Is limited to flimsy generalizations	- Uses only simple obvious statements
Writing Strategies	Effectively uses writing strategies to enhance reflection.	- Uses a variety of writing strategies; - uses specific, concrete details.	- Uses few purposeful writing strategies; - uses some details and sensory language.	Does not attempt to elaborate ideas or elaborates only through repetition of the initial statement.
Coherence and Style	- Consistently uses appropriate language; - Shows deep insight through a natural flow of ideas and an effective conclusion.	- Achieves unity through a natural progression of ideas; - uses precise language	- Uses only simple generic language; - has lapses in coherence; - has tendency to digress.	-Does not have coherence in writing; - is not organized

Grammar Study

Parsing

Review the grammar you have studied so far by parsing the following sentences. Remember that when you parse a sentence you tell the part of sentence and grammatical function of each word. You then explain the words and construction, giving all the information that is known about the word. This week we will add gender to the nouns. Tell whether each noun is nominative or objective case, singular or plural, masculine, feminine, or neuter. Your explanation may be done orally.

										Adv	
										(Prep phrase)	
	Sub	**Pred**		**DO**			**pred DO**				
Adj	**N**	**V**	**adj**	**N**	**C**	**adv**	**V**	**PN**	**P**	**adj**	**N**
Example: The	dog	caught	the	ball	and	obediently	set	it	(on	the	porch).

Explanation: *Dog* is the subject of the sentence (nominative, singular, neuter); *caught* and *set* are compound predicates (indicative mood, past tense, active voice). *Ball* is the direct object (objective case, singular, neuter) of the verb *caught*; *it* (3rd person pronoun, objective case, singular, neuter) is the direct object of the verb *set*. *Obediently* is an adverb modifying *set*. *On the porch* is a prepositional phrase used as an adverb modifying *set*. *Porch* (objective case, singular, neuter) is the object of the preposition *on*.

1. Our avenue is strewn with the whole crop of autumn's withered leaves.

2. Such companions befit the season of frosted window-panes and crackling fires,

when the blast howls through the black-ash trees of our avenue.

Week 16

Day 1
Read the following saint story.

Always Move Forward; Never Turn Back

Mexico: 1760's

The sun was setting, and Father Serra and his fellow priest were in the middle of nowhere. The two Franciscan priests were missionaries, and hardships were commonplace for them, but they bore these hardships with patience and good humor. They had conducted a parish mission in a distant village, and they were traveling on foot back to the seminary of San Fernando in Mexico City. The journey took many days. They had expected to make it to shelter before nightfall, but traveling in the wilderness of Mexico had taken longer than they had expected. The two priests were caught in the open with no shelter for the night. This was happened many times before in a country that was rich in wide open spaces, and the Franciscans were used to it. In the gathering dark, Father Serra began looking for a good place to spend the night in the open when he spotted what looked like a small dwelling in the distance.

As they made their way closer, they saw a small house standing behind three cotton wood trees. Would it offer them shelter? Knocking on the door, they were welcomed by a small family inside: a courteous man, his young wife, and their young son. The home was very poor by clean and tidy, and with humble dignity, the family offered the priests a simple meal and a place to sleep. The priests felt a deep peace as they watched the small boy play on the well-swept floor. Arising the next morning, they thanked the family for their kind hospitality, and went on their way.

Before long, they saw some men in a mule train. The gray robes of the Franciscan priests were a familiar sight in Mexico, and the muleteers greeted the priests amiably. But something puzzled them.

"Where did you spend the night, Fathers?" one of the men asked.

"In that small home over there, behind those three cottonwood trees," Father Serra gestured toward the tall tress in the distance behind them.

"I know this area well, Father," said the man. "There are no homes here for many miles around." So the muleteers and the Franciscans made their way to the three cottonwood trees. When they arrived, they were in for a surprise. There was no home there at all. Only the three cottonwoods stood as sentinels in the wilderness. Father Serra was astonished.

"Perhaps it was the Holy Family who offered us shelter," he said to his companions. He walked on to Mexico City with renewed vigor.

Father Junipero Serra was a man who had remarkable trust in God to help him in his difficulties as a missionary. Never seeking himself, he lived only to bring the joy of a life lived in Christ to the Indians of Mexico and California. He knew that God loved these people enough to give His Son to them, and to bring them to the faith in His Son as member of His church was Father Serra's goal. Father Serra placed complete trust in God as he took resolute steps to reach this goal, never looking back. He exemplified the virtue of perseverance in his life as a missionary.

Father Serra was from the Island of Mallorca, off the coast of Spain. He had joined the Franciscans while still in his teens, and after becoming a priest he rose to the rank of Doctor of Theology, and taught future priests in the Franciscan seminary. He was born to teach. He combined excellent scholarship and a true love of God and neighbor in a warm and outgoing personality. He seemed to make real the love of Christ to everyone he met.

He always wanted to be a missionary, but he had to wait, because he was much in demand as a professor and preacher. One day, news came that some missionaries had changed their minds, and some replacements had to be found in a hurry, for the ship headed for the New World was to sail soon. Father Serra and some of his former students, now Franciscan priests, volunteered immediately. They sailed for Mexico, and landed in Vera Cruz in 1749. Father Serra was thirty-six years old.

He spent nine years in the Sierra Gorda region as pastor to the Pame Indians, nine years as a traveling parish missioner, and two years managing the missions of Baja, California. But when he was asked to join an expedition to establish missions in Alta California (the present state of California), Father Serra accepted with joy: this was why he came to the New World! After a journey of over 600 miles, Father Serra finally reached California. He scouted a good site for a mission near the sea, and erected his first California mission cross on July 16, 1769 at Mission San Diego.

Curious Indians watch this ceremony, but missionary progress was slow. The Indians were at first uninterested in the teachings of the Franciscans, and stole whatever they could. Disease claimed many lives. Provisions ran out. A ship loaded with supplies never arrived. Nearly a year passed. Portola, the governor of Baja, California who was the leader of the expedition, decided that if a ship did not arrive by St. Joseph's Day (March 19), the expedition would go back to Mexico for good.

Go back? Father Serra wanted to go forward instead, so he began a novena, which is nine days of special prayer. He and his companions asked St. Joseph to pray for the success of their mission efforts. Then on the feast of St. Joseph, they spotted a sail! Two days later, a supply ship landed, and Father Serra gave thanks that the mission could go onward at last. Always, he persevered in prayer.

There were many difficulties in California. At first converts were few, and illness took its toll among the priests. But in time, Father Serra's persistence paid off, and soon groups of Indians asked for Baptism consistently each year. To safeguard the faith of the Indians, Father Serra established missions along the California coast so that their faith could grow in a Catholic environment.

Father Serra found the first nine missions in California: San Diego, San Carlos Borromeo, San Antonio, San Gabriel, San Luis Obispo, San Francisco, San Juan Capistrano, Santa Clara, and San Buenaventura. They were linked by a road called El Camino Real—The Royal Road. Father Serra traveled this road many times to serve his Indians during the fifteen years he spent in California, and one of his companions estimated that he traveled more than 24,000 miles over the years. He baptized over 6,000 Indians, almost ten percent of all the

California Indians.

Worn out from his work, Father Serra died in 1784 at age seventy at the Mission of San Carlos Borromeo in Carmel, and he is buried there. He is considered to be the father of the state of California. Beatified by Pope John Paul II in 1988, his life is an exemplary illustration of perseverance and abiding trust in God. His motto rings through the ages: "Always move forward, never turn back."

—Elaine Woodfield

Write you first impression of the essay. Consider the example of Father Serra for our lives. Consider the style of writing and the use of sentence variety.

Serra's Viaticum by Mariano Guerrero

Grammar Study

Sentence Structure

Find the following constructions in the essay about Father Serra and write the sentence in which the construction appears:

1. Compound sentence joined by "and."
2. Compound sentence joined by "but."
3. Adverb clause
4. Adjective clause
5. Noun clause
6. Participle phrase
7. Infinitive phrase

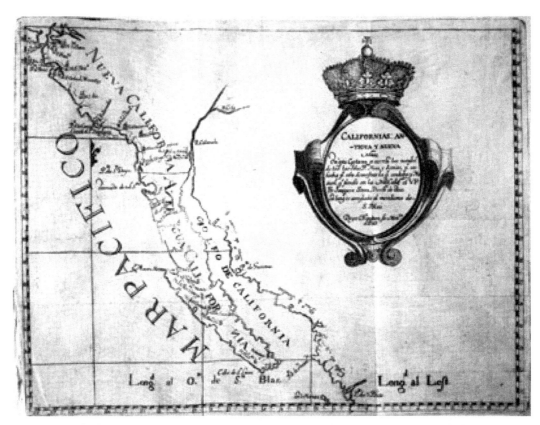

Map of California, 1787

Day 2

Guided Response

Reread the essay on Blessed Junipero Serra. This is an example of expository writing. Even though the author uses story telling techniques, the aim of the essay is to inform. Notice the structure of the essay. The author begins with an anecdote (a small story) to introduce us to the priest. Then the main part of her essay begins. She tells the life story of Father Serra chronologically choosing the events in his life that best exemplify her thesis and those which are necessary to lead us to those events. (For example, that he was a teacher does not directly support the thesis but it is included because we need to see how he became a missionary.)

What do you think is the thesis of the essay?

Copy the following outline on your paper and create an outline for the essay.

I.   Introduction
    A. Anecdote:
    B.
    C. Thesis statement:

II.   Body
    A. Early life
          1.
          2.
          3.
    B. Early Missionary experience
          1.
          2.
    C. Work in California
          1. Mission San Diego
               a.
               b.
               c.
          2. Other Missions
               a.
               b.

III. Conclusion
    A. End of life
          1.
          2.
    B.
    C.

Grammar Study

Sentence Combining

Combining sentences is an effective way to increase the maturity of your prose. Consider this student example:

> *He moved to the United States to play minor league baseball. Now he plays for the New York Mets.*

This sentence can be changed from sounding like an elementary student wrote it to sounding like a more mature writer composed it by simply combining the two sentences with a conjunction.

> *He moved to the United States to play minor league baseball, and now he plays for the New York Mets.*

Sentences can also be combined by changing one sentence into a word, phrase or clause.

> *Although he now plays for the New York Mets, he first moved to the United States to play minor league baseball.*

> *He first moved to the United States to play minor league baseball but now plays for the New York Mets.*

Exercise A

Combine the following sentences by changing one of the sentences into a word, phrase, or clause or by connecting the two sentences with a conjunction. Be sure to use proper punctuation. (Remember that two independent clauses joined with a conjunction must have a comma after the first clause before the conjunction.)

1. They burst out of the clouds into a shaft of light. All of this happened abruptly.
   —Madeleine L'Engle, *A Wrinkle in Time*

2. By afternoon, Perrault returned with three more dogs. He was the one who was in a hurry to be on the trail to Dawson.
   —Jack London, *The Call of the Wild*

3. He ate slowly. As he ate, he was hoping that in the days to come he'd be able to remember how good each mouthful had been.
   —Irene Hunt, *Across Five Aprils*

4. The thing one immediately noticed about him was his beautiful, crinkly, snow-white beard. I once heard a missionary say it was like the beard of an Arabian sheik. His bald crown only made it more impressive.

—Willa Cather, *My Antonia*

5. This boy was well dressed, too—well dressed on a week-day. This was simply astounding.

—Mark Twain, *Tom Sawyer*

6. The great shops of Boston which had been bringing wealth for over a hundred years were idle in their berths. Not one might come and go.

—Esther Forbes, *Johnny Tremain*

Exercise B

Imitate the structure of the new sentence you created in Exercise A to write a new sentence of your own topic.

For example,

> *Although he now plays for the New York Mets, he first moved to the United States to play minor league baseball.*

Imitation: *Although she now has many dolls, her first doll remains the dearest in her heart.*

Day 3

Writing

This week you will begin to write an expository essay for which you will do research. Although, your main purpose is to inform, you may use story telling anecdotes in your writing.

Today you will decide on your topic, begin your research, and decide on a thesis statement or controlling idea about your topic. Follow the steps listed below.

Prewriting

1. First, you must pick a topic. You may research an American saint, as Mrs. Woodfield did in the essay "Always Keep Going; Never Turn Back." Or, you may choose any topic that interests you or that you have always wanted to find out about. If you play the violin, perhaps you'd research the origin of the instrument. If you love football, perhaps you'd research the development of the game. If you love knitting, perhaps you'd choose one fiber to research and explain how yarn is made from it.

2. Once you have your topic, create a "Know, Question, Learn" chart. (See sample on the next page.) In the "Know" column, list all the things that you already know about your topic. In the "Question" column list the things you'd like to find out. These will be the things that you will search for in your research. As you learn things about the topic, or answer your questions, fill in the "Learn" column. You may need more space for what you learn than is on the chart, so feel free to use the whole back side of you paper to take notes. Find at least 2 sources for your information.

3. You may find that your topic is too broad and that you will need to narrow it down. For example, if you want to report on Medieval knights, perhaps you would narrow it to the process for becoming a knight, or to the equipment that a knight used.

4. After you have researched and answered the questions you had about the topic, you must decide on a focus for your paper. In Mrs. Woodfield's essay about Blessed Serra, she decided to focus on his perseverance and trust in God. This focus becomes the controlling idea or thesis of her paper. Your paper is ordered to presenting information that supports your thesis, not as a strict proof as in a persuasive paper, but as parts to a whole. The parts of your paper complete a whole picture with the thesis statement as its caption.

Citing Your Sources

As you take notes keep track of where you get your information. Here is an easy way: Write your sources at the top or bottom of your note taking chart. Number each source. Next to each fact you write down, put the number of your source next to it.

If you use the Internet, do not copy and paste information from a website into your paper—that's plagiarism! Take notes of what you find on the Internet, noting the website and date you visited the site. Then when you go to write your paper, write from *your* notes.

Avocado

KNOW	QUESTION	LEARN
grows in California has "good" oils grows on trees (smallish trees) used to make guacamole soft green flesh	What are the health benefits? Where did it originate? What are the main varieties?	Avocado is a fruit (2) Fuerte main CA avocado until Hass variety in 1935 (2) -contains 81 mg of lutein for healthy eyes (1) -contain 20 vitamins and minerals (1) -contains 76 mg beta-sitosterol to maintain healthy cholesterol levels (1) -nutrient booster allows body to absorb more fat-soluble nutrients (1)

Sources

① www.avocado.org/healthy-living/nutrition

② Encyclopedia Britannica

Thesis Statement: Avocadoes are a nutritious addition to any diet.

Day 4

Writing

Today you will continue to research your topic for the expository paper. At a certain point in your research, the idea for your thesis statement will become clear to you. Please note the thesis statement about avocadoes on the previous page. I chose that thesis because as I researched avocadoes, I was amazed at their nutritional benefits.

Once you have your research complete and have selected a thesis statement (focus for your paper), you can begin to outline your paper. For now, simply write "introduction" for that part of your paper, and focus on outlining the body of the paper.

For the body, begin by grouping the information you found into categories.

Avocadoes

What they look like

How they are grown

The nutritional benefits

These groupings will become the major divisions of your outline. Create an outline from your research following the basic structure of the outline in Day 2. In your outline, jot notes from the facts you have gathered. Keep the number of the source of your information right with the fact. Study the sample below. Notice that if the fact is copied directly from the source, it is put in quotes. The number in parenthesis at the end of the fact corresponds to the source list.

> C. Nutritional benefits of avocadoes
>   1. fatty oils
>   a. one serving contains 165 mg omega-3 fatty acids; 2534 mg omega- 6 fatty acids 2534 mg (1)
>   b. why fatty acids are important
>   1. essential to body, but the body can't make them (4)
>   2. control blood pressure, cholesterol, prevent heart disease (4)
>   2. Lutein
>   a. One serving contains 81 mg of lutein (1)
>   b. Importance of lutein
>   1. antioxidant improving health of eyes and skin (3)
>   2. research shows it may reverse symptoms of macular degeneration. (3)

3. other research show "higher levels of lutein in the serum may be linked with less thickening of arterials walls" lessening risk of heart attack. (3)
3. Vitamins and Minerals
    a. fruit contains over 20 (1)
       1. list of most important nutrients (1)
    b. contains 76 mg beta-sitosterol which maintains healthy cholesterol levels (1)
    c. nutrient booster (1)

Once you have your outline complete, set it aside until next week.

Grammar Study

Sentence Combining

Find at least three places in the any of the stories and essays in this text where you can combine sentences. Write the new sentence on your paper.

Sample: *Only the three cottonwoods stood as sentinels in the wilderness. Father Serra was astonished.*

Revision: Father Serra was astonished to see only the three cottonwoods standing as sentinels in the wilderness.

Be sure to tell from which story you took your sentences.

Week 17

Day 1

Read the following expository essay and reflect about it.

A Confident Humility: Venerable Father Solanus Casey

Detroit, Michigan: 1920s

When the young mother walked into the waiting room, she was looking for a miracle. Her baby boy had an infection of the mastoid bones at the base of the skull, and his fever was 108 degrees. In those days, there was little anyone could do to cure this disease. The baby was not expected to live. His mother's journey to the waiting room was a journey of faith because the waiting room was not that of a doctor, but of a Capuchin monastery. She was seeking Father Solanus.

Father Solanus was the doorkeeper, or porter, of the monastery. He was so kind that people made special trips to the monastery just to visit him. The waiting room was full of these people, each with a problem: illness, unemployment, alcoholism, lack of faith, worries about a loved one. Finally it was her turn to see him. The woman took a seat next to his desk, holding her baby on her lap, and told him all about her baby's illness. Father Solanus gave her his undivided attention, and his gaze was kind and patient.

"My baby is going to die. Can you help?" She asked. When she finished speaking, the priest recommended enrolling the baby boy in the Seraphic Mass Association. He filled out the membership card and accepted the woman's fifty cents as dues. Members of the SMA

 share in all the masses said by all Capuchin missionaries throughout the world, and the dues go to help the lepers whom the missionaries serve.

"After all, there is great power in the Mass," he said, smiling at the woman. He blessed the baby boy, and said to the mother, "Have confidence in God's mercy. He'll be better by morning." Her worries eased a little, and the woman went home. Just a few hours later, the baby boy's fever disappeared. The woman was so overjoyed that she returned to the monastery that same evening to thank Father Solanus in person. Father told her to thank God instead because man has a duty to thank God for all His blessings, and he spoke to her about the power of the Mass. He seemed to have no idea that he had anything to do with the cure. But the woman believed, as many people did, that Father Solanus's prayers also were very powerful in obtaining the miracle for her son. In Father Solanus's waiting room, miracles were constant.

Father Solanus was a man of great humility because he was unaware that he was instrumental in so many cures, miracles, and favors from Heaven. He would never take any credit for any miracle, believing himself to be merely a servant of God. He also was a man of complete confidence in God, and was sure that God would answer prayer, especially prayer associated with the Mass. Father Solanus would urge people seeking "favors" to "thank God ahead of time" as an act of faith in God's answer to prayer.

Father Solanus was so humble that nothing shocked or offended him; as a result, he could be an instrument of grace. One man fought a losing battle with alcoholism. He had been a successful accountant, but he became addicted to alcohol. His life fell apart, and he found himself living in a seedy hotel, living only for drink. He heard a talk by Father Solanus which inspired him to give up drinking for good. But his body fought back, and he went through a terrible withdrawal. Wandering the streets, he ended up at Father Solanus's door. Father noticed his condition and took him to a private office, where the man poured out his trouble to him. In those days, alcoholism was considered to be a moral failing, and shame nearly paralyzed the man. But Father Solanus was kindly.

"When did you get over your sickness?" he asked compassionately. This surprised the man, who had never heard alcoholism described this way.

"My sickness? You mean my drunk, Father," he replied. They both laughed at this and the man felt his terrible feeling disappear, and peace take its place. He never took another drink. Returning to normal life, he practiced accounting again, and became a generous donor to charities run by the Capuchins.

Father Solanus had humility enough to pray to God for every need, and confidence enough to believe that every prayer is heard. Father Solanus established the Capuchin Soup Kitchen to feed the many poor people who came to the monastery. One day, they ran out of bread. "Let's pray a Hail Mary," suggested Father Solanus, and everyone joined in prayer. As they finished, a man with a huge basket of bread walked in the door. He had a whole truckful from a bakery that had baked more than they needed that day.

He learned humility and confidence through deep disappointment. He was born Barney Casey in 1870 in Wisconsin, one of ten children of a close-knit Irish farming family. He quit school early to support the family farm by working a variety of jobs: prison guard, logger, streetcar motorman. But he wanted to be a priest, and finally entered the seminary at age 21 in Milwaukee. Classes were taught in German and Latin, and Barney did not know either language. He struggled to learn them and to keep up in class, but he was not successful, and after four years, he returned home; his superiors suggested that he apply to a religious order.

A priest friend suggested that Barney write to the Jesuits, the Franciscans, and the Capuchins (a stricter branch of the Franciscans), and then make a choice. Barney made a novena to prepare for the Feast of the Immaculate Conception, and asked Our Lady to guide his choice. Attending Mass on the feast, he heard the words, "Go to Detroit," and he knew that he should join the Capuchins, who had a novitiate there. He received the Capuchin habit and the name Francis Solanus, after a famous missionary in Latin America.

Solanus struggled with his studies, and some of his superiors did not think that he was prepared for the priesthood, but none doubted his goodness. He was ordained on July 24, 1904 as a simplex priest—one who can say Mass but cannot hear confessions or preach a formal sermon. Father Solanus never complained, but this was a humiliating cross for him. But he decided to make the best of whatever happened to him, and have confidence in God to use him however He wanted. His superiors assigned him to be the monastery doorkeeper and news of the "holy priest" spread. Father Solanus enrolled nearly everyone in the SMA, and miracles became so constant that his superiors suggested that he keep a notebook of petitions and answers. These notebooks are now being studied by those involved in Father Solanus's cause for sainthood.

Father Solanus served in New York, Michigan, and Indiana, leaving a trail of miracles, healings, and love for the Mass behind him. He died in Detroit on July 31, 1957 at age eighty-seven, his dying words a final testimony to his confident humility: "I give my soul to Jesus Christ."

—Elaine Woodfield

Write your first impression of this essay. Include what you think we can learn from the life of Venerable Solanus Casey. How is his way to holiness similar to other saints about which you have heard?

*I'm offering my suffering that all might be one. If only I could see
the conversion of the whole world.*
—Father Francis Solanus

Grammar Study

Sentence Variety Using Phrases

Review the phrases we have discussed so far in this text: prepositional, infinitive, gerund, participle, and appositive. How is each one used? Remember that the preposition, infinitive, gerund, participle and appositive can have an object.

Exercise A
Label each of the following underlined phrases indicating what kind of phrase it is. What is the object of each phrase.

1. Sam showed us how to get to his house by <u>drawing a map in the sand.</u>
2. The boys <u>in the choir</u> competed at the state competition.
3. <u>Munching a piece of straw,</u> the boy ambled down the road.
4. Mr. Humboldt, <u>the teacher of our environment class,</u> was interviewed on the nightly news.
5. Whenever we want <u>to swim a lap or two,</u> we just walk across the road to the pool.

Exercise B
Identify the phrases underlined in each of the following sentences. Then imitate the sentence by writing one of your own topic.

Example: The woman took a seat next to his desk, <u>holding her baby on her lap,</u> and told him all about her baby's illness.

Participle phrase, used as an adjective modifying *woman*

Imitation: The boy shuffled slowly out the door, holding his puppy in his arms, and wished he didn't have to take a bath.

1. <u>Attending Mass on the feast,</u> he heard the words, "Go to Detroit," and he knew that he should join the Capuchins, who had a novitiate there.

2. His mother's journey <u>to the waiting room</u> was a journey of faith because the waiting room was not that of a doctor, but of a Capuchin monastery.

3. But he decided <u>to make the best of whatever happened to him,</u> and have confidence in God to use him however He wanted.

4. He quit school early to support the family farm by <u>working a variety of jobs: prison guard, logger, streetcar motorman.</u>

5. Father Solanus was the doorkeeper, <u>or porter,</u> of the monastery.

183

Day 2

Guided Response

Reread the essay "A Confident Humility: Venerable Father Solanus Casey" and discuss the following questions with your teacher.

1. What parts of the life of Father Solanus described in this essay do you think are the most interesting? How could you implement his style of holiness in your life?

2. How does the author *show* the "confident humility" of Father Solanus? Find specific places in the text and explain them.

3. Think carefully about the biography of Fathers Serra and Casey. What do Father Junipero Serra and Father Solanus Casey have in common?

4. Consider the organization of the essay. Notice the chronological order of the events Mrs. Woodfield reports. She begins with stories that take place while Father Solanus is a Capuchin. Then she goes back and tells the story of how he became a priest. What is the effect of this mixing up the order of events? Do you think it is an effective way to organize the paper? Explain your answer.

5. Listed below are the various patterns normally used in an expository paper. Which pattern is used in this essay? Which pattern is used in the essay about Father Serra in Week 16? Which pattern is used in the essay about beavers in Week 6? Explain how you can tell.

   Description: The author describes a topic listing features, characteristics, and examples, using words such as *for example, characteristics are.*

   Sequence: The author lists items or events in chronological order, using words such as *first, second, third, next, finally.*

   Compare and Contrast: The author explain how two or more things are alike or different, using such words as *different, in contrast, alike, same as, on the other hand.*

   Cause and Effect: The author list one or more causes and the resulting effects, using words such as *reasons why, if . . . then, as a result, therefore, because.*

   Problem and Solution: The author states a problem and lists one or more solutions, using words such as *problem is, dilemma is, is solved, question answered, can be resolved.*

   Narrative Interspersion: The author includes narration within the expository text to clarify, elaborate, or link the subject to personal experience.

Writing

If you have not finished the research and outline for the topic that you chose last week, complete that work. Then you will move on to writing the introduction of the paper.

The Introduction

The purpose of the introduction is to present your topic and main idea to the reader. You need to capture your reader's attention, give background on the topic, develop interest in the topic, and guide your reader to the thesis—all neatly packaged in one or two paragraphs. Here are a few ways to being the introduction:

- **Anecdote** (like the essays about Father Serra and Father Solanus Casey)
  Be sure the anecdote is short and leads directly to your thesis. Otherwise your reader may get lost in the story and not get the point of your paper.
- **Dialogue**
  You do not have to identify the speakers. Keep it short with only a few exchanges and then elaborate on the dialogue in two or three sentences.
- **Summary**
  You can use general information about your topic and then narrow it, gradually becoming more specific, as your lead the reader to your thesis statement.
- **Startling information or fact**
  This information must be true and you must elaborate on it showing how it fits with your thesis.
- **A question**
  Sometimes students overuse this method. Be sure that the question will generate interest. Elaborate in a few sentences and then move to your thesis.
- **A quotation**
  Choose a quote by someone with experience with your topic. Elaborate in a few sentences. It must be clear to the reader how this quote fits with your topic and your thesis.

Do not reference yourself in the introduction or say something like "I'm going to tell you about . . . "

Write several versions of your introduction and set them aside until tomorrow.

Day 3

Writing

Today you will write the body of your expository essay. Review the patterns of expository essays on the previous page and decide what pattern your paper follows. Remember that the purpose of an expository essay is to deliver information. You do not have to develop an argument or prove anything; you only have to understand your topic and present it to the reader in an understandable way.

Using the outline you have made, write the essay. Make a new paragraph for each division in your outline. Remember to use transitions to move the reader logically through your points. Please see the transition chart in the appendix when choosing words to begin and end your paragraphs. You can use story telling as Mrs. Woodfield does in her saint biographies. But, this is not the time for emotional appeals or personal opinion; just report on the facts in a concrete and expressive way. Remember the this will be a first draft of your essay. Try to make your thoughts understandable and write without worrying about spelling and punctuation.

When you are done, read the body of the essay out loud to yourself. Make any changes that come to your mind as you read. You may share it with someone if you want to get input.

Then save your draft for Day 4.

Day 4

Writing

Reread the introductions to your paper that your wrote on Day 2. Reread the body of your essay that your wrote on Day 3. Decide which introduction goes best with your essay. You may find that you need to rewrite your introduction to match what you wrote in the body of the essay.

Transitions
Check for transitions in the body of your paper. Review the "hook" transition. The first sentence of the paragraph includes something from the previous paragraph.

> **Sample #1** "hook" transition which links key ideas from one paragraph to another.
> The War of Independence or the American Revolution saw Anglo-Americans desiring to be free from British rule and to form their own nation. Would such a desire spread to the French in Quebec? Would Britain lose all its colonies in North America?

As history has shown, *in a rather ironic way, Canada did remain British because it was French.*
To begin to understand the irony of these events in Canadian history, one must ask the question, why did the French in Quebec, known as les Canadiens, not support the American Revolution? After all, it would have been an opportunity for them to be liberated from their British conquerors.

Sample #2 "Hook" transition

Habitats for animals were not drastically changed; indeed, *the tropical ecosystems* were much the same as before because the small coffee trees growing near the ground didn't require any forests to be cleared or plants eliminated.
These ecosystems were changed forever with an American innovation. In 1970, agricultural scientists decided to develop a new, high-yield coffee plant that grew only in the full sun. Farmers were easily convinced to adapt to this modernization because they could produce five times more coffee than before.

Sentence Combining
Check your sentence structure throughout the essay. Is there any place where sentences can be combined to make the writing flow more easily? Can one sentence be added as a clause or phrase to another? Are some sentences better short and choppy to make a point?

Conclusion
Today you will write the conclusion to your paper. Sometimes the conclusion is the most difficult part of your paper to write. You want to remind your reader of your thesis in a graceful way, leaving the reader satisfied, but you don't want to simply reiterate what you wrote in the introduction. Keep in mind that the closing is also probably what the reader will remember most from your paper. Keep it short!

Possible Strategies for closing up the paper:

Echoing the introduction (do not simple repeat the thesis, but tie the ending into your
    Introduction)
Challenge the reader to find out more
Look to the future (talk about consequences or implications)
State what action needs to be taken
Explain why the topic is important
Pose a question
Give a *short* anecdote
Describe a powerful image
Give a thought-provoking quotation
Give an interesting thought, something profound for the reader to consider

You should not introduce any totally new ideas in the conclusion; however, you should not merely repeat your thesis either. You want to synthesize your ideas, not summarize them.

Strategies to avoid
Do not begin with unnecessary, overused phrases such as "in conclusion," "in summary," or "in closing."
Do not state the thesis for the very first time in the conclusion.
Do not introducing a new idea or subtopic in your conclusion.
Do not end with a rephrased thesis statement without any changes.
Do not make sentimental, emotional appeals that are out of character with the rest of an analytical paper.
Do not include evidence (quotations, statistics, etc.) that should be in the body of the paper.

Look at the closing paragraphs of the two saint biographies you have read the last two weeks:

Father Solanus served in New York, Michigan, and Indiana, leaving a trail of miracles, healings, and love for the Mass behind him. He died in Detroit on July 31, 1957 at age eighty-seven, his dying words a final testimony to his confident humility: "I give my soul to Jesus Christ."

Worn out from his work, Father Serra died in 1784 at age seventy at the Mission of San Carlos Borromeo in Carmel, and he is buried there. He is considered to be the father of the state of California. Beatified by Pope John Paul II in 1988, his life is an exemplary illustration of perseverance and abiding trust in God. His motto rings through the ages: "Always move forward, never turn back."

Once you have written your conclusion and are satisfied with it, file your paper in your drafts folder.

Grammar Study

Parse the following sentences using the format you have learned. You may give the explanation orally with your teacher. Go in this order

1. Identify part of speech of each word.
2. Identify the parts of the sentence (As you tell the parts of the sentence give the case, number and gender of nouns and the tense, mood, and voice of verbs.)
3. Identify clauses and their subjects, predicates, and complements.
4. Identify verbals and phrases and their objects and modifiers and tell how they are used.
5. Explain the modifiers.

Example: The baby was not expected to live.

					Infintive
	Sub	**pred**		**pred**	
Adj	**N**	**V**	**adv**	**V**	**V**
The	baby	was	not	expected	to live.

Explanation: *Baby* (nominative, singular, neuter) is the subject, *was expected* (past progressive, indicative mood, active voice) is the predicate. *To live* is an infinitive used as the direct object of the verb *was expected. Not* is an adverb modifying *was expected.*

1. His superiors assigned him to be the monastery doorkeeper and news of the "holy priest" spread.

Challenge:
2. He quit school early to support the family farm by working a variety of jobs: prison guard, logger, streetcar motorman.

Week 18
Review Unit 2

Day 1

Study the following painting.

On His Holidays by John Singer Sargent

Free write: Think about the painting and write freely on whatever you are inspired by the painting to write. You may write a story, a description, or a poem.

Grammar Study

Review

Review the following grammatical forms. Explain each one and demonstrate it in a sentence.

Nouns
1. Concrete and abstract nouns
2. Collective nouns
3. Appositives

Verbs
1. Verb phrases
2. Mood
3. Tense
4. Voice

Phrases
1. Appositive
2. Gerund
3. Participle
4. Infinitive

Day 2

Writing

This week you will choose one of the papers you have written in the unit to make a final copy. This is the last step in the writing process: publishing. You will want to revise your paper to improve the writing and then finally correct for spelling and punctuation.

Review the papers in your drafts folder. Discuss them with your teacher and decide which one represent your best writing or has the best potential for a perfected final draft.

- Tall Tale/Legend
- Description (mood)
- Reflection
- Expository (research)

Once you have selected your paper, begin by reading it carefully. Try to be objective and make changes that you think will improve the paper. Then you will seek feedback about your paper. Find someone who will read or listen to you read your paper. After reading or listening to the paper, ask your reader/listener the following questions:

1. What do you think is the best thing about this paper?

2. **Tall Tale**: Do you think this story seems like an "authentic" American tall tale or legend?

   Description: Can you tell what mood I was trying to convey through this description?

   Reflection: Can you tell what I thought about this event?

   Expository: Do you know what my thesis statement is in this paper?

3. What questions remain in your mind after reading the paper?

4. What suggestions do you have that might improve the paper?

After reading or discussing your reader/listener's comments, make any changes that you think are appropriate. Set your paper aside until Day 3.

Grammar Study

Parse the following sentence.
1. Identify the part of speech of each word.
2. Identify the parts of the sentence (As you tell the parts of the sentence give the case, number and gender of nouns and the tense, mood, and voice of verbs.)
3. Identify subordinate clauses and their subjects, predicates, and complements. (When labeling the words on your paper, label the subject, verb, and complement of the subordinate clause *under* the sentence so that it's not confused with the subject and verb of the main clause.)
4. Identify verbals and phrases and their objects and modifiers and tell how they are used.
5. Explain the modifiers.

After we watch the movie, we will walk down the street, looking in the fancy shop windows.

Day 3

Writing

Today you will make a final copy of the paper you have chosen from this unit. Review your revisions from Day 2. Decide if any other revisions need to be made. Then go over each line on the Revision Checklist on the following page to be sure you have thought about every area.

One item on the checklist has not yet been addressed in this course: the comma splice. A comma splice occurs when two independent clauses are joined with a comma but no conjunction. (I wanted to eat some ice-cream, we had no ice-cream.) It's basically a punctuated run-on sentence. It can be corrected in several ways.

Semi-colon
I wanted to eat some ice-cream; we had no ice-cream.

Conjunction
I wanted to eat some ice-cream, but we had no ice-cream.

Create two sentences
I wanted to eat some ice-cream. We had no ice-cream.

Once you have checked your paper for everything on the list, make a final copy. You may type it or write it in your best handwriting.

File it in your writing portfolio.

Revision Checklist

Organization/Structure

Does the paper seem appropriate to the audience—your peers)? (What makes it so?)

Have the ideas been adequately developed?

Are all paragraphs unified and coherent?

Is there an inherent logical order evident in the placement of each paragraph? (Paragraph location is purposeful and logical.)

Do the paragraphs flow smoothly from one to another?

Does each paragraph serve a logical purpose?

Could any of the sentences be written more concisely without losing meaning? Could any of the sentence be combined to introduce more variety?

Are the sentences clear and complete?

Are there sentences that announce what you are going to say or that sum up what have already said, ***and therefore could be cut***?

Style and Voice

Minimal use of passive voice

Use of specific details ("Showing" language with action verbs and concrete nouns)

Consistency of verb tense

Minimal use of forms of "to be"

Varied sentence structure, rhythm, and length

Word choice: clear, effective, concise

Grammar, Punctuation, Spelling

Pronoun-antecedent agreement
Subject-verb agreement
No sentence fragments or run-ons
Quotations places correctly
No comma splices
Correct spelling

Day 4

Grammar Study

Parse the following sentences.

1. Identify the part of speech of each word.
2. Identify the parts of the sentence (As you tell the parts of the sentence give the case, number and gender of nouns and the tense, mood, and voice of verbs.)
3. Identify subordinate clauses and their subjects, predicates, and complements. (When labeling the words on your paper, label the subject, verb, and complement of the subordinate clause *under* the sentence so that it's not confused with the subject and verb of the main clause.)
4. Identify verbals and phrases and their objects and modifiers and tell how they are used.
5. Explain the modifiers.

1. Studying the notations carefully is the job of the interpreter, Dr. Revel.

2. Scattered by the fierce wind, the leaves found their way into every crack and crevice that had been left by the workers.

3. If we knew the future, we could be peaceful about our lives.

Unit 3

Week 19

Day 1
Read the following essay and reflect upon it.

The Duty and Value of Patriotism

Patriotism is love of country, and loyalty to its life and weal—love tender and strong: tender as the love of son for mother, strong as the pillars of death; loyalty generous and disinterested, shrinking from no sacrifice, seeking no reward save country's honor and country's triumph.

Patriotism! There is magic in the word. It is bliss to repeat it. Through ages the human race burnt the incense of admiration and reverence at the shrines of patriotism. The most beautiful pages of history are those that count its deeds. Fireside tales, the outpourings of the memories of peoples, borrow from it their warmest glow. Poets are sweetest when they reecho its whisperings; orators are most potent when they thrill its chords to music.

The human race pays homage to patriotism because of its supreme value. Patriotism is the vital spark of national honor; it is the fount of the nation's prosperity, the shield of the nation's safety. Take patriotism away, the nation's soul has fled, bloom and beauty have vanished from the nation's countenance.

The human race pays homage to patriotism because of its supreme loveliness. Patriotism goes out to what is among earth's possessions the most precious, the first and dearest,—*country*; and its effusion is the fragrant flowering of the purest and noblest sentiments of the heart.

Patriotism is innate in all men; the absence of it betokens a perversion of human nature; but it grows its full growth only where thoughts are elevated and heart-beatings are generous.

Man is born a social being. A condition of his existence and of his growth to mature age is the family. Nor does the family suffice to itself. A larger social organism is needed, into which families gather, so as to obtain from one another security to life and property, and aid in the development of the faculties and powers with which nature has endowed the children of men. The whole human race is too extensive and too diversified in interests to serve those ends; hence, its subdivisions into countries and peoples. Countries have their providential limits—the waters of the sea, a mountain range, the lines of similarity of requirements for all methods of living.

In America the government takes from the liberty of the citizen only so much as is necessary for the weal of the nation, which the citizen by his own act freely concedes. In America there are no masters who govern in their own right, for their own interest, or at their own will. We have over us no Louis XIV, saying, "The State, it is I"; no Hehenzollern,* announcing that in his acts as sovereign he is responsible only to his conscience and to God. Ours is the government of the people, by the people, and for the people. The government is our own organized will.

Our Republic is liberty's native home—*America*. The God-given mission of the Republic of America is not only to its own people; it is to all the peoples of the earth, before whose eyes it is the symbol of human rights and human liberty, toward whom its flag flutters hopes of future happiness for themselves.

Is there not for Americans a meaning in the word *Country?* Is there for Americans reason to live for country, and if need there be, to die for country? Whatever the country, patriotism is a duty; in America the duty is thrice sacred. The duty of patriotism is the duty of justice and of gratitude. The country fosters and protects our dearest interests,—our altars and hearthstones. Without it there is no safety for life or property, no opportunities for development and progress. All that the country is, she makes ours, and today how significant the world over are the words: *I am a citizen of America.*

The days when patriotism was a duty have not departed. The safety of the Republic lies in the vigilant and active patriotism of the American people. Day by day the spirit of Americanism waxes strong; narrowness of thought and increasing strife cannot resist its influences.

Noblest Ship of State, sail on over billows, and through storm, undaunted, imperishable! Sail thou on, peerless ship, safe from shoals and malign winds, ever strong in keel, ever beauteous in prow and canvas, ever guided by heaven's polar star! Sail thou on, I pray thee, undaunted and imperishable!

—Archbishop John Ireland, 1896 (Abridged by Emma Serl)

*The family name of the kings of Prussia

Write your first response to this essay. What do you like best about it? What thoughts came in to your mind as you read? Does this sound like something you would hear a bishop say today? Explain.

Grammar Study

In this unit, you will be studying the most common grammar usage errors and how to avoid them. One special feature of that study is practicing the correct usage of these forms. Each week you will write the following sentences and work toward memorizing them. At the end of the unit, you will be required to write them from memory. As you progress through this unit, you will learn the reasons these sentences are correct.

For today, copy these sentences into your notebook.

1. I hope I did as well as he.
2. It was George who saw you and whom I saw.
3. I wanted to read the book myself.
4. Neither of her books was lying on the desk.
5. There was a conflict between him and me.
6. John likes skiing, skateboarding, and bicycling.
7. Does either of you know where the manual is?
8. The door's being locked created problems.
9. Don't just try to do it; be sure to do it.
10. Running along the curb, he tripped.

See if you can figure what common errors people might make with some of these sentence parts.

Day 2

Guided Response

Reread the essay "The Duty and Value of Patriotism" and discuss these questions with your teacher.

1. What do you think is the overall main idea of the essay? Give the reasons you think this is the main idea.

2. Highlight your favorite parts of the essay and explain why you like them.

3. Find several places where the author uses abstract nouns and ideas. Find several places where he uses concrete nouns and descriptions. Which is more prevalent in this essay?

4. Find an example of figurative language in the essay and say what kind of figurative language it is.

5. Why does the author think that patriotism is important?

6. Do you agree that in America our duty to patriotism is thrice-fold and involves justice and gratitude? Explain.

7. What does this statement mean? (Look at its place in the text for the context)

   In America the government takes from the liberty of the citizen only so much as is necessary for the weal of the nation, which the citizen by his own act freely concedes.

8. Write a paragraph in which you explain whether or not you agree with the thoughts presented in this essay. Be sure to give your reasons whether you agree or not.

Grammar Study

Adjective and Adverb Usage

The most common mistake with adjective and adverb usage is to use an adjective when an adverb is required.

In each of these cases, an adjective is being used incorrectly as an adverb, modifying the verb or an adjective.

He ran quick.
He painted too slow.
You baked a real nice cake.

Here the adverb is used appropriately:

He ran quickly.
He painted too slowly.
You baked a really nice cake.

In one prominent instance, people use an adverb when they should use an adjective:

Incorrect:	**Correct:**
I feel badly for you.	*I feel bad for you.*

Feel is a state of being verb in this instance and needs an adjective.
To say you *feel badly* means that you are not good at feeling, which seems a bit silly.

Good/Well

Even though it seems quite simple to tell whether to use "good" or "well" in a sentence, people still confuse their use regularly.

Good

"Good" is an adjective and so is used to describe a noun. It can be used as predicate adjective.

He ate a good apple.
That apple is good.

Remember that other words beside *is, are, was* and *were* can take a predicate adjective.
The flower smelled good.

Well

"Well" is an adverb. It cannot be used as a predicate adjective.

I did well on the test.

"Well" is also an adjective in one usage only: *I have not been well since my cold last month. Mary was sick, but now she is well.*

Exercise A

Write an explanation in your own words of how to use "good" and "well" correctly. Give examples.

Exercise B

Select the appropriate word in each sentence below.

1. Sandra speaks English very (good, well). She has very (good, well) pronunciation.
2. It was (really, real) important to reach the bank before closing.
3. The dog ran (quick, quickly) to the door.
4. The children ran (happy, happily) out of the car to the water's edge.
5. That sounds (good, well).
6. Those cupcakes are (awful, awfully) good.
7. Edward did not perform (good, well) on the test.
8. He was (real, really) happy to get such a great seat at the game.

Exercise C

Explain why the adverb or adjective is used in each sentence.

1. He turned pale
2. The moon shone brightly
3. Roses smell fragrant.
4. He handled the boy roughly.

5. The work remains unfinished.
6. He grew old in the service.
7. The board feels rough.
8. She dresses neatly.
9. The dress looks neat.
10. The speaker arose, calm and dignified.

Day 3

Writing

There is an interesting program called "This I Believe" sponsored by National Public Radio in which ordinary citizens write an essay about one of their strongest beliefs. It's based on a radio program of the same name that was popular in the 1950s. People who submit essays explain what is important to them by writing about an event that changed their view of things, or a virtue they have come to appreciate based on their experiences. A few years ago, I heard an essay submitted to this program about how important it is to attend funerals. The author had just experienced the death of her father and was truly amazed at the amount of people who came to his funeral and how comforting that was to her family. Prior to that experience she had avoided going to funerals, but after experiencing the awe and solace of having her father remembered by so many people, she decided that this was an important thing to do for other people. In a recently submitted essay, the author explains how singing is important to the quality of life—not professional singing, but everyday singing with friends.

This week you will write a "This I Believe" essay. And in the end, I encourage you to submit it to NPR for possible inclusion in their program. Visit www.npr.org and search "This I believe" to find out more about that. You can read sample essays—even essays from the 1950s! Here is a sample

December 23, 2007

I've been moved by the magic of Christmas music since the nuns in grammar school etched the words of the carols into my brain. That magic persists despite the memory of our pre-pubescent male voices that sounded more like a pond of bullfrogs than the Vienna Boys Choir. The music rose above us. Even our childhood rivalries and petty differences were no match for the spell of that music. I believe that Christmas music can touch the spirit.

Those nuns taught me the music and the lyrics, but I would learn of the real magic about 10 years later.

On Christmas Eve 1968, I was a patient in a military hospital in Yokota, Japan. My leg had been shattered by a couple of machine gun bullets in a five-hour battle in Vietnam. My body was full of shrapnel and my hands had been badly burned. For three weeks, Army doctors in Vietnam struggled to save my leg. They sent me to Japan on that Christmas Eve to give a new team of surgeons a chance to work their magic.

And I was in desperate need of magic. Somewhere it was Christmas but it didn't feel like it to me—at least not until I heard the music piped through the PA system.

A chorus sang of "peace on earth and mercy mild" and promised "God and sinners reconciled." Another voice called to "let us all with one accord sing praises to our heavenly Lord" and another, to "sleep in heavenly peace" but heaven and peace seemed so distant to me.

My misery was interrupted by a low moan coming from the next bed. All I could see was a white cast shaped like a body; cutouts for his eyes, nose and mouth were the only breaks in the cast. Even as the music inched me toward comfort, the reality of pain anchored me in the present. But looking at my neighbor enclosed in God-knows-what-kind-of-pain, mine didn't seem nearly as important.

The soft strains of "Silent Night" were filling the air of the ward when the nurses made final rounds with our medications. When my nurse approached, I asked her to push my bed closer to the man in the cast. I reached out and took my new friend's hand as the carol told us "all is calm, all is bright."

We spoke no words to each other. None were needed. The carol revived the message of hope and the triumph of love for me. I felt a slight tightening on my hand and for the first time that Christmas I felt I would survive my ordeal, and for the first time in a long time, I wanted to.

I believe there is magic in Christmas and the music that celebrates it, because it brings us closer together and closer to our own hearts.

—Steven Banko

This style of essay is expository, not autobiographical, even though you relate your belief through your own experiences and thoughts. To begin you must decide on something about which you have a strong belief. One idea that the NPR website suggests is to consider a list of values (abstract nouns) and see if you have an experience (concrete experience) that relates to one of the values. Decide on a value that's important to you and find a concrete experience you've had that made you think it's important. Here is list of values:

reliability	faith	respect
dedication	self-control	patience
hope	compassion	cooperation
honesty	loyalty	prudence

Perhaps you have come to believe in one of these values based on an experience in your life. Perhaps there is something in your life that you love and you believe it is important for everyone. After thinking about these values and other things that you have strong belief in, decide on the belief that you will write about in this essay.

You must state your belief in one sentence. You may use this sentence as the opening line of your essay, or you may write an introductory explanation first.

Here is the opening to Jackie Robinson's essay in the 1950s:

At the beginning of the World Series of 1947, I experienced a completely new emotion when the National Anthem was played. This time,

I thought, it is being played for me, as a much as for anyone else. This is organized major league baseball, and I am standing here with all the other, and everything that takes place includes me.

About a year later, I went to Atlanta Georgia to play in an exhibition game. On the field, for the first time in Atlanta, there were Negroes and white. Other Negroes, besides me. And I thought: What I have always believed as come to be.

And what is it that I have always believed? First of all, that imperfections are human . . .

Write the first draft of your "This I Believe" essay. Use first person and be sure to focus only on the belief you have chosen. Don't spend time saying what you don't believe. Think of your audience as the radio listening public. What would say to them?

After you have written your draft, set it aside until Day 4.

Grammar Study

Subject Verb Agreement

A common mistake that students make is to confuse verb agreement by making a verb agree with a noun that is not the subject.

Example: One of these shoes are yours. (Incorrect)
            One of these shoes is yours.   (Correct)

In this case the word "one" is the subject and so requires a singular verb. The word "shoes," while plural, is the object of the preposition, not the subject of the sentence. This mistake is most often made when the subject is an indefinite pronoun.

Exercise A
Determine if the sentences below are correct. If not, supply the word/words that will correct them.

1. The weather in the southern states gets very hot during the summer.
2. At least three-quarters of that book on famous Americans are about people who lived in the nineteenth century.
3. Some of the desks in the classroom are broken.
4. Making pies and cakes are Mrs. Vanders specialty.
5. Where does your parents live?
6. Only the black widow spider, of all the spiders in the United States, has caused death among human beings.

7. Each of the kinds of fruit were new to the exchange students.
8. A group of students are absent today because they are attending the philharmonic.
9. Every one of the players were present to accept the team's trophy.
10. The boys who skated at the pond were very excited.

Day 4

Writing

Reread the first draft of the "This I Believe" essay you wrote on Day 3. Read it aloud. It should be long enough to fill about 3 minutes of reading-aloud-time. Make any changes in it that come to your mind as your read. Read it out loud to someone else and ask the following questions:

1. Is it clear what belief I am writing about?
2. What were the most interesting or most effective parts of the paper?
3. Are there any places that I could make the writing more interesting?
4. Do you have any other suggestions for the paper?

Make any changes in your paper based on this conversation. Then file your paper in your drafts folder.

Grammar Study

Parse the following sentences.
1. Identify the part of speech of each word.
2. Identify the parts of the sentence (As you tell the parts of the sentence give the case, number and gender of nouns and the tense, mood, and voice of verbs.)
3. Identify subordinate clauses and their subjects, predicates, and complements. (When labeling the words on your paper, label the subject, verb, and complement of the subordinate clause *under* the sentence so that it's not confused with the subject and verb of the main clause.)
4. Identify verbals and phrases and their objects and modifiers and tell how they are used.
5. Explain the modifiers.

1. To be a soldier in Washington's army was his greatest desire.

2. Each of the boys was happy when he heard the great news.

Week 20

Day 1

Read the poem below several times and reflect upon it.

O Captain! My Captain!

O Captain! my Captain! our fearful trip is done,
The ship has weathered every rack, the prize we sought is won,
The port is near, the bells I hear, the people all exulting,
While follow eyes the steady keel, the vessel grim and daring;

       But O heart! heart! heart!
       O the bleeding drops of red,
         Where on the desk my captian lies
         Fallen cold and dead.

O Captain! My captain! Rise up and hear the bells;
Rise up—for you the flag is flung—for you the bugle trills,
For you bouquets and ribboned wreath—for you the shores a-crowding
For you they call, the swaying mass, their eager faces turning;

       Here Captain! dear father!
       This arm beneath your head!
         It is some dream that on the deck
         You've fallen cold and dead.

My captain does not answer, his lips are pale and still,
My father does not feel my arm, he has no pulse nor will,
The ship is anchored safe and sound, its voyage closed and done,
From fearful trip the victor ship comes in with object won;

       Exult, O shores, and ring, O bells!
       But I with mournful tread
         Walk the deck my Captain lies,
         Fallen cold and dead.

—Walt Whitman

Write your first response to the poem. What is effective about this poem? What does it make the reader feel?

Grammar Study

Imitation Sentences

Copy the practice sentences into your notebook:

1. I hope I did as well as he.
2. It was George who saw you and whom I saw.
3. I wanted to read the book myself.
4. Neither of her books was lying on the desk.
5. There was a conflict between him and me.
6. John likes skiing, skateboarding, and bicycling.
7. Does either of you know where the manual is?
8. The door's being locked created problems.
9. Don't just try to do it; be sure to do it.
10. Running along the curb, he tripped.

Word Usage

Loose and *lose*

These two words are often confused because they sound similar. Here is the correct usage:

> The bolt that held the door in place was *loose*.
> I hated to *lose* the race.

Your and *you're*

At one time, the misspelling of "you're" was listed as the number one spelling error in America. How easy it is to accidentally write *Your Welcome* instead of *You're Welcome*!

> *Your* purse was found on the counter top.
> *You're* privileged to be able to own a computer.

Effect and *affect*

Some people use these words interchangeably and arbitrarily. *Affect* is primarily used as a verb that takes an object (unless it is in passive voice). It is also used as a noun in psychological or psychiatric descriptions as a noun meaning *feeling* or *emotion*. Any other use of it as a noun is not correct. *Effect* can be used as a noun or a verb.

> Your attitude will *affect* your acceptance to the program.

He *affected* an English accent for his part in the play.

The *effects* of the landslide had yet to be felt when the rumbling stopped.
Her prayers for her son finally *effected* his conversion.

Exercise

Create a set of sentences which demonstrated the proper use of each of the words described above.

Day 2

Guided Response

Reread the poem "O Captain! My Captain" by Walt Whitman and discuss these questions with your teacher.

1. Did you know that Walt Whitman has written this entire poem in figurative language? You could say that the poem is a *figure* of something else. In this poem he is talking about the death of Abraham Lincoln, not the death of a sea captain. Reread the poem with that in mind and find the figures.

2. For each stanza, explain how the figure works out. (What is represented in each stanza?) Review the kinds of figurative language defined in Lesson 14. What type of figurative language is used in this poem?

3. Give your opinion of the poem. What works well in it? Is it a poem that you like? Explain why or why not.

4. Read the poem aloud and try to express the rhythm of the poem in your reading. What effect do the repeating words have on the reading, especially the O Captain, my captain?

5. What is the tone of the poem? What emotions does he convey? How does Whitman create this tone?

6. Write in paragraph form your interpretation of the poem.

"Sic semper tryrannus, The South is avenged" Harper's Weekly, 1864

Grammar Study

Word Usage

Lie and lay

Despite the presence of exercises on these two words in every English book ever written, people still confuse their usage. *Lay* means to set something down; one thing is acting upon another. It is a transitive verb and will always have an object. *Lie* means to put oneself in a prone position; nothing or no one is acting upon another. However, what *really* confuses their usage is that they are irregular verbs with forms that are similar to each other.

Present	Past	Past Participle
Lie	lay	lain
Lay	laid	laid

Lay the books on the table when you enter the room
He wanted to *lie* down after the long day's march.

Could have/Should have/Would have

It seems to have slipped into our spoken language to say *could've* instead of *could have* (or even in some cases *coulda*). When students go to write that construction, they unfortunately write *could of*, I suppose because that is what it sounds like. But that usage is incorrect.

I *could have* been a contender.
Mary Anne found out that she *should have* read the recipe.
The driver *would have* come to pick you up if you had asked.

There, their and they're

Once again, these words are often confused despite relentlessly drill pages in English workbooks. *They're* is the contraction for *they are* and should only be used as the subject/ verb of a sentence or clause. *Their* shows possession and should only be used as an adjective or as a pronoun (see sample below). *There* has several uses. It is used as an adverb to show place. It is also used as pronoun to introduce a sentence in which the verb comes before its object. In this usage it is called an *expletive*. (Definition of expletive used in this sense: A word or other grammatical element that has no meaning but is needed to fill a syntactic position, such as the words *it* and *there* in the sentences *It's raining* and *There are many books on the table.*)

Please put the groceries *there* on the table. (adverb)
There aren't enough cookies left for the whole team. (expletive)
They're not quite happy with the test results.
We left *their* change on the counter near the toaster. (adjective)
The money is *theirs*. (pronoun)

Exercise A

Create sentences that show the proper use of each of the words described above.

Exercise B

Correct the usage mistakes in the following paragraph.

After a wild and windy day on the lake, the boys laid down in there bunks. It was a shame to loose the race in the end after they're valiant efforts to stay in the lead for so long. The sailed swift and steady, but the affects of they're ripped sail could not be overcome. Laying there and chatting about the day, they decided they had performed good and would of done better if they hadn't had to battle one of the best teams on the lake in the final stretch. Exhausted from the day's labor, each of the boys were asleep before the night curfew had sounded.

Day 3

Writing

Today you will create a poem using "O Captain, My Captain" as a sample. In Week 14 you wrote a copy change of a paragraph. This week you will do a copy change of Whitman's poem. Here is a sample written by a student. Her poem "Workbooks" is based on a stanza from a Keats poem. First read the original by Keats:

Minnows
(an excerpt from "I stood tip-toe upon a little hill" by John Keats)

Where swarms of minnows show their little heads,
Staying their wavy bodies 'gainst the streams,
To taste the luxury of sunny beams
Temper'd with coolness. How they ever wrestle
With their own sweet delight, and ever nestle
Their silver bellies on the pebbly sand.
If you but scantily hold out the hand,
That very instant not one will remain;
But turn your eye, and they are there again.
The ripples seem right glad to reach those cresses,
And cool themselves among the em'rald tresses;
The while they cool themselves, they freshness give,
And moisture, that the bowery green may
live . . . .

And now the copy-change:

Workbooks
(by Agnes, age 12)

Where swarms of workbooks rear their ugly heads,
Shoving their papery thickness 'gainst our brains,
To feel the drudgery of printed plains
Temper'd with graphite. How they ever wrestle
With all our sanity, and ever nestle
Their bulk upon our desks (they weigh a ton).
If you but scantily think, "Oh, I'm done!"
You'll notice that more questions will remain;
Yet turn the page, and there they are again.
The workbooks seem right glad to bore and burden,
All for the sake—they say—to foster learnin';
The while they make us toil, they headaches give,
And suffering, that no free time may live . . . .

You will write your poem following the pattern of "Oh Captain! My Captain!" As in the sample above, you may borrow some words, or just follow the phrasing and rhythm. Although Whitman's poem is serious, your poem may be humorous or serious.

O Muffin! My Muffin !   O Kitten! My Kitten!
O Dancer! My dancer!   O Clarinet! My Clarinet!
O Computer! My Computer   O Mother! My Mother!

Brainstorm topics for a few minutes and then decide on one to try. You can discard it and try another if you find it isn't working. Try to write a poem as long as Whitman's but at least get 8 lines done. Then set aside your poem for Day 4

Day 4

Writing

Reread the poem Oh Captain! My Captain! Read it a second time out loud. Then see how much of it you can say from memory.

Read your own poem out loud. Make any changes in your text based on your reading of it. Ask someone to read it and give his or her suggestions for improvement. Then file it in your drafts folder.

Exercise

Do a copy change of each of the following sentences using your own topic. Match phrases and clauses, following the pattern of the sentence.

1. Sure enough, when the fresh tapers were burning well, the gold flowers on Sainte Anne's cloak began to show; not entire, but wherever there was a fold in the mantle, the gold seemed to flow like a glistening liquid.
   —From *Shadows on the Rock* by Willa Cather

2. The deep scattering layer is an astounding new problem of oceanography, a mystifying physical mezzanine hovering above the bedrock of the sea. The phenomenon rises and falls with the cycle of sun and dark, leading some scientists to believe it is a dense blanket of living organisms, so vast as to tilt the imagination.
   —From *The Silent World* by Jacques Cousteau

Grammar Study

Parse the following sentences.
  1. Identify the part of speech of each word.
  2. Identify the parts of the sentence (As you tell the parts of the sentence give the case, number and gender of nouns and the tense, mood, and voice of verbs.)
  3. Identify subordinate clauses and their subjects, predicates, and complements. (When labeling the words on your paper, label the subject, verb, and complement of the subordinate clause *under* the sentence so that it's not confused with the subject and verb of the main clause.)
  4. Identify verbals and phrases and their objects and modifiers and tell how they are used.
  5. Explain the modifiers.

1. The professor was amazed by the number of students who suffered the effects of the flu.

2. Health officials were keeping records of students affected by the flu.

Week 21

Day 1

Read the following nature observation and reflect on it.

An Encounter with an Owl

Well, what an exciting experience we had yesterday evening! We finally got a close up look at a bird we've long admired, and just recently studied in depth—the owl. This was an encounter we won't soon forget . . .

It was nearing dusk, and the sun was just starting to set, when I noticed a large brown shape perched in the large maple across the street. The creature was well camouflaged by its coloring, but as it moved along the branch I realized it was some kind of bird. Its size suggested a variety of raptor, but after staring through the windows a few moments more, I realized I would need a closer look to determine its precise identification.

I immediately called out for my boys to come to me quickly with the camera, hoping that the bird would stay still long enough for us to get a shot. Within moments we were, all five of us, tumbling out the door, and rushing down the steps - eager to solve this latest nature mystery. In our excitement and haste, we ran out into the yard, not even grabbing our coats! The air was crisp and cold, and the fading light was golden and soft. It was, truly, a beautiful late winter evening.

As we neared the tree, we slowed our pace and quieted our footsteps as much as we could. The snow was crunching beneath our feet and we feared the bird would be frightened off by our approach. Thankfully, he held his position, and soon we were standing at the base of the maple tree.

Five pairs of eyes were fastened steadily on the bird, and within moments we realized we were in fact looking at an owl! We exchanged excited grins, but with a meaningful glance, I reminded the boys to keep still.

As I began snapping pictures, our attention was drawn to a male cardinal who was singing loudly and hopping around on a branch to the left of the owl. His aggressive behavior led us to believe he was sounding an alarm to the songbird community. Certainly the appearance of an owl, a bird of prey, and a rare sight so far outside of the woods, would cause a commotion—and not just among the birds! Before long we were joined by several other neighbors, all similarly armed with cameras and equally awed by the owl's presence.

He was awake and alert—not asleep as we originally thought. (He may have been napping and woke at our approach, but he certainly didn't't seem to mind our attention.) The owl stared down at us, occasionally preening his feathers, and at one point he rotated his head almost entirely! (We later learned that this particular species of owl can only rotate his head about 270 degrees, not 360 as is commonly believed.)

The winter chill soon became too much for me, and, with one last long glance at our magnificent owl, I headed back home to begin some research. Just a few minutes later the boys joined me inside and together we found a name for our bird: *the Barred Owl*.

According to *Birds of New England*, the Barred Owl is a fairly common year-round resident in these parts. It prefers coniferous and mixed-wood forests, especially such areas that are situated beside a water source. We realized the river that runs through the deep woods behind our home makes our little corner of the world a perfect habitat for the Barred Owl! Last summer, during one of our hikes out back in the woods, we found an old tree with a large open cavity on one side. It was too high up for us to see inside, but we felt sure it was a nest of some kind. When the snow melts in another week or two we will trek back out to that tree and look around for signs of the owl. Feathers would be a clue, but even more telling would be the presence of owl pellets near the base of the tree.

Just last week the boys had the opportunity to dissect owl pellets during a class at a wildlife refuge not far from here. We learned that owls cannot digest the fur, feathers or bones of the creatures they eat, and that this matter is collected in their gullet. Once the gullet is full, the owl regurgitates a pellet. By examining the bones left behind, one can identify the owl's most recent meal. It was a fascinating experience!

Here at home we spent a little time on-line, reading about the Barred Owl and its behaviors. According to one site, the mating season of the Barred Owl begins in February with potential mates calling to each other near evening. Nesting gets underway beginning in March and carries on throughout the summer. At one website we found, we were able to actually listen to the calls of Barred Owls! The familiar call

(*Who cooks for you? Who cooks for you?*) had us remembering summer nights and the sounds of the woods after dark …

This particular memory led me to ponder another question: if owls are thought to be nocturnal creatures, then why was this one out and about during the day? I voiced a hope that his appearance was not some sign of distress, but the boys remembered learning in their class that while owls are indeed primarily nocturnal, they can occasionally be seen during the daytime. This would occur most often during courtship and mating. The Barred Owl does, however, hunt mostly at night.

And speaking of hunting, we can't help but fret a bit for the many, small, furred and feathered friends that visit our feeders every day. After all, these songbirds and squirrels are the prey that make up an owl's main diet. As rare as an owl sighting is, however, I think an owl's hunting would be even more unlikely to witness. We'll just keep track of our favorite red squirrels and hope that their visits do not dwindle at all anytime soon.

What an amazing experience this was, our very first encounter with an owl! Within the space of an hour we had pictures to show and new information to digest— as well as a wonderful memory to share through the years.

Just as darkness overtook the neighborhood, the owl swept off into the night. We may never get the opportunity to see him again, but we're grateful he chose to stop last evening, in that tree across the street. It was a chance meeting we'll never forget.

—Dawn Hanigan
Nature Journal Entry 2/22/2009

Write your first impressions of this observation. What are its strengths? What questions remain in your mind after reading it?

Grammar Study

Imitation Sentences

Copy the practice sentences into your notebook:

1. I hope I did as well as he.
2. It was George who saw you and whom I saw.
3. I wanted to read the book myself.
4. Neither of her books was lying on the desk.
5. There was a conflict between him and me.
6. John likes skiing, skateboarding, and bicycling.
7. Does either of you know where the manual is?
8. The door's being locked created problems.
9. Don't just try to do it; be sure to do it.
10. Running along the curb, he tripped.

Word Usage

This week we will take a look at pronouns and how to use them properly. Today the exercises focus on using the correct case. Reread sentences #1 and #5 above. In sentence #1, the word *he* is used instead of *him* because the pronoun is the subject of a clause, thereby taking the nominative form of the pronoun. The whole clause is not printed in the sentence, but really it would be like saying

> *I hope I did as well as he* did.

Many people would use the word *him* instead of *he* in sentence #1 because they don't understand the implied verb *did*. The objective form of the pronoun (him) is not called for.

In sentence #5, the objective case *is* called for since the pronouns are the objects of the preposition *between*. Unfortunately, many people say *between he and I* thinking that they are being more grammatically correct.

Lastly, when the pronoun is used as the predicate nominative it must be in the nominative case.

> It is I
> That is he.
> If ever there were happy men, the discharged soldiers were they.

Review the chart of the personal pronouns in the Appendix.

Exercise A

Read each of the following sentences and choose the correct word to complete the sentence. Give the reason for your choice.

1. Mother left Tom and (I or me) at home.
2. I am sure that is (he or him).
3. Fred, Harry, and (I or me) have formed a club.
4. Between you and (I or me) I think he has made a great mistake.
5. My classmates did not do as well on the test as (I or me).
6. Invitations were sent to Tom and (she or her).
7. Every week my friend and (I or me) gather flowers for the Mary grotto.
8. Without the help of Susan and (she or her), I never would have finished.
9. Before you and (he or him) wash the car, please take out the trash.
10. We found out that the thief was (he or him).

Barred Owl, sleeping

Day 2

Guided Response

Reread the nature observation on Day 1 and discuss these questions with your teacher.

1. While the writing in a record of an observation is expository, it is filled with descriptive writing. Word choice becomes important as the author attempts to accurately describe the event either to remember it better himself, or to place a picture in the reader's mind. Highlight the places in the observation where the descriptive language the author chooses is vivid and effective. Discuss what makes these particular passages effective.

2. This author also sprinkles in information that she has heard or learned since making the observation. Underline the places where she does that. How do those additions enhance the observation?

3. Often times, a naturalist will close the observation with a reflection of some kind, a thought that the observation put in his head. What do you think of the way this author closes her piece? Would you have ended it differently? Explain.

4. Make an outline of the observation.

5. Make a list of things in nature around your house, in the backyard, or at the local park that you have observed or noticed.

Grammar Study

When used as the subject, the following indefinite pronouns always take a singular predicate.

Each, either, neither, one, everyone, anyone, someone, no one, everybody, anybody, somebody, nobody

Incorrect: *Everyone brought their best piece of writing to the meeting.*
Correct: *Everyone brought his best piece of writing to the meeting.*

Note on using *he* or *she* and *his* or *her*: Common traditional use is to always use the masculine form to refer to mankind generally. In these times, that isn't so politically correct. Some writers will always say *his or her* to be sure not to offend anyone. Some will alternate between *his* and *her*. If you know the gender of the group is one or the other, use the pronoun that matches it.

Everyone brought his best piece of writing
Everyone brought his or her best piece of writing.

Another common mistake you will hear and see everywhere, especially on the nightly news, is to use the singular verb for the expletives *there* and *here* when it has a plural subject. This happens because people contract the verb *is* with the word *there* (*there's*) and they've forgotten that *there* isn't really the subject of the sentence in that construction. With these constructions (called expletive constructions), the subject follows the verb but still determines the number of the verb. The verb must agree with what *appears* to be the complement in the sentence. I catch myself making this mistake while speaking sometimes.

> Incorrect: There's too many cows grazing on the plains.
> Correct: There are too many cows grazing on the plains.

In this example, the verb must agree with *a lot*, not with cows, since cows is the object of the preposition.

> Incorrect: There are a lot of cows grazing on the plains.
> Correct: There is a lot of cows grazing on the plains.

Exercise A
Analyze the subject-verb agreement of the following sentences. If it is correct, explain why it is correct and leave it as is. If not, correct the sentence.

1. Here's two apples that I picked right off the tree yesterday.
2. Anybody who wants to come is invited.
3. Each of the soldiers are required to carry enough provision for the march.
4. Neither the mother nor the father were able to convince the boy to come down from the tree.
5. Everyone at the races was sure they saw the other horse win.
6. There's no reason why you shouldn't come along.
7. Either you or your mother are required to sign the release form.
8. Someone in the rescue party was supposed to pick up his backpack.
9. There's surely many false reports about what happened.
10. Near here are a flock of Canadian geese.

Exercise B
Write a sentence using each of the following correctly.

1. There with a plural subject
2. Here with a singular subject
3. Everybody
4. Each

Day 3

Writing

This week you will observe something in nature and write an observational record of it. Today, choose something to observe. It can be anything in nature or perhaps a family pet. Observe the creature carefully and take notes on what you see. Be as specific as you can in your notes and even record any thoughts that come into your head about the creature as you watching. For example, you might question why it does something. Write the question down. Draw a sketch, or a series of sketches, of the creature. Even if you don't think you are a good artist, attempting to draw it will help with your observation. It requires you to notice details and consider them with respect to the whole. As a sample sketch for your reference, please look carefully at the sketch by the author in the journal entry on Day 1.

Save your notes and your sketches for Day 4.

Grammar Study

Who and Whom

In order to know which pronoun is correct, you need to know how the word is used in the sentence. *Who* and *whoever* are always used in the nominative case, and *whom* and *whomever* are used in the objective. That seems easy, but it's not always easy to tell which case is called for in the sentence, particularly if the sentence is a question or the pronoun introduces a clause.

Here is the simple example that most people will get right:

Who came to your concert? (Subject)
To whom did you give the book? (Object)

Here are the more difficult cases:

It was Sally *who* was last in line. (*Who* is the subject pronoun of the clause)
Sally was a girl *whom* I met at the game. (*Whom* does not have a verb. *I* is subject of *met*.)

One method suggested by many an English teacher is to substitute the personal pronoun "he/him" or "she/her" for "who/whom." If he or she would be the correct form, the proper choice is who." If "him" or "her" would be correct, use "whom."

It was Sally. She was last in line.
Sally was a girl. I met her at the game.

223

Although this trick will help you use the right word, it's best to know *why* it works.

There is one case that really confuses people:

> We wanted to vote for *whoever* seemed the best candidate.
> Give the book to *whoever* will use it most effectively.

Whoever is the proper choice in both of these sentences. Even though you might think that since it follows the preposition, it ought to be in the objective case as the object of the preposition, actually, the *entire clause* is the object of the preposition. Since the pronoun has a verb of which it is the subject, the nominative case is used.

So, if you're unsure which case to use, follow these simple rules:

1. Try substituting "he/him" or "she/her": If either "he" or "she" works, then it's "who;" if "him" or "her" works, then it's "whom."

2. Every verb with a tense in a sentence must have a subject. That word is always in the nominative case, so use "who." For example: In this sentence, *Pete wanted to choose whoever got to the game first.*
    - "Pete" is the subject of "wanted"
    - "he" (whoever) is the subject of the verb "got."

    In the sentence, *Give it to whoever deserves it* ([You] give it to whoever deserves it.)
    - "he" (whoever) is the subject of the verb "deserves."

This rule supersedes the first rule as it relates to "who" and "whom."

Exercise A

Select the appropriate pronoun for each sentence below. Explain your reason for each choice.

1. He is the freeman (who, whom) the truth makes free.
2. There was one philosopher (who, whom) chose to live in a tub.
3. He will present a trophy to (whoever, whomever) can name all fifty state and their capitals in less than 3 minutes.
4. Conquerors are a class of men with (who, whom) for the most part, the world could well dispense.
5. He bowed to every man (who, whom) he met.
6. The general (who, whom) was appointed immediately resigned.
7. These men (who, whom) you see standing about are waiting for work.
8. (Who, Whom) is to blame for these atrocities?
9. (Who, Whom) do you see in the street?
10. The girl (who, whom) you saw is my sister.
11. (Whoever, Whomever) left this pile of shoes here must come and distribute them.

12. They (who, whom) remember the year 1800 will remember also the great controversy, whether it was the beginning of a century or the end of one.

Exercise B
Write a declarative sentence for each word listed below demonstrating its proper use.

1. Whomever
2. Whoever
3. Who
4. Whom

Day 4

Writing

Today you will write your nature observation. Using the notes you made on Day 3, write a record of your observation. You may use the first person if you like. Include as much description as you can with details about the creature you observed. At the end you may include a conclusion you have drawn about the creature based on your observation. Perhaps the observation brought questions to your mind about the creature. You may state those and provide your speculation on how they would be answered.

There is no set format to writing an observation, but begin with some sort of action to grab the attention of your reader. Include a conclusion that closes your observation in a satisfying way for the reader.

When you have completed your draft, share it with your teacher or a family member and ask if the observation record makes sense and if the writing adequately brings the creature to life.

File the draft in your drafts folder.

Grammar Study

Reflexive Pronouns

Reflexive pronouns have two distinct uses. The first is for emphasis, used as an appositive:

The captain *himself* replied to my question.
He *himself* was present.

Secondly, it is used in the objective case to *refer back* to the subject (noun or pronoun).

The defeated general killed *himself* in despair. (direct object)
He betrayed *himself* by his folly. (direct object)
He was upset with *himself* for his cowardice. (object of the preposition)
He gave *himself* a blow. (indirect object)

Many people mistakenly use the reflexive pronoun as a subject in the nominative case. This is grammatically incorrect. (See the Pronoun Chart in the Grammar Appendix.)

Pete, Sam, and myself will be attending the ordination.

Exercise
In each of the following sentences, identify the reflexive pronouns. Tell how it is used—for emphasis or as an object. If it is used as an object, say whether it is the direct object, indirect object, or object of the preposition.

1. The story itself was scarcely credible.
2. She amused herself with walking and reading.
3. Envy shoots at other and wounds herself.
4. Jack sat by himself in a corner.
5. The men themselves carried no provisions except a bag of oatmeal.
6. I will hardly know myself in the party gown.
7. The prisoner threw himself into the sea and swam for the shore.
8. Every guilty deed holds in itself the seed of retribution.

Parsing
Parse the following sentence.

1. Identify the part of speech of each word.
2. Identify the parts of the sentence (As you tell the parts of the sentence give the case, number and gender of nouns and the tense, mood, and voice of verbs.)
3. Identify subordinate clauses and their subjects, predicates, and complements. (When labeling the words on your paper, label the subject, verb, and complement of the

subordinate clause *under* the sentence so that it's not confused with the subject and verb of the main clause.)

4. Identify verbals and phrases and their objects and modifiers and tell how they are used.
5. Explain the modifiers.

He is the freeman whom the truth makes free.

Observing Nature

Week 22

Day 1
Study the following landscape paintings and reflect on them.

Mountain and Lake by Thomas Doughty

Mount Washington from the Saco River by Samuel Lancaster Gerry

Write your first impressions of each painting. What does each painting make you think of?

Grammar Study

Copy the imitation sentences into your notebook. Today, try to write as much as you can without looking back at the book.

1. I hope I did as well as he.
2. It was George who saw you and whom I saw.
3. I wanted to read the book myself.
4. Neither of her books was lying on the desk.
5. There was a conflict between him and me.
6. John likes skiing, skateboarding, and bicycling.
7. Does either of you know where the manual is?
8. The door's being locked created problems.
9. Don't just try to do it; be sure to do it.
10. Running along the curb, he tripped.

Mistakes with Modifiers

This week you will be studying mistakes that people make with modifiers: adjectives and adverbs and the phrases and clauses that act as adjectives and adverbs.

1. I hope / hopefully: Reread sentence #1 above. Many people today use the word "hopefully" instead of saying *I hope*. In some ways, this usage is like a conjunction or interjection. *(Hopefully, we'll get the right answers on the test.)* However, the grammatical use of *hopefully* is as an adverb that modifies a verb.

We turned the key *hopefully.*

2. all ready / already: *All ready* means completely prepared and *already* means previously.

He was *all ready* to wait for his dessert.
She had *already* served it.

3. everyday / every day: If *every-* is used as a prefix, the meaning shifts to "common" or "average" instead of the adverbial *every* as in "all" of something.

No one likes *everyday* chores, like washing dishes.
Doing them *every day* is even worse!

4. some time / sometime / sometimes: *Some time* is an adverbial phrase meaning an interval. *Sometime* is an adverb indicating an indefinite event. *Sometimes* indicates a probability.

After *some time*, the dancer said, "My feet are *sometimes* sore."

Sometime later, the dancer soaked her feet.

Exercise

Use each of the following words correctly in a sentence.

1. Hopefully   2. sometime
3. everyday   4. already

Day 2

Guided Response

Study the pictures from Day 1 again and complete the following activities.

1. To what is your eye drawn when you first look at each painting?

2. Is this the focal point of the painting? If not, what do you think is the focal point? How is this achieved in each painting? *

3. How does the artist of each painting use light in his painting? What is the effect of the light in each painting?

4. Explain the tone or mood that you think each painting conveys. What in the painting helps to convey the mood?

5. In two columns on your paper, make a list of details that you see in each painting.

6. Write a paragraph for each painting that explains what is going on in the painting.

*A focal point is the element in a painting that pulls in the viewer's eye, that is the center of attention or the main subject. An artist emphasizes a focal point through the painting's composition, through color, and through the range of tones used. Often called the *center of interest*, a focal point could very well be a small portion of the painting.

Grammar Study

Misplaced Modifiers

To avoid confusion, a modifier should be placed right next to the word it modifies. These words are often misplaced: *only, often, almost, nearly, just, barely.*

For example, see how the meaning of the sentence changes when you change the position of these words in the sentence.

> *Charlie almost bought the car as soon as he saw it.*

This sentence says that he didn't buy the car, but that that he wanted to. Maybe he just strolled around the lot.

> *Charlie bought the car almost as soon as he saw it.*

Charlie buys the car soon after seeing it.

Phrases can also be misplaced. Here is a famous example:

> *"One morning I shot an elephant in my pajamas. How he got into my pajamas I'll never know."*
> —Groucho Marx)

Here are a few others.

> *I was told that I had won first prize at the fair by my 4-H leader.*

Correction: My 4-H leader told me that I had won first prize at the fair.

> *The young girl was walking the dog in a blue snowsuit.*

Correction: The young girl in a blue snowsuit was walking the dog.

Exercise A
Correct the modifier placement errors in the following sentences.

1. "Mr. Clinton acknowledged the role played by the men who subdued the gunman when he spoke at a dinner on Saturday night." (*The New York Times*)

2. "Historians have been kept guessing over claims [that] Dr James Barry, Inspector General of Military Hospitals, was in fact a woman for more than 140 years." (The Daily Telegraph, March 5, 2008)

3. The heiress donated a pair of shoes to a charity that sold for over $20,000.

4. "Burk is headquartered in a small room on the tenth floor of an aging Washington office building; she is not paid by the council, and her only full-time paid employee is a pleasant young woman with a nose ring named Rebecca, who sits at the front desk." (reprinted in The New Yorker)

5. Daria went to the party wearing a full length gown.

6. My cousin went on and on, describing the details of the party in the elevator.

7. Kitty and Frank found the flowers hiking up the mountain.

8. "Plastic bags are a favorite of grocers because of their price, about 2 cents per bag compared to 5 cents for paper. Used widely since the 1970s, environmentalists now estimate between 500 billion to a trillion bags are produced annually worldwide." (Associated Press, "Environmental Concerns Force Grocers, Bag Makers to Rethink the Plastic Bag," *Savannah Morning News*, January 30, 2008)

9. The photojournalist took a picture of a demonstrator with a long lens camera.

10. A young woman entered the room wearing a clown suit.

Exercise B
Use each of the following words correctly in a sentence.

1. only   2. almost
3. barely   4. just

Day 3

Writing

This week you will be writing a compare and contrast essay about the two painting featured on Day 1.

Begin by studying the paintings again. Look over the list of details for each one that you made on Day 2. Group the lists by similarities and differences. Think about the tone or mood of each painting. Is it the same? Think about the focal point of each painting. How does each artist emphasize the focal point? Think about the color. Think about the use of light. Think about the style of painting.

Choosing a Format

Study the following outlines for a compare and contrast essay. You will need to choose one to use for this paper.

1. First compare, then contrast, or vice versa. Place the one you want to emphasis last. This most basic structure focuses the paper on the comparing and contrasting and not so much on the ideas.

   > Paragraph 1: Introduction
   > Paragraph 2: Similarities of the two paintings
   > Paragraph 3: Differences in the two paintings
   > Paragraph 4: Conclusion

2. First discuss one painting and then the other. The similarities and differences don't come out until you are done with the 3rd paragraph. This is also a basic structure that most beginning writers choose. It focuses on the items themselves and not so much on the comparing and contrasting.

   > Paragraph 1: Introduction
   > Paragraph 2: Discuss/Describe one painting
   > Paragraph 3: Discuss/Describe the other painting
   > Paragraph 4: Conclusion.

3. Writers compare and contrast by taking important specific elements and looking at the way those elements are the same or different in object compared. This more sophisticated method requires real control over your subject. You will want to choose elements in the paintings that are explicitly comparable or contrasting.

   > Paragraph 1: Introduction
   > Paragraph 2: Element 1 (discuss the similarities and differences of the two paintings in this element, for example, use of light)
   > Paragraph 3: Element 2

Paragraph 4: Element 3
Paragraph 5: Conclusion

Choose the method you feel most comfortable trying. Then you must have a thesis statement for your paper.

Creating a Thesis Statement

Your thesis statement needs to be more than simply *These two painting have many similarities and differences.* That does not focus the paper enough, and is not very engaging for the reader. Here are some samples of weak theses that you should avoid:

> This paper will compare and contrast two restaurants.
> Denny's and Perkins are similar in some ways and different in others.
> Denny's and Perkins are similar in many ways, but they have one major difference.

Here is a stronger thesis based on what will be actually discussed in the paper:

> Denny's and Perkins have similar prices and menu items, but their atmospheres and their ability to provide service are strikingly different.

And a stronger one:

> Denny's and Perkins both offer a variety of modestly priced food, but the service at Denny's makes it a better place to treat your family to a casual night out.

In this last one, you are not only comparing and contrasting, but you have given a judgment, answering for your reader why the similarities and differences should be of any concern.

Making an Outline

Make an outline for your paper using the structures listed above. Include as much detail in your outline as you can so that when you go write your draft, all your thoughts about the paintings are in order. Here is a sample of the third option.

I. Introduction
    A. Introduce the painting and the artists and speak generally about them.
    B. Thesis statement
II. Body
    A. Element 1 to be compared/contrasted– topic sentence
        1. Doughty
          a. support
          b. support
        2. Gerry
          a. support
          b. support

B. Element 2 – topic sentence
     1. Doughty
        a. support
        b. support
     2. Gerry
        a. support
        b. support
C. Element 3 – topic sentence
     1. Doughty
        a. support
        b. support
     2. Gerry
        a. support
        b. support

III. Conclusion
    Restate thesis and give the judgment.

Create your outline and set it aside for Day 4

Day 4

Writing

Today you will write a first draft of the compare and contrast essay about the two paintings. Using your outline, write your draft. If you've taken your time to make a detailed outline, the drafting will be a breeze.

After you write the draft, check the transition chart (see the Appendix) to be sure you have included efficient transitions between your paragraphs. The use of the "hook" transition is especially effective in a compare and contrast essay.

Get some feedback on your essay by asking your teacher or a family member to read it. Ask if the thesis is strong enough and if the paper flows logically. Make changes in your paper based on your conversation.

File your paper in your drafts folder.

Grammar Study

Dangling Modifiers

A dangling modifier is a word or phrase that modifies a word not clearly stated in the sentence.

Here is the correct way to use a modifier:

> *Having finished chores*, Sam ate a big dinner.

Having finished the chores is a participle phrase modifying Sam. The word modified is placed *directly after* the modifying phrase. The golden rule is to place the modifier right next the word it modifies.

Here is the same modifier left dangling without the word it's supposed to modify.

> *Having finished chores*, a big dinner was eaten.

Did the dinner finish the chores? Obviously not, but if the modifier is left as it is, that is what the sentence is saying.

So how do you fix the dangling modifier?

Strategies for revising dangling modifiers:
1. Name the appropriate or logical doer of the action as the subject of the main clause:

> *Having finished chores*, Sam ate a big dinner.

2. Change the phrase that dangles into a complete introductory clause by naming the doer of the action in that clause:

> *When Sam finished his chores*, he ate a big dinner.

3. Combine the phrase and main clause into one:

> Sam finished his chores and then ate a big dinner.

Exercise

Correct the dangling modifiers in the following sentences using one of the three strategies listed above. You may add words to the sentences if needed.

1. Walking to church on a subzero morning, my left foot became frozen.
2. Without knowing the correct answer, it was difficult to do well on the test.
3. To bake a proper tiramisu, the directions must be followed exactly.
4. When just three years old, Nancy's mother took her to her first horse show.
5. Without giving much effort, there is no way to learn a foreign language.

Sunset – Little Miami Valley (Ohio) by Charles Wilson Knapp

Week 23

Day 1

Read the following newspaper article and write your first response to it.

Laundry Car Over Cliff

Laundry strike sympathizers drove a Walker Laundry Company motor truck over Cliff Drive hill at Hardesty Avenue late this afternoon, after capturing the car and routing the driver and two special officers at Fourteenth Street and Euclid Avenue. One of the special officers fired a shot into the crowd before fleeing from the rain of bricks and stones. No one was injured. Homer Maze, 5106 East Twenty-fourth Street, was driving the laundry truck. Guarding him were two special officers, Sam Seaman, 2700 East Twenty-seventh Street, and C.L. Winner, 717 East Eleventh Street.

Maze was making a delivery at Fourteenth Street and Euclid Avenue when a crowd of about twenty-five men and women approached from the west and opened fire of rocks and stones on the standing car. Maze came from the house and made a run to join the special officers. After several minutes of fusillading stones, the officers and Maze deserted the car and reported the disturbance at the Flora Avenue Police Station. Seaman, one of the special officers, told of firing a shot toward the crowd, attempting to disperse the strike sympathizers. Re-enforcements joining the attacking party seemed to arrive steadily, they said, so they gave up the car to the crowd.

When the police arrived at the scene of the disturbance, a part of the crowd was yet there. Six men and one woman were arrested. The men could not be identified by Maze or the special officers as having thrown stones. The woman, Julia Anderson, 1711 West Prospect Place, was identified by them and was held on a $51 cash bond. She denies having thrown anything.

The truck was found after a search, but is practically demolished.

A second wrecking party was reported from Eleventh Street and Chestnut Avenue.

B. L. Ferguson, 6424 Lee Street, driver of a Kansas City Laundry Company truck, and a special officer, Salvator Schira, 1911 Missouri Avenue, were attacked by fifteen men and twelve women. A stone thrown by one of the striking laundry workers struck Ferguson on the cheek, another on the right hand. His injuries are not severe.

—Ernest Hemingway in the *Kansas City Star*,
January 20, 1918

Write your first response to this news item. What were you thinking as you read it? Was it clear or confusing?

Grammar Study

Parse the following sentences.
1. Identify the part of speech of each word.
2. Identify the parts of the sentence (As you tell the parts of the sentence give the case, number and gender of nouns and the tense, mood, and voice of verbs.)
3. Identify subordinate clauses and their subjects, predicates, and complements. (When labeling the words on your paper, label the subject, verb, and complement of the subordinate clause *under* the sentence so that it's not confused with the subject and verb of the main clause.)
4. Identify verbals and phrases and their objects and modifiers and tell how they are used.
5. Explain the modifiers.

1. When the police arrived at the scene of the disturbance, a part of the crowd was yet there.
2. One of the special officers fired a shot into the crowd before fleeing from the rain of bricks and stones.

Day 2

Guided Response

1. There are three styles of writing in journalism: news, features, and editorials. Which style is used in this article? How can you tell?

2. Even though Hemingway went on to become a famous novelist, he spent some years in his youth as a reporter for the *Kansas City Star* newspaper. Do you think there is evidence in this article that he has the makings of a Nobel prize winning writer? Explain.

3. Review the elements of voice in Week 15 (diction, details, imagery, syntax, and tone). Find examples of each of these elements in Hemingway's article. Consider what kind of tone a news article ought to have.

4. Based on your experience of today's newspapers, do you think this is the style used in newspapers today? Explain.

5. A news article must answer the following questions: who, what, when, where, why, and how, otherwise known as the . Make a list of these categories on your paper and then say how each one is answered in the article.

6. Make a list of topics and/or events that you know about that would make good news articles. Choose one and list the 5 W and the H for it.

Copy the imitation sentences into your notebook. Today, try to write as much as you can without looking back at the book. By this time you should have some of them memorized.

1. I hope I did as well as he.
2. It was George who saw you and whom I saw.
3. I wanted to read the book myself.
4. Neither of her books was lying on the desk.
5. There was a conflict between him and me.
6. John likes skiing, skateboarding, and bicycling.
7. Does either of you know where the manual is?
8. The door's being locked created problems.
9. Don't just try to do it; be sure to do it.
10. Running along the curb, he tripped.

Use the following words correctly in a sentence. You may add a suffix of or if needed. Explain to your teacher how and why your usage of these words is correct.

1. hopefully   2. affect   3. myself
4. whom   5. everyone   6. one

Ernest Hemmingway, 1918

240

Day 3

Straight news writing requires attention to detail and presenting the facts objectively without personal opinion. The writer needs to be able to sift through available information and determine what is most important to report. News articles should have the following characteristics:

1. Attention getting headline
2. A strong lead containing 5 W's and H (who, what, when, where, why, and how)
3. Use of quotes (we like to hear what others have to say about the topic of the story)
4. Real facts (the truth and accuracy matter)
5. A strong summary
6. Arrangement of the story (presenting information from most to least important)

Reread the article by Hemingway printed on Day 1. Identify each of the characteristics listed above.

Not all events are "newsworthy," that is, important or compelling enough to be of interest to a wide group of people. Some key elements when considering "newsworthiness" are:

1. Timing: if it happened today, it's news, if it happened last week, it's not.
2. Significance: how many people are affected.
3. Proximity: the closer a story hits to home, the more newsworthy it is.
4. Prominence: when famous people are affected, the story matters (i.e. car accident involving your family vs. a car accident involving the President).
5. Human Interest: because these stories are based on emotional appeal, they are meant to be amusing or to generate empathy or other emotions. They often appear in special sections of the newspaper or at the end of the newscast as a "feel good" story or to draw attention to something particularly amusing, quirky, or offbeat.

Consider Hemingway's article with respect to these elements of newsworthiness. Which of these elements does it have?

The structure of a news article is often described as an upside-down pyramid. You want all the pertinent information right in the beginning of the article and as you continue, less and less important information is given. This is for two reasons. First, many people only read the headlines and the first few sentences of news articles. They need to get all the facts in those few sentences. Then, if they choose to read on, they can get more details, or read quotes by people involved. The second reason is that often an editor must chop an article to make it fit in the newspaper and you wouldn't want the most important facts to be missing.

So, your lead paragraph, called the "lead" is the most important part of the article. The author attempts to answer the 5Ws and the H all in that paragraph. Reread Hemingway's piece with that in mind.

Today you will write a news article about an event you have witnessed or were a part of.
You can base it on a humorous scene from your family

Desperate Mother Breaks Rolling Pin
Dog Upsets Garden Party

or base it on an event from a book you have read

Girl Foils Wolf in Deadly Attack (Little Red Riding Hood)
Traffic Jam in Downtown Boston (Make Way for Ducklings).

Once you have decided upon your event, make a list of the 5Ws and the H. Write your lead based on that information. Then continue to explain the event using quotes and further details. Just because you are writing objectively without inputting your opinion, doesn't mean you can't include colorful details. Use strong action words and specific nouns just as you would for narrative writing. You might include what happened after, how it was resolved, or what the people involved plan to do next. When you are done, write your headline.

Share your paper with your teacher and show where you have included the characteristics of a news story listed at the beginning of today's assignments.

File the paper in your drafts folder.

Day 4

Writing

Now that you have taken a stab at writing a news article, consider all the types of writing that make up the styles you'd find in newspapers and magazines.

Hard news: This is how journalists refer to news of the day. It is a chronicle of current events/incidents and is the most common news style on the front page of your typical newspaper. It starts with a summary lead. What happened? Where? When? To/ by whom? Why? It must be kept brief and simple, because the purpose of the rest of the story will be to elaborate on this lead.

The hard news writer must keep the writing clean and uncluttered and give the readers the information they need.

Soft news: This is a term for all the news that isn't time-sensitive. Soft news includes profiles of people, programs or organizations. These types of articles would appear later in the newspaper.

Feature: A news feature takes one step back from the headlines, exploring what's going on behind the news. News features are less time-sensitive than hard news but no less newsworthy. They can be an effective way to write about complex issues too large for the terse style of a hard news item. The pieces are generally longer and go deeper into a story, looking at it from several angles. You would find this style in the "lifestyle" section of the newspaper, for example, or in a magazine.

A feature takes a certain angle and explores it by interviewing the people involved and drawing conclusions from that information. The writer explores an important issue of the day and explains it to the reader through comments from people involved in the story. It's basic good storytelling.

Although the style is more narrative, no personal opinions are allowed. Present the opinions of others through quotes. The writer is the narrator in the truest sense, outside the story.

Editorial: The editorial expresses an opinion. The editorial page of the newspaper lets the writer comment on issues in the news. All editorials are personal but the   topics must still be relevant to the reader.

Next week you will be writing a feature story. Take some time today (at least 15 minutes) to brainstorm a list of possible topics you could use. A feature story may be about a person who has contributed to the community, the history of a particular event or tradition, a sports team, a 4-H event, a youth music concert, or a current issue like the pro-life debate, the death penalty, or pay raises for politicians. You may browse your local paper to see the kinds of features they have.

Make the list as comprehensive as possible so you have a lot to choose from. Get input from others in your family or class. Then make a decision about your topic. The reason you should choose your topic this week is so that you will have time to mull it over and decide on your angle. When I have a writing assignment I think about it for days and days before I start to write.

Parse the following sentences.
1. Identify the part of speech of each word.
2. Identify the parts of the sentence (As you tell the parts of the sentence give the case, number and gender of nouns and the tense, mood, and voice of verbs.)
3. Identify subordinate clauses and their subjects, predicates, and complements. (When labeling the words on your paper, label the subject, verb, and complement of the subordinate clause *under* the sentence so that it's not confused with the subject and verb of the main clause.)
4. Identify verbals and phrases and their objects and modifiers and tell how they are used.
5. Explain the modifiers.

Remember that a clause may be inside a phrase and a phrase inside a clause.

Wiping his tears as he spoke, the little child told us his story.

Although he had originally been kind, the coach was angry with us quite often.

Week 24

Day 1

Read the following news feature and record your first reaction.

The Long Road Home
In New Orleans, families struggle to return to normal one
year after Hurricane Katrina.

Chakia Boutte, 12, surveys what she has lost in the year since Hurricane Katrina devastated the Gulf Coast. The playground where she once spent afternoons is closed. Her block is full of stormwrecked homes, many abandoned. A pile of charred debris sits in front of what used to be Chakia's house. The home was looted and burned after her family evacuated in a rescue boat.

"I cried when I saw my house," she says, remembering the first time she returned home after the storm. "[Looters] took everything, even my jar of pennies."

Chakia and her cousin Mikia Kirton, 8, have lived in Houston since the storm forced their families to move. The girls dreaded returning to school this fall. They say other kids sometimes make fun of them. "They say, 'You used to have a home, now you live in the Astrodome,'" says Mikia. After Hurricane Katrina, thousands of evacuees had to take shelter at the Houston Astrodome.

After spending time in Arkansas, Oklahoma, and Texas, Toye Domino is happy to be starting fifth grade in New Orleans. "We had to travel halfway around the country to get back here," says Toye, 10. "I want to stay here because it's my hometown."

For kids in New Orleans, the start of school is a welcome sign of normalcy. One year ago, their lives were forever altered by Hurricane Katrina. More than 1,300 people died because of the Aug. 29, 2005, storm. About 770,000 people were displaced and evacuees scattered across the country.

"New Orleans has changed a lot," says Myeisha McDaniels, 13, whose family has moved back to the city. "Almost everyone I knew is gone."

This fall, about 56 of the city's 128 public schools will be open. Officials expected about 30,000 students, down from pre-Katrina enrollment of 60,000. The routine of the school day seems to help returning students cope, says Desmond Moore, an English teacher at Harriet Tubman Elementary School. "The kids are adjusting," he says. "It really feels normal to them to be back in school."

Still, there are challenges. The school doesn't have Internet access. Even basic supplies, such as textbooks and paper, can be scarce. "It forces you to do a little bit more with less," says Moore.

Rebuilding—slowly

Government spending for relief and recovery is nearing $100 billion, but the pace of rebuilding has been uneven. In some places, such as the Mississippi coast, progress is evident. Piles of debris have been cleared, and homes and businesses are being repaired or rebuilt. Hotel casinos have reopened, boosting the economy.

The picture is different in New Orleans. Parts of the city look as though Katrina passed through one month, rather than one year, ago. Neighborhoods that were hardest hit by floods, such as the Lower Ninth Ward, remain in ruins. The stench of mold and rotting garbage (locals call it "the Katrina smell") hangs in the air. Rusted cars and uprooted trees line the streets.

Gutted homes bear the scars of Katrina: watermarks and spray-painted symbols left by search teams. The remnants of people's lives—a high school volleyball trophy, water-damaged family photos, a lone sneaker—are strewn about the mostly deserted streets.

About half of the former population of 450,000 has returned to the city. Because few housing options are available, rents have risen an estimated 25 to 30 percent. To encourage more people to come back, Louisiana developed a $9 billion hurricane recovery program. However, the federal government only recently allocated enough money to fully fund the program.

In July, New Orleans officials announced the Unified New Orleans Plan. It calls for each city neighborhood to devise a rebuilding plan. Those plans will be combined with a citywide infrastructure plan to create a final rebuilding strategy. Meanwhile, the roads are full of potholes, and street signs point in every direction. Power outages are frequent. Many hospitals, banks, churches, and grocery stores remain shuttered.

"We're recovering slowly," New Orleans City Councilmember Cynthia Hedge-Morrell says with a sigh. "Like a cancer patient."

Strong roots

For those who lived through it, the memories of Hurricane Katrina remain fresh. Myeisha recalls being stuck in traffic trying to leave New Orleans before the storm. "The wind started blowing. The car started shaking. I thought we were going to die." Even now, Myeisha says, "I get scared when it rains."

Teachers and students draw strength from a poster in the Sophie B. Wright Charter School office. It shows a storm-damaged tree and includes a quote from the poet George Herbert that reads, "Storms make the oak grow deeper roots." That's the way many returning New Orleanians say they feel. "We want to think about how we survived, how we overcame," says Moore, "and how we're overcoming."

Write your first impressions of this news feature. What do you think is done effectively? How does it include the facts of the situation? Notice the beginning and ending. Is the opening engaging? Is the ending satisfactory?

Grammar Study

Imitation Sentences

Copy the imitation sentences. Write as many as you can from memory.

1. I hope I did as well as he.
2. It was George who saw you and whom I saw.
3. I wanted to read the book myself.
4. Neither of her books was lying on the desk.
5. There was a conflict between him and me.
6. John likes skiing, skateboarding, and bicycling.
7. Does either of you know where the manual is?
8. The door's being locked created problems.
9. Don't just try to do it; be sure to do it.
10. Running along the curb, he tripped.

Exercise

Edit this passage, correcting the mistakes.

Walking through the door at the top of the stairs Nora noticed that there was a strange dog between Stanley and I. She screamed even though neither of us were scared. I tried to quiet her saying, "Stanley, Rupert, and myself found this dog by the creek. He's our dog."

"There are a ton of reasons you should get rid of him," Nora cried, "not the least of which is that mom will have a fit. You can't keep him."

I picked up the dog and sat him on the coffee table. "See, he's nice," I said. The dog barked and tried to lay down on the table. Panting and licking, his face was friendly and gentle. Stanley ran to get some food to feed the dog in the kitchen. I caressed him and spoke gently to him. *Hopefully mom will let us keep him,* I thought.

Day 2

Guided Response

Reread the news feature printed on Day 1 and discuss the following questions with your teacher.

1. Reread the description of a feature story on Day 4 of Week 23. How well does this article fit the description? Explain.

2. A feature story should have an attention grabbing opening that draws a reader in. Identify the introduction. Where is the thesis or the line that tells the reader what the article is about? How far into the article does this line appear?

3. The ending of a feature should leave the reader with a profound thought or some idea about the future in other words, a somewhat "happy" ending. How effective is the ending of this news feature?

4. Notice the use of quotes in the article. How many different people are quoted? How are the quotes used in the story (where do they appear)?

5. Do you think this is a feature that would be interesting to someone your own age? Explain. What makes it interesting or not interesting?

6. Create an outline for the article.

Grammar Study

Possessive Modifiers for Gerunds

Recall that gerunds are verbals used as nouns (subjects, objects, predicate nominatives, and appositives). Often a gerund will have a word in front of it that modifies it. This modifier should be in the possessive case.

I did not know about *their* coming.

The word coming is the object of the preposition and a gerund. So its modifier there is in the possessive case. Some people make the mistake of using the objective form of the word as is,
I did not know about *them* coming.

Other examples:

Incorrect: I can understand *him* not wanting to fight the champ.

Correct: I can understand *his* not wanting to fight the champ.

This same rule applies if the modifying word is a noun; it's not just a rule for pronouns.

Incorrect: The *pitcher* hitting that batter caused the loss.
Correct: *The pitcher's* hitting that batter cause the loss.

Exercise A
Underline the correct choice in each sentence.

1. I am pleased about (he, him, his) taking over the chorus.
2. Mr. Johnson complained about (Jan, Jan's) listening to records after nine o'clock.
3. Mr. Pine never objected to (we, our, us) whistling in the halls.
4. We couldn't listen to (Tom, Tom's) complaining any longer.
5. He objects to (your, you) using company funds for private purposes.
6. Many people were afraid of (he, his, him) becoming a dictator.
7. (Mary's, Mary) joining the club was the subject of the discussion.
8. We were surprised at (their, them, they) raising hamsters.
9. The most important item is (we, us, our) needing shorter hours.
10. (Red Deer, Red Deer's) growing so fast created problems.
NOTE: Exceptions to the rules about the possessive case used with a gerund can occur when
  1. the noun or pronoun is to be stressed.
        I can't understand walking out in the middle of a rehearsal.
  2. the noun is plural.
        He disapproves of women working after marriage.
  3. the noun is modified.
        I approve of a well-trained adult playing football.

Exercise B
Select the correct choice in each sentence, using the instructions in brackets when applicable.
1. I heard about the (car, car's) failing to brake.
2. When we heard about the (girls, girls') losing the quiz bowl on a technicality, we were sad.
3. Have you heard about the (twins', twins) being suspended.
4. I enjoyed (your, you) singing in the concert.
5. Philip? I didn't know about (him, his, he) dropping the course. (emphasize pronoun)
6. A clever (lawyer, lawyer's) pleading a case is fascinating to hear.
7. The (boys', boys) whistling was improved.
8. The dance class was spoiled by the (record, record's) jumping.
9. We need to discuss (you, your) balancing the check book.
10. We all noticed the (table, table's) wobbling.

Day 3

Writing

Today you will begin to write a news feature story. Perhaps you have been thinking about a topic since last week. Here is a little more information about feature stories.

Features are interesting stories about people, places, and events. They aren't as concerned with conveying basic facts as in conveying a mood, feeling, or theme. Unlike writing news articles, there are no hard and fast "rules" for composing features. Features, common in newspapers, are even more common in magazines.

Tips for writing feature stories:

1. Many feature stories are biographical sketches of individuals. Often interviews with public figures (athletes or entertainers) or compelling people (such as a homeless person) can make for interesting feature stories.

2. Unlike in a news article, the feature writer is allowed much creativity in the story's composition. The order of presentation is based solely on the criteria of what makes for the most interesting read.

3. Pretend you are telling a story. Draw on storytelling techniques from other media, such as movies, theater, fiction, and music. This may include visualization of the scene you are creating. Sounds, smells, and textures can even be a viable means of expression. Paint a picture with words.

4. Metaphors and comparisons are fair game in feature stories. Your impressions can be communicated. For example, a feature on a political candidate can include the following: "Decked out in his garish jumpsuit, Greg Samsar bears a greater resemblance to a professional wrestler than a serious gubernatorial candidate."

5. Although personal insights are allowed in a feature, strive for objectivity. Tell both sides of the story: "Samsar responds to critics of his apparel by noting that Abraham Lincoln would go weeks without shaving." If you are featuring a homeless man and include comments critical of the police for enforcing loitering violations, give a police spokesman a chance to respond.

Source: http://www.cuw.edu/

Getting Ready to Write

Lead

Unlike a hard news lead, the feature lead can be much more creative, telling a story or setting the stage before getting to the purpose of the article. The *purpose* of the article is somewhat like the thesis in an essay. It is the main point you want to make. It is included in the lead, but you can lead up to it gradually. Notice in the sample on Day 1, the author does not get to the purpose (.) until the 4th paragraph. First she quotes students commenting on the storm and describes the scene.

Content

The writer presents the human side of the news along with the facts by using feature writing techniques such as quotes, vivid verbs and descriptive writing. Make an outline of your article before you begin to write a draft so you will know where you are going when you begin to write.

Notice the transitions that the author uses in the sample. . Here the author is shifting from the positive things talked about in the previous paragraph to greater problems in the second. This sentence indicates a shift in focus. These kinds of transitions help the reader move logically through the article.

Ending

A news feature is the skilled telling of a complete story and needs a strong feature conclusion where the writer makes or reinforces a point. There are several types of feature endings.

: summarizes the points made in the story. It usually focuses on impact,   effects or outcome.
: plants a fact, idea or scene in the lead and completes it at the end.
: ties up loose ends, answers questions or solves problems posed in the lead.
: provides a natural ending to a story told in chronological order.

> **Unending**: leaves a key question unanswered. It is used to stimulate reader thinking—to get the reader involved with the situation posed in the story.

: provides a surprise ending designed to jolt the reader.
: combines two or more of the above.

Begin by reading the sample feature story printed on the next page. Notice the comments in the right hand column. Once you have studied the sample, make an outline for your article. Then write your lead and will decide which kind of ending is best suited to your topic.

Go over your outline and lead with your teacher and explain your choice of endings. Then save your outline for Day 4.

Brief Analysis of a News Feature

Children polish writing at camp   **Headline**

Penmanship suffers in computer age   **Subhead**

By Lini S. Kadaba

Knight Ridder News Service   **Byline**

Friday, August 27, 1999

PHILADELPHIA -- Welcome to Camp   **Lead**
HandRIGHTing Ink., a place to mind one's p's   For hard news, the lead should be just
and q's and other details of proper penmanship.   one line. A feature like this one can
This is a place for children to practice putting   afford to play a little bit in order to
pencil to paper -- something that has become a   attract the reader.
necessity in the age of computers.

Poor penmanship costs U.S. businesses perhaps   Even though this is a light story, this
as much as $200 million a year in lost time and   author still supplies facts and cites
revenue, according to American Demographics   sources.
magazine. The American Medical Association
has urged physicians to dot their i's and cross
their t's, noting the scribble of doctors has
caused medication errors, even patient deaths.

In other words, the handwriting is on the   This author is having fun with
wall, and it's clearly a scrawl that needs swift   language. Coming after a paragraph
attention.   with hard facts, this sentence is a
                                                         refreshing contrast.

"In plain English, it's a mess," said Rose   Now that the author has gotten
Toomey, a graphologist near San Diego who   the point across, we see a series of
analyzes handwriting. "It's illegible. (With)   quotations to personalize the story,
computers, who wants to take the time to pick   make it more vivid... direct quotations
up a tool and write?"   from eyewitnesses and experts are
                                                         vital to a good news story.

Not John Hanes, 13, who lives in Paoli, Pa. "I   Now we start moving into some
don't like writing," he said of the mechanics of   general background. This isn't
cursive.   necessary for you the reader to

His mother, Susan Hanes, wants him to   understand the main point of the story,
improve his scratchy, hard-to-read script. She   but it does help flesh out the motives
also wants her daughter Hilary, 8½, to learn the   and goals of the people involved.
correct way to form cursive letters.

Both children happily attend HandRIGHTing
Ink., where the order of the day is righting
writing.

"I've seen kids struggling with their grip,
with their posture, with their attention, and
with their writing," said Amy Carroll, an
occupational

therapist who cofounded the company earlier this year with Sandy Purvis, also an occupational therapist.

"We really have a very structured approach that can help people change their bad habits," said Carroll, who herself struggled as a child.

On a recent Monday four children, ages 8 to 11, started the 2½-hour morning session with a review of perfectly printed rules (Do not push, trip or insult, says one that Purvis wrote) and then launched into warm-up exercises for fingers.

The kids clapped to "Miss Mary Mack/All dressed in black" and learned to sign their names. Later they would bounce on the trampoline and ride scooter boards on bellies through an obstacle course of cones.

The activities may seem like fun and games, adding to the camplike atmosphere, but in reality they hone ruler-straight posture and coordination, visual acuity and attention spans -- some of the problems faced by sloppy scribes.

"The underlying conditions are the ones that are fueling the dysfunction," Purvis said. "We are providing foundation skills that let the children improve lots of areas."

The actual handwriting lessons span two 30-minute periods. The teachers provide the children with all sorts of aids, including rubber pencil grips, slant boards, special cushions to accommodate fidgeters and even Twizzlers, this last to get kids to stop chewing on their nails.

"The idea is to find more appropriate ways to meet these needs," Carroll said. "It's all fine-tuning."

Each child is assessed for his or her special needs. Rickey, for one, sat on the fidgeter's cushion and leaned into his workbook atop a slantboard. As he gripped his pencil and wrote i-c-e in cursive, Purvis offered instruction and encouragement.

"That's right -- i, travel, c, bump top line, travel,

Now that we've got the basics, some reaction from participants, and some commentary on the significance of the whole thing, we zoom in on a little scene in which we watch the students at work.

The author has saved some very specific details until the end of the article... only a reader who was extremely interested in the subject (perhaps because they already have some knowledge in the area) will read all the way until the end... so the author me very specific details which mddetailesight interest readers

253

e, bump the top line, travel. Awesome!" she said, stamping the page with a star as Rickey smiled. A few weeks earlier, his print was almost impossible to read.

HandRIGHTing Ink., favors Jan Z. Olsen's Handwriting Without Tears approach to script over traditional standbys because of the method's flexibility. Palmer's method, with its loops and slants -- what most boomers learned -- is losing favor, it seems.

"We tolerate a lot of variation," Purvis said. For one, none of the children had to slant their script to the right unless the slant came naturally.

"Slant versus straight is overrated," Carroll added. According to her, slanted script came into fashion because of fountain pens. "It wouldn't work if they did up and down."

Instead of model script, the goal here is legibility. "Is it functional? Is it clear? Is it fast?" Carroll said.

—Source: setonhill.edu

Day 4

Writing

Reread the feature story from Day 1. Reread the annotated feature from Day 3. Then take your outline and lead and write the first draft of your feature story. Check for transitions and be sure your ending is appropriate to the topic.

Read your draft out loud to yourself to see if you have made any obvious errors. Then read the article to someone else. Ask you listener the following questions:

1. Is the lead interesting enough to grab your attention?
2. Could you tell what the focus of the article is? (See if they can tell you what the focus is.)
3. Is there enough detail to cover the topic? What parts did you find most interesting?
4. Was the ending satisfying? (Ask your listener to explain his answer.)
5. What suggestions do you have to improve the article?

Parse the following sentences.

1. Identify the part of speech of each word.
2. Identify the parts of the sentence (As you tell the parts of the sentence give the case, number and gender of nouns and the tense, mood, and voice of verbs.)
3. Identify subordinate clauses and their subjects, predicates, and complements. (When labeling the words on your paper, label the subject, verb, and complement of the subordinate clause *under* the sentence so that it's not confused with the subject and verb of the main clause.)
4. Identify verbals and phrases and their objects and modifiers and tell how they are used.
5. Explain the modifiers.

(Remember that a clause may be inside a phrase and a phrase inside a clause.)

Piles of debris have been cleared, and homes and businesses are being repaired or rebuilt.

Hurricane Katrina over the Gulf of Mexico, 2005

Week 25

Day 1

Read the following piece and comment on it.

O Shenandoah

O Shenandoah I long to hear you,
Away, you rolling river.
O Shenandoah I long to hear you
Away, I'm bound away, across the wide Missouri.

O Shenandoah I long to see you
Away, you rolling river.
O Shenandoah I long to see you
Away, I'm bound away, across the wide Missouri.

O Shenandoah, I love your daughter
Away, you rolling river.
I'll take her 'cross the rolling water
Away, I'm bound away, across the wide Missouri.

'Tis seven years since I have seen you
To hear your rolling river
O Shenandoah I long to see you
Away, I'm bound away, across the wide Missouri.

For seven years, I've been a rover,
Away, you rolling river.
O Shenandoah, I've been a rover,
Away, I'm bound away, across the wide Missouri.

Farewell, goodbye, I shall not grieve you
Away, you rolling river.
O Shenandoah I'll not deceive you
Away, I'm bound away, across the wide Missouri.

O Shenandoah I'll not forget you
I'll dream of your clear waters.
O Shenandoah you're in my mem'ry
Away, I'm bound away, across the wide Missouri.
                                    —Traditional, American

Write you first response to this piece. What does it make you think of? Have you heard other words used in it? (In folk poems and songs, many different variations appear based on the geographic area or the interpretation of the poet/singer.) Sing it if you know the tune.

Grammar Study

Copy the imitation sentences. Write as many as you can from memory.

1. I hope I did as well as he.
2. It was George who saw you and whom I saw.
3. I wanted to read the book myself.
4. Neither of her books was lying on the desk.
5. There was a conflict between him and me.
6. John likes skiing, skateboarding, and bicycling.
7. Does either of you know where the manual is?
8. The door's being locked created problems.
9. Don't just try to do it; be sure to do it.
10. Running along the curb, he tripped.

Parallel Structure

Parallel structure refers to the matching of grammatical elements within a sentence. When things are listed in a series or a conjunction is used, all the grammatical forms must match. For example, sentence number 6 above, John is doing 3 things: skiing, skateboarding, and bicycling. All three things in the series are *ing* verbs. *The items in a series must be all nouns, all infinitives, all prepositional phrases, all gerunds, or all clauses.*

For example, this sentence is incorrect:

Sandy is only interested in fishing for frogs and cookies.

To correct it, the two elements being connected have to be the same grammatical form:

Sandy is only interested in fishing for frogs and eating cookies.

In a series of clauses, all verbs must be in the same voice.

This sentence is incorrect:

The news reporter expected that he would pitch his idea to the editor, that he would win the assignment, and that he would be admired by all for snagging the story.

The last clause switches to the passive voice. Here is the corrected version:

The news reporter expected that he would pitch his idea to the editor, that he would win the assignment, and that all would admire him for snagging the story.

Other Examples:

Parallel phrases: I intend to climb the mountain and to ski down.
The children scrambled under the table, across the floor, and into the secret cubby hole.

Parallel clauses: He wanted the be the best not because he thought it was right, but because he was proud.

Exercise
The following sentences have parallel structure errors. Write the corrected sentence on your paper.

1. Solving puzzles is beneficial to children by helping them in future jobs, for logic reasons, and in developing problem solving strategies.

2. All the runners bounced, stretched, and were practicing their starts.

3. Rachel was unsure of the recipe, the ingredients, and to know if the oven was ready.

4. The children became hungry on the trail, were frightened by strange noises and they felt overcome with fatigue.

5. Bernie hates to cultivate, to weed, and harvesting the plants, but she loves to eat the food.

Day 2

Guided Response

Reread the poem *O Shenandoah* printed on Day 1 and discuss the following questions with your teacher.

1. Do you think it is a song or a poem? Explain your answer. What makes something a poem? What makes it a song?

2. What tone or mood does the poem/song have? Explain your answer.

3. Like many folk songs, the words may be different depending on the book in which you find it, or the person you hear singing it. Some people believe that *O Shenandoah* began as a "chanty" sung by boatmen on the Missouri river and then traveled through other seamen around the world.

   There have been various theories about the song's meaning. Some say it's about the boatman's love for the river and/or the Shenandoah valley in Virginia. Some say it's a metaphor for a woman that the boatman left behind. Some say it did not originate with the boatmen at all, but was either a slave song or about a Civil War soldier. Write what you think the poem is about. Use evidence from the poem to support your idea.

4. Write a copy change poem (as you did in Week 20) using *O Shenandoah* as your poem of origin.

Grammar Study

Usage Problems with Infinitives

Many people use the following improper construction:

> I wish you would try and keep this room clean.

The speaker uses a conjunction as if there are two things he wants the listener to do. (First that *you would try* and secondly that *you would keep*.) He really intends one thing, though, and that is that the room be clean. Here is the proper construction:

> I wish you would try to keep this room clean.

The same mistake is made when using the word "be sure"

> Incorrect: You must be sure and fasten your seat belt.
> Correct: You must be sure to fasten your seat belt.

These mistakes are easy to make while you are speaking, but should be avoided in formal writing.

A word about split infinitives: It is long been a "law" of English that the infinitive shall not be split up by a modifier, as in *He hopes to sincerely express his love*. This is because when rules about English were being made, Latin was the model language. In Latin you don't split an infinitive because an infinitive is one word. That idea carried over into English.

While splitting should *generally* be avoided for proper English usage, sometimes the meaning of sentence is changed if you move the modifier. Consider the sentences below and see which one best expresses the thought of the sentence.

> He hopes to sincerely express his love.
> He sincerely hopes to express his love.
> He hopes to express his love sincerely.
> He hopes sincerely to express his love.

Exercise A
There is one error in each of the following sentences. (It could be any usage errors that have been discussed in this unit so far.) Find the error and correct the sentence.

1. We were really surprised to find that the dessert tasted like it had no sugar in it.
2. Unable to lift the heavy crate alone, two friends helped me.
3. If you can't bake the pastry like I told you, I cannot be responsible for the results.
4. Throughout the entire ordeal, Dan lay quiet on the couch.
5. It was obvious that the coach felt badly about the way the team had played.
6. I'll check the essay when you finish for spelling mistakes.
7. That test was harder than I thought; hopefully the teacher will be lenient.
8. They had a lot of fun acting like they knew what they were doing.
9. I've told you a hundred times to not talk with your mouth full.
10. If you really care about him, you won't object to him making little mistakes once in a while.
11. I am not sure who she had in mind.
12. We didn't know about them being lost until we read the story in the newspaper.

Exercise B
Use the following words correctly in a sentence.

1. lie   2. set
3. effect   4. like

Day 3

Writing

The Definition Essay

This week you will write a definition essay. In a definition essay, the writer takes an abstract concept and explains what it means, making it concrete for the reader. The definition essay provides a personal, extended definition of these abstract terms by various methods. Listed below are some approaches that can be used in any combination in a definition essay.

Analysis: Divide the subject into parts and define each part separately.
Classification: Describe what classes the subject belongs to according to dictionary definitions.
Comparison: Show the term's likeness to or difference from something familiar.
Details: Describe the physical characteristics, traditional thoughts, and other distinguishing attributes that describe the term.
Examples and Incidents: Narrate incidences that can bring to life a group, theory, or object.
Negation: Mention what it is not so that it's easier to see what it is.
Origins and Causes: Explain the history of the term (Where did the it come from? What is the background information?
Results, Effects, and Uses: Discuss the consequences and uses of the term.

Choosing a topic

You will need to choose a "debatable" topic, that is something that is not overly obvious. For example, it wouldn't be too interesting to read about the definition of the word *student*, but the definition of a *good student* would be open for debate. Choose a general topic instead of a specific one. The more general or abstract your topic, the more room for debate about it exists.

   Here are some suggested topics:
Define a good poem (or good music or art)
Define patriotism
Define gluttony
Define holiness
Define "home"
Define the perfect basketball (or any other sport) fan
Define the perfect chocolate confection
Define perfection
Define success
Define contrition

You may choose any term you like, but discuss it with your teacher before beginning to write.

Prewriting

Free write: Write about your chosen term for 15-20 without stopping. Explore your thoughts about it completely. Take longer if you need more time to think.

Extended Thinking: In order to solidify your thinking about the term, use your free-write to write the answers to the following questions.

Consider 2 different ways to describe the term you're defining.

What sorts of examples would best illustrate it?

What kind of conflict might the word involve?

What is it similar to?

What metaphor could be used with this term?

Are there any other words that must be understood in order to understand this one?

What events or conditions might cause your word?

What thoughts and feelings are generally associated with your word?

List three synonyms for your word:

—Adapted from www.successlink.org/GTI/l

Formulating a thesis: You must be able to write your definition of the term you have chosen in one sentence. Go over your free-write and the answers to the questions above and determine what you really think about the term. Your thesis may have several parts to it. Do not use the first or second person in your thesis. Saying "I think" or "I believe" weakens the thesis. Simply state your definition as a fact.

Outline: Before creating an outline, review the approaches listed on the previous page. Decide which ones you will use in your paper, which ones are most appropriate to the term you have chosen. Then you may create an outline using a formula like this outline:

I. Introduction

    A. Attention getter

        1. You may want to include what the traditional or common meaning of the term is, but avoid using a dictionary definition in your introduction (not much of an attention getter!).

        2. You may want to describe a scene in which the term is being illustrated.

        3. You may want to open with a image of the word opposite to the one your paper will show.

    B. Thesis: State how you define the term. The definition may have several parts.

II. Body
    A. Background information:
        1. Not completely necessary, but if you need to, use this part of your paper to provide it.
    B. Point one
        1. The first part of your definition of the term.
        2. Example to illustrate that point.
        3. Analysis of how the example illustrates the point.
    C. Point two
        1. The second part of the definition of the term or say what it is *not*.
        2. Example to illustrate that point.
        3. Analysis of how the example illustrates the point.
    D. Point three
        1. The third part of the definition (if there is one)
        2. Example to illustrate that point.
        3. Analysis of how the example illustrates the point.
    E. Point four, etc.

III. Conclusion
    A. Review your definition's main points
    B. You may want to explain how your definition has affected you.
    C. Closing attention getter: Refer back to something in your introduction to tie the paper together.

Writing

Write the introduction for your definition essay. Be creative in the way you introduce your word. Here is a sample:

> A word of advice for the untrained fashionists of the world: jeans have evolved. Two inch rises are in, pleats are out, and the only way those old Levis will fly is if they are the original, 501's bought at a trendy vintage store. Jeans are no longer pants made of heavy, twilled cotton for uniforms and work clothes (Dictionary.com); they are a subculture of style. Infinite brands, ever-changing styles, and rising prices create the world of denim. Each pair is classified by the mood of the owner, saved for particular situations in which they will be perfectly utilized. Jeans have created their own definition; they are confidence, comfort, and contentment.

Notice how this student writer works in the conventional definition from a dictionary source without saying something more trite, as in, *The dictionary defines jeans as pants made of heavy, twilled cotton for uniforms and work clothes.*

Save your outline and introduction for Day 4.

Day 4

Writing

Today you will write the definition essay. Reread the introduction you wrote yesterday and see if you want to make any changes in it. Then write the body and conclusion of your essay following the outline you made on Day 3. When you are done think of a clever title, one that reveals something about the approach you are taking or the thesis. (You don't want to call The Definition of _____.)

Ask someone to you read your essay and tell you what they think of the way you presented your word. Check your paper for proper parallel construction. To do this, look for any place in your paper where you used conjunctions and see if the grammatical forms are parallel. Then file your essay in your drafts folder. Correct them as needed

Grammar Study

Parse the following sentence.
1. Identify the part of speech of each word.
2. Identify the parts of the sentence (As you tell the parts of the sentence give the case, number and gender of nouns and the tense, mood, and voice of verbs.)
3. Identify subordinate clauses and their subjects, predicates, and complements. (When labeling the words on your paper, label the subject, verb, and complement of the subordinate clause *under* the sentence so that it's not confused with the subject and verb of the main clause.)
4. Identify verbals and phrases and their objects and modifiers and tell how they are used.
5. Explain the modifiers.

(Remember that a clause may be inside a phrase and a phrase inside a clause.)

He ran away as if a ghost were after him.

Week 26

Day 1

Read the following essay and reflect on it.

Electric Lighting Becomes a Reality

Have you ever wondered what people used for lighting their homes before electric lights were widely used? When did that happen? What did it take for it to become a reality? In the early nineteenth century, gas lamps were commonly used in American homes. The later varieties used a screen that was heated until it glowed, producing a steadier light. Electric lighting did not become generally available until near the end of the nineteenth century, after a development period of nearly a hundred years.

English scientist Sir Humphrey Davy demonstrated arc lamps, the earliest electric lamps, during a series of lectures very early in the nineteenth century. He produced light by passing a current between two pointed carbon electrodes, causing arcing between them, rather like lightning. As you can imagine, these lamps were too bright and hot for normal indoor use, although they were used for street lighting in a few locations. They also burned out rather quickly. In 1802, Davy demonstrated the possibility of a filament light by passing a current through a thin platinum wire until it glowed. This, too, burned out very quickly; it was also very expensive.

Scientists on both sides of the Atlantic continued work to develop practical electric lamps. Soon they realized that when the filament was heated in air, it oxidized rapidly. If the filament could be placed in an evacuated bulb instead of in air, it would last much longer. Starting in the 1840s, several different filament bulbs were developed and patented. However, the vacuums that could be achieved at the time were not very good; there was still too much oxygen in the bulbs, so they burned out rather quickly. In addition, electricity itself was too

expensive for the lamps to be widely used. Sir Joseph Swan was one of the scientists who worked on the problem; however he abandoned it soon after 1860.

American technologist and inventor Thomas Alva Edison took up the challenge in the late 1870s. His team sought a design that would be long lasting, safe, reliable, and inexpensive. The goal was to create a light bulb that would replace the gaslights and kerosene lamps that were then widely used. Edison's work improved on the previous work of many others. His vision was also broader in scope than theirs: he realized that to make electric lighting a reality, he must not only develop a worthy light bulb, but also the whole system that would enable it to work. Edison took his idea to financiers Morgan and Vanderbilt, who agreed to underwrite the costs of his experiments. Edison then assembled his team, forming the Edison Electric Company.

Edison once said, "Genius is 1% inspiration and 99% perspiration." This was certainly true for the development of the lighting system. Over a period of years, Edison's team performed thousands of experiments. They tried all kinds of materials, from fine metal wires to animal hairs and plant fibers. (They even tried tungsten, which is used in incandescent bulbs today, but they could not make it work with the technology of the time.) Edison said that his team had tried over 6000 different materials for filaments. They also worked on improving the bulbs in a glass-blowing shop as well as on improving the vacuum. Experiment after experiment failed. Yet, Edison urged his team to keep on trying: he felt they had learned something valuable with each failed experiment.

Finally, in 1879, their hard work paid off: their platinum-filament bulb lasted for a few hours. Unfortunately, it was too expensive, so they went back to work. With a lower current, better vacuum, and a filament of carbonized thread, they made a bulb that lasted 13½ hours. By the time of the public demonstration on the last day of 1879, the carbon filament bulb lasted 40 hours. Edison applied for a patent on the light bulb, which was granted early in 1880. However, Sir Joseph Swan had again taken up work on the light bulb in about 1875 and had independently demonstrated and patented his bulb in England. Thus, Edison offered him a partnership in order to avoid patent infringement problems.

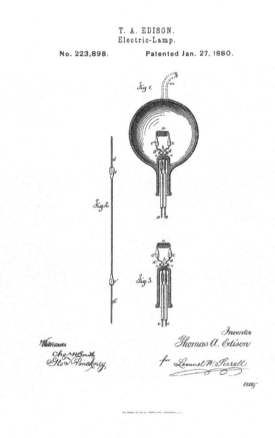

Meanwhile, Edison's team continued to work on the other parts needed to complete the system. This included equipment to generate and regulate electric current, and to safely and effectively transmit the electric power to users. They even had to develop the sockets and on/off switches! Another Edison innovation was the development of the parallel circuit for his light bulbs. Until this time, lights had been wired in series, so that if one burned out, all the lights would go off. Not only that, but it was difficult and time-consuming to determine which bulb was burned out, since a fault in any one of them would cause all to switch off. The parallel circuit solved these problems. Finally, in 1882, the Edison Electric Company brought the world's first central electric generating station online in New York City, making electric lighting a reality for homes and businesses.

This, of course, was only the start of the electric lighting revolution. Within a few years, the lamps had been improved to last up to 1200 hours. And, once Edison had proven the concept, electric generating stations began springing up across the nation and in other parts of the world as well. About a decade later, Willis Whitney invented a treatment for the filament to prevent the bulbs from blackening over the lifetime of the bulb. And within a decade after that, William Coolidge developed a method for making tungsten filaments, and inert gases rather than a vacuum began to be used within the bulb. This essentially completed the development of the incandescent light bulb.

Thanks to Edison's perseverance, we have much more than just light bulbs today. Edison's continued experiments with bulbs led to the discovery of the Edison effect, which in turn led to the development of vacuum tubes and the first computers.

—Suchi Myjak

Write your first reaction to this essay. Was there anything surprising? What did you find most interesting? What further questions do you have about Edison?

Grammar Study

1. I hope I did as well as he.
2. It was George who saw you and whom I saw.
3. I wanted to read the book myself.
4. Neither of her books was lying on the desk.
5. There was a conflict between him and me.
6. John likes skiing, skateboarding, and bicycling.
7. Does either of you know where the manual is?
8. The door's being locked created problems.
9. Don't just try to do it; be sure to do it.
10. Running along the curb, he tripped.

This week, instead of copying these sentences, say what rule is used in each one. Explain why the sentence is correct.

Day 2

Guided Response

Reread the history of electric lighting essay printed on Day 1 and complete the following activities.

1. Identify the three main parts of an expository essay: introduction, body, and conclusion. Underline or copy the thesis statement.

2. List in order the major events that made electric lighting a reality.

3. Which of the those events do you think was most important in the development of electric lighting? Explain why you think it is the most important. Then order the remaining events in order of their importance.

4. Why do you think Edison was so successful in his projects? (There may be more than one reason.)

5. What is the significance of electric lighting becoming a reality? (Why does it matter? What did it mean for science and for human life?)

6. Evaluate the opening and the closing of this essay. What is effective about each part?

Grammar Study

Subject-Predicate Agreement Revisited

The words *some, most, all, none* and *a lot* can change from plural or singular depending on the sentence in which they are used.

These are correct:

None of the students are big enough
A lot of the cookies were from the Mid-town Bakery.

Most of us were quite happy with the election results.
All of the band members were ready on time, but their instruments never arrived.
Some of the men were waiting for the train instead of walking to the bus station.

This may seem to contradict what we said earlier about the object of the preposition not determining the verb form, but with these few words, the sense of the preposition influences the meaning of the subject. The verb still agrees with the subject (verbs never agree with prepositions). It may seem as though the predicates are agreeing with the objects of the prepositions, but the sense of the subject can change from singular to plural depending on the object of the preposition.

Remember that these words always have a singular predicate: *Each, either, neither, one, everyone, anyone, someone, no one, everybody, anybody, somebody, nobody.*

Exercise A
Tell whether the following sentences are correct or incorrect. If incorrect, change it to make it correct.

1. Neither of the proposals were accepted by finance committee.
2. Are there any old books you want to donate to the library sale?
3. Each of the books has an exciting plot.
4. None of those papers were left on the shelf.
5. The number of florists attending the flower show were surprising.
6. Everybody who saw the movie was sure it would win first place in the festival.
7. Each of the players were sure that their team would win.
8. None of the players were sure that their team would win.

Exercise B
Review Clauses
Identify the dependent (subordinate) clauses in the sentences below. Say whether they are adjective, adverb, or noun clauses. There may be more than one in each sentence.

1. Edison applied for a patent on the light bulb, which was granted early in 1880.

2. As the landscape changed from brown to green, the army awakened, and began to tremble with eagerness at the noise of rumors. (*Red Badge of Courage* by Stephen Crane.)

3. Neighborhoods that were hardest hit by floods, such as the Lower Ninth Ward, remain in ruins.

4. Hoping to impress the lesson more deeply, Mrs. March, who had a good deal of humor, resolved to finish off the trial in an appropriate manner. (*Little Women* by Louisa May Alcott)

5. Whether she wanted to admit it was beside the point.

6. He rode on until he reached the city, where all the people stood in exactly the same positions.

Day 3

Writing

Today you will write a summary of the article printed on Day 1.

A summary is a condensed version, in your own words, of the writing
of someone else; a condensation that reproduces the thought, emphasis,
and tone of the original. It abstracts all the significant facts of the original—
overall thesis, main points, important supporting details—but, unlike a
paraphrase, it omits and/or condenses amplifications such as descriptive
details (McAnulty 1981;50).

Here are the steps to writing a summary:

1. Read the text and think about it as a whole to determine the main point. (Look at your answer to number 1 in the Guided Response from Day 2).
2. Determine the main idea of each paragraph or section. Find the most important supporting details. You can write them in an outline fashion, or just list them. (Reread your answers to number 2 and 3 in the Guided Response from Day 2.)
3. Read the text again to be sure you have captured the author's main ideas.
4. Write the summary in your own words (don't look back to the original article as you write) conveying the author's tone and emphasis. To begin, the first sentence should name the article and give the main idea of the article. Example:

    In the feature article "Four Kinds of Reading," the author, Donald Hall, explains his opinion about different types of reading.

5. Do not make personal comments or judgements about the value of the author's point.
6. Use third person, present tense.

Write a first draft of your summary and save it for Day 4.

Day 4

Writing

Reread the article on electric lighting printed on Day 1. Reread your summary of the article. Ask yourself these questions about your summary:

1. Is the main idea stated clearly in the first sentence?
2. Are all important details included?
3. Are the details in a logical order?
4. Are the ideas connected by transitions to make the writing flow?
5. Is the main idea restated in the conclusion tying the ending back to the beginning?

Make changes in your paper based on your observations. Ask someone to read your paper and ask them the same questions. Discuss the summary with you reader and then make changes in your paper based on your conversation. Before you file it, check for parallel construction in any sentence where you used a conjunction.

File the summary in your drafts folder.

Grammar Study

Parse the following sentence.
1. Identify the part of speech of each word.
2. Identify the parts of the sentence (As you tell the parts of the sentence give the case, number and gender of nouns and the tense, mood, and voice of verbs.)
3. Identify subordinate clauses and their subjects, predicates, and complements. (When labeling the words on your paper, label the subject, verb, and complement of the subordinate clause *under* the sentence so that it's not confused with the subject and verb of the main clause.)
4. Identify verbals and phrases and their objects and modifiers and tell how they are used.
5. Explain the modifiers.

(Remember that a clause may be inside a phrase and a phrase inside a clause.)

Mrs. March, who had a good deal of humor, resolved to finish off the trial in an appropriate manner.

Week 27

Day 1
Study the picture below and think about it.

Westward, the Course of Empire Takes its Way (a.k.a *Westward Ho!*) by Emmanuel Gottleib Leutze

1. Study the painting and then close your book and try to remember as much detail as you can from the painting. You can try and sketch it or write down the things you noticed in it.

2. Imagine that you are aboard a wagon train heading west. Either write a journal entry about one day of your trip or write a letter about your journey to an imaginary family member back in the East.

Grammar Study

This unit focused on correcting the most common grammar errors that people make. While it is good to know that something is an error, it is even better to understand why it is an error. That shows your mastery of grammar.

Here are the ten sentences you have been practicing each week in this unit, but this time they have the error included instead of the correct sentence. Find the error in each one and tell why it must be changed (what is the grammatical concept behind each correction).

1. I hope I did as well as me.
2. It was George whom saw you and who I saw.
3. Sally and myself wanted to read the book.
4. Neither of her books were lying on the desk.
5. There was a conflict between he and I.
6. Sally likes dancing, racquet ball, and skating.
7. Do either of you know where the manual is?
8. The door being locked created problems.
9. Don't just try and do it; be sure and it.
10. Running along the curb he tripped.

Day 2

Guided Response

Review the painting printed on Day 1. The artist, Emmanuel Leutze, was commissioned by the U.S. Congress in 1861 to decorate a stairway in the Capitol Building with the theme: Westward the Course of Empire. This reproduction shows the way the mural appears on the wall. The body of water in the bottom section is the Pacific Ocean. The mural represents the idea of Manifest Destiny.

Discuss the following questions with your teacher.

1. Name the things in the painting that you think represent the idea of Manifest Destiny. (If you are not sure what Manifest Destiny is, look it up so you can discuss it with regard to this painting.) How well do you think Leutze captured the sense of westward expansion? Explain your answer.

2. In what poses are the women portrayed? In what poses are the men portrayed? What if any conclusion can you draw about the painter's view of the movement west?

3. What is the tone or mood of the painting? What things in the painting help to convey the tone or mood?

4. Why do you think Congress wanted this subject for the Capitol Building?

5. The title of the painting is taken from a poem written in 1724 by Bishop Berkeley of Ireland. The poem is entitled: "Verses on the Prospect of Planting Arts and Learning Is America." Berkeley believed in a philosophic way of looking at the history of empires of the world, and he concluded that the general trend that power tended west would end with America. America would be the last great empire.

   > Westward the course of Empire takes its way
   >   The first four acts already past.
   > A fifth shall close the drama with the day.
   >   Time's noblest offspring is the last.

This may seem to flatter America, but really, Bishop Berkeley did not like America. Still, his conclusions, as represented in his poem, seem to have come true. Explain this verse with regard to the painting and with regard to American history. What do you think the verse means and how can it applied to the painting?

Grammar Study

Review the usage rules for the following words. Use each properly in a sentence. (This can be done orally with the teacher.)

1.	good/well	7.	hopefully
2.	loose/lose	8.	all ready/already
3.	effect/affect	9.	some time/sometimes/sometime
4.	lie/lay	10.	every day/everyday
5.	there/their/they're	11.	your/you're
6.	who/whom	12.	myself

Day 3

Writing

This week, you will take one of the drafts that you have written in the Unit, revise it, and make a final copy for your writing portfolio. Choose the writing that you like the best, or the one that you think best shows your writing skill. Here is a list of the papers that you have written:

This I Believe	Nature Observation	Compare/Contrast
News Article	Feature Article	Definition Essay
Summary		

No paper, even one written by a professional writer, is perfect the first time it is written! So take your time in the revision stage to find places where you can improve. Today's revision will focus on style and voice.

Style
This unit concerned expository style. Here are the characteristics of good expository style:

- ✓ focus on main topic
- ✓ logical supporting facts
- ✓ details, explanations, and examples
- ✓ strong organization
- ✓ clarity
- ✓ logical order
- ✓ smooth transitions

Reread the essay you have chosen to revise and evaluate it based on each of these categories.

Use the chart below to help you think about them. The point of reviewing your paper this way is to find places that need improvement, so judge critically. If you find something done wonderfully or something lacking, make a note of it in the chart.

Then, ask someone else to read your essay and listen to his or her suggestions for improving your paper. You may ask that person to judge you on each of the style categories.

Score yourself in each category, with 5 being the highest score and 1 the lowest. Then explain your score below it

Focus on main topic	
Logical supporting facts	
Details, explanation,examples	
Strong organization	
Clarity	
Logical order	
Smooth transitions	

Final note on style: In all but the "This I believe" paper you should avoid the words *believe*, *know*, and *think*. These words weaken the point you are trying to make. So instead of saying

> *I think the painting captures the hopeful attitude of the saint,*

say

> *The painting captures the hopeful attitude of the saint.*

Instead of saying,

> *As you know, this author spent many years developing his characteristic descriptions,*

say,

> *This author spent many years developing his characteristic descriptions.*

Voice

Review the 5 elements of voice discussed in Week 15:

Diction: Word choice is the most basic and important element.

Details: Facts, individual incidents.

Imagery: Brings the senses to life in words.

Syntax: Syntax is the grammatical structure of a sentence, the way words are arranged. Various sentence structures pace the writing and determine the focus.

Tone: Tone is the attitude of the speaker or writer as revealed in the choice of vocabulary or the intonation of speech.

Evaluate your paper based on these categories. Use the chart below to record your evaluation.

Diction	List some words that you chose particularly for their effectiveness. Say why they are effective as you have used them.
Details	What details are included to help get your point across?
Imagery	What kinds of imagery do you use?
Syntax	Check your sentence variety. Are there too many of one kind of sentence? Do you have a mix of simple, complex, and compound? (Count them if you need to find out.)
Tone	What is the tone of your paper? What helps to bring about that tone?

After you have evaluated your paper using this chart, makes changes in your paper to improve the elements of voice.

Set your paper aside until Day 4.

Day 4

Writing

Review the changes you made in your paper on Day 3 and make any last minute improvements that come to your mind as your read the paper. Now make a final copy of your paper. A final copy is done in your best handwriting in ink, or typed.

When you are done, ask yourself the following questions. The more serious you are about reflecting on your writing process and progress, and the more aware of yourself of as a writer you become, the more your writing will improve.

Final Copy Reflection

1. What I think I did well in this paper:

2. What I tried to improve on in this paper:

3. What I liked least about my writing on this paper:

4. What I want the teacher to address when reviewing my paper:

5. What I want to work on in my next paper:

6. The most important thing to me about my writing right now is:

Unit 4
Short Story

Week 28

Day 1

Read the following short story. As you read, highlight passages that you particularly like or that evoke strong images. When you are done write your initial response to the story.

The Ransom of Red Chief

It looked like a good thing: but wait till I tell you. We were down South, in Alabama--Bill Driscoll and myself-when this kidnapping idea struck us. It was, as Bill afterward expressed it, "during a moment of temporary mental apparition"; but we didn't find that out till later.

There was a town down there, as flat as a flannel-cake, and called Summit, of course. It contained inhabitants of as undeleterious and self-satisfied a class of peasantry as ever clustered around a Maypole.

Bill and me had a joint capital of about six hundred dollars, and we needed just two thousand dollars more to pull off a fraudulent town-lot scheme in Western Illinois with. We talked it over on the front steps of the hotel. Philoprogenitiveness, says we, is strong in semi-rural communities therefore, and for other reasons, a kidnapping project ought to do better there than in the radius of newspapers that send reporters out in plain clothes to stir up talk about such things. We knew that Summit couldn't get after us with anything stronger than constables and, maybe, some lackadaisical bloodhounds and a diatribe or two in the Weekly Farmers' Budget. So, it looked good.

We selected for our victim the only child of a prominent citizen named Ebenezer Dorset. The father was respectable and tight, a mortgage fancier and a stern, upright collection-plate passer and forecloser. The kid was a boy of ten, with bas-relief freckles, and hair the colour of the cover of the magazine you buy at the news-stand when you want to catch a train. Bill and me figured that Ebenezer would melt down for a ransom of two thousand dollars to a cent. But wait till I tell you.

About two miles from Summit was a little mountain, covered with a dense cedar brake. On the rear elevation of this mountain was a cave. There we stored provisions.

One evening after sundown, we drove in a buggy past old Dorset's house. The kid was in the street, throwing rocks at a kitten on the opposite fence.

"Hey, little boy!" says Bill, "would you like to have a bag of candy and a nice ride?"

The boy catches Bill neatly in the eye with a piece of brick.

"That will cost the old man an extra five hundred dollars," says Bill, climbing over the wheel.

That boy put up a fight like a welter-weight cinnamon bear; but, at last, we got him down in the bottom of the buggy and drove away. We took him up to the cave, and I hitched the horse in the cedar brake. After dark I drove the buggy to the little village, three miles away, where we had hired it, and walked back to the mountain.

Bill was pasting court-plaster over the scratches and bruises on his features. There was a fire burning behind the big rock at the entrance of the cave, and the boy was watching a pot of boiling coffee, with two buzzard tailfeathers stuck in his red hair. He points a stick at me when I come up, and says:

"Ha! cursed paleface, do you dare to enter the camp of Red Chief, the terror of the plains?"

"He's all right now," says Bill, rolling up his trousers and examining some bruises on his shins. "We're playing Indian. We're making Buffalo Bill's show look like magic-lantern views of Palestine in the town hall. I'm Old Hank, the Trapper, Red Chief's captive, and I'm to be scalped at daybreak. By Geronimo! that kid can kick hard."

Yes, sir, that boy seemed to be having the time of his life. The fun of camping out in a cave had made him forget that he was a captive himself. He immediately christened me Snake-eye, the Spy, and announced that, when his braves returned from the warpath, I was to be broiled at the stake at the rising of the sun.

Then we had supper; and he filled his mouth full of bacon and bread and gravy, and began to talk. He made a during-dinner speech something like this:

"I like this fine. I never camped out before; but I had a pet 'possum once, and I was nine last birthday. I hate to go to school. Rats ate up sixteen of Jimmy Talbot's aunt's speckled hen's eggs. Are there any real Indians in these woods? I want some more gravy. Does the trees moving make the wind blow? We had five puppies. What makes your nose so red, Hank? My father has lots of money. Are the stars hot? I whipped Ed Walker twice, Saturday. I don't like girls. You dassent catch toads unless with a string. Do oxen make any noise? Why are oranges round? Have you got beds to sleep on in this cave? Amos Murray has got six toes. A parrot can talk, but a monkey or a fish can't. How many does it take to make twelve?"

Every few minutes he would remember that he was a pesky redskin, and pick up his stick rifle and tiptoe to the mouth of the cave to rubber for the scouts of the hated paleface. Now and then he would let out a warwhoop that made Old Hank the Trapper, shiver. That boy had Bill terrorized from the start.

"Red Chief," says I to the kid, "would you like to go home?"

"Aw, what for?" says he. "I don't have any fun at home. I hate to go to school. I like to camp out. You won't take me back home again, Snake-eye, will you?"

"Not right away," says I. "We'll stay here in the cave a while."

"All right!" says he. "That'll be fine. I never had such fun in all my life."

We went to bed about eleven o'clock. We spread down some wide blankets and quilts and put Red Chief between us. We weren't afraid he'd run away. He kept us awake for three hours, jumping up and reaching for his rifle and screeching: "Hist! Pard," in mine and Bill's ears, as the fancied crackle of a twig or the rustle of a leaf revealed to his young imagination the stealthy approach of the outlaw band. At last, I fell into a troubled sleep, and dreamed that I had been kidnapped and chained to a tree by a ferocious pirate with red hair.

Just at daybreak, I was awakened by a series of awful screams from Bill. They weren't yells, or howls, or shouts, or whoops, or yawps, such as you'd expect from a manly set of vocal organs—they were simply indecent, terrifying, humiliating screams, such as women emit when they see ghosts or caterpillars. It's an awful thing to hear a strong, desperate, fat man scream incontinently in a cave at daybreak.

I jumped up to see what the matter was. Red Chief was sitting on Bill's chest, with one hand twined in Bill's hair. In the other he had the sharp case-knife we used for slicing bacon; and he was industriously and realistically trying to take Bill's scalp, according to the sentence that had been pronounced upon him the evening before.

I got the knife away from the kid and made him lie down again. But, from that moment, Bill's spirit was broken. He laid down on his side of the bed, but he never closed an eye again in sleep as long as that boy was with us. I dozed off for a while, but along toward sun-up I remembered that Red Chief had said I was to be burned at the stake at the rising of the sun. I wasn't nervous or afraid; but I sat up and lit my pipe and leaned against a rock.

"What you getting up so soon for, Sam?" asked Bill.

"Me?" says I. "Oh, I got a kind of a pain in my shoulder. I thought sitting up would rest it."

"You're a liar!" says Bill. "You're afraid. You was to be burned at sunrise, and you was afraid he'd do it. And he would, too, if he could find a match. Ain't it awful, Sam? Do you think anybody will pay out money to get a little imp like that back home?"

"Sure," said I. "A rowdy kid like that is just the kind that parents dote on. Now, you and the Chief get up and cook breakfast, while I go up on the top of this mountain and reconnoitre."

I went up on the peak of the little mountain and ran my eye over the contiguous vicinity. Over toward Summit I expected to see the sturdy yeomanry of the village armed with scythes and pitchforks beating the countryside for the dastardly kidnappers. But what I saw was a peaceful landscape dotted with one man ploughing with a dun mule. Nobody was dragging the creek; no couriers dashed hither and yon, bringing tidings of no news to the distracted parents. There was a sylvan attitude of somnolent sleepiness pervading that section of the external outward surface of Alabama that lay exposed to my view. "Perhaps," says I to myself, "it has not yet been discovered that the wolves have borne away the tender lambkin from the fold. Heaven help the wolves!" says I, and I went down the mountain to breakfast.

When I got to the cave I found Bill backed up against the side of it, breathing hard, and the boy threatening to smash him with a rock half as big as a cocoanut.

"He put a red-hot boiled potato down my back," explained Bill, "and then mashed it with his foot; and I boxed his ears. Have you got a gun about you, Sam?"

I took the rock away from the boy and kind of patched up the argument. "I'll fix you," says the kid to Bill. "No man ever yet struck the Red Chief but what he got paid for it. You better beware!"

After breakfast the kid takes a piece of leather with strings wrapped around it out of his pocket and goes outside the cave unwinding it.

"What's he up to now?" says Bill, anxiously. "You don't think he'll run away, do you, Sam?"

"No fear of it," says I. "He don't seem to be much of a home body. But we've got to fix up some plan about the ransom. There don't seem to be much excitement around Summit on account of his disappearance; but maybe they haven't realized yet that he's gone. His folks may think he's spending the night with Aunt Jane or one of the neighbours. Anyhow, he'll be missed to-day. To-night we must get a message to his father demanding the two thousand dollars for his return."

Just then we heard a kind of war-whoop, such as David might have emitted when he knocked out the champion Goliath. It was a sling that Red Chief had pulled out of his pocket, and he was whirling it around his head.

I dodged, and heard a heavy thud and a kind of a sigh from Bill, like a horse gives out when you take his saddle off. A niggerhead rock the size of an egg had caught Bill just behind his left ear. He loosened himself all over and fell in the fire across the frying pan of hot water for washing the dishes. I dragged him out and poured cold water on his head for half an hour.

By and by, Bill sits up and feels behind his ear and says: "Sam, do you know who my favourite Biblical character is?"

"Take it easy," says I. "You'll come to your senses presently."

"King Herod," says he. "You won't go away and leave me here alone, will you, Sam?"

I went out and caught that boy and shook him until his freckles rattled.

"If you don't behave," says I, "I'll take you straight home. Now, are you going to be good, or not?"

"I was only funning," says he sullenly. "I didn't mean to hurt Old Hank. But what did he hit me for? I'll behave, Snake-eye, if you won't send me home, and if you'll let me play the Black Scout to-day."

"I don't know the game," says I. "That's for you and Mr. Bill to decide. He's your playmate for the day. I'm going away for a while, on business. Now, you come in and make friends with him and say you are sorry for hurting him, or home you go, at once."

I made him and Bill shake hands, and then I took Bill aside and told him I was going to Poplar Cove, a little village three miles from the cave, and find out what I could about how the kidnapping had been regarded in Summit. Also, I thought it best to send a peremptory letter to old man Dorset that day, demanding the ransom and dictating how it should be paid.

"You know, Sam," says Bill, "I've stood by you without batting an eye in earthquakes, fire and flood—in poker games, dynamite outrages, police raids, train robberies and cyclones. I never lost my nerve yet till we kidnapped that two-legged skyrocket of a kid. He's got me going. You won't leave me long with him, will you, Sam?"

"I'll be back some time this afternoon," says I. "You must keep the boy amused and quiet till I return. And now we'll write the letter to old Dorset."

Bill and I got paper and pencil and worked on the letter while Red Chief, with a blanket wrapped around him, strutted up and down, guarding the mouth of the cave. Bill begged me tearfully to make the ransom fifteen hundred dollars instead of two thousand. "I ain't attempting," says he, "to decry the celebrated moral aspect of parental affection, but we're dealing with humans, and it ain't human for anybody to give up two thousand dollars for that forty-pound chunk of freckled wildcat. I'm willing to take a chance at fifteen hundred dollars. You can charge the difference up to me."

So, to relieve Bill, I acceded, and we collaborated a letter that ran this way:

Ebenezer Dorset, Esq.:
We have your boy concealed in a place far from Summit. It is useless for you or the most skilful detectives to attempt to find him. Absolutely, the only terms on which you can have him restored to you are these: We demand fifteen hundred dollars in large bills for his return; the money to be left at midnight to-night at the same spot and in the same box as your reply—as hereinafter described. If you agree to these terms, send your answer in writing by a solitary messenger to-night at half-past eight o'clock. After crossing Owl Creek, on the road to

Poplar Cove, there are three large trees about a hundred yards apart, close to the fence of the wheat field on the right-hand side. At the bottom of the fence-post, opposite the third tree, will be found a small pasteboard box. The messenger will place the answer in this box and return immediately to Summit. If you attempt any treachery or fail to comply with our demand as stated, you will never see your boy again.

If you pay the money as demanded, he will be returned to you safe and well within three hours. These terms are final, and if you do not accede to them no further communication will be attempted.

TWO DESPERATE MEN.

I addressed this letter to Dorset, and put it in my pocket. As I was about to start, the kid comes up to me and says:

"Aw, Snake-eye, you said I could play the Black Scout while you was gone."

"Play it, of course," says I. "Mr. Bill will play with you. What kind of a game is it?"

"I'm the Black Scout," says Red Chief, "and I have to ride to the stockade to warn the settlers that the Indians are coming. I 'm tired of playing Indian myself. I want to be the Black Scout."

"All right," says I. "It sounds harmless to me. I guess Mr. Bill will help you foil the pesky savages."

"What am I to do?" asks Bill, looking at the kid suspiciously.

"You are the hoss," says Black Scout. "Get down on your hands and knees. How can I ride to the stockade without a hoss?"

"You'd better keep him interested," said I, "till we get the scheme going. Loosen up."

Bill gets down on his all fours, and a look comes in his eye like a rabbit's when you catch it in a trap.

"How far is it to the stockade, kid? " he asks, in a husky manner of voice.

"Ninety miles," says the Black Scout. "And you have to hump yourself to get there on time. Whoa, now!"

The Black Scout jumps on Bill's back and digs his heels in his side.

"For Heaven's sake," says Bill, "hurry back, Sam, as soon as you can. I wish we hadn't made the ransom more than a thousand. Say, you quit kicking me or I'll get up and warm you good."

I walked over to Poplar Cove and sat around the post office and store, talking with the chawbacons that came in to trade. One whiskerand says that he hears Summit is all upset on account of Elder Ebenezer Dorset's boy having been lost or stolen. That was all I wanted to know. I bought some smoking tobacco, referred casually to the price of black-eyed peas, posted my letter surreptitiously and came away. The postmaster said the mail-carrier would come by in an hour to take the mail on to Summit.

When I got back to the cave Bill and the boy were not to be found. I explored the vicinity of the cave, and risked a yodel or two, but there was no response.

So I lighted my pipe and sat down on a mossy bank to await developments.

In about half an hour I heard the bushes rustle, and Bill wabbled out into the little glade in front of the cave. Behind him was the kid, stepping softly like a scout, with a broad grin on his face. Bill stopped, took off his hat and wiped his face with a red handkerchief. The kid stopped about eight feet behind him.

"Sam," says Bill, "I suppose you'll think I'm a renegade, but I couldn't help it. I'm a grown person with masculine proclivities and habits of self-defence, but there is a time when all systems of egotism and predominance fail. The boy is gone. I have sent him home. All is off. There was martyrs in old times," goes on Bill, "that suffered death rather than give up the particular graft they enjoyed. None of 'em ever was subjugated to such supernatural tortures as I have been. I tried to be faithful to our articles of depredation; but there came a limit."

"What's the trouble, Bill?" I asks him.

"I was rode," says Bill, "the ninety miles to the stockade, not barring an inch. Then, when the settlers was rescued, I was given oats. Sand ain't a palatable substitute. And then, for an hour I had to try to explain to him why there was nothin' in holes, how a road can run both ways and what makes the grass green. I tell you, Sam, a human can only stand so much. I takes him by the neck of his clothes and drags him down the mountain. On the way he kicks my legs black-and-blue from the knees down; and I've got two or three bites on my thumb and hand cauterized.

"But he's gone"— continues Bill— "gone home. I showed him the road to Summit and kicked him about eight feet nearer there at one kick. I'm sorry we lose the ransom; but it was either that or Bill Driscoll to the madhouse."

Bill is puffing and blowing, but there is a look of ineffable peace and growing content on his rose-pink features.

"Bill," says I, "there isn't any heart disease in your family, is there?"

"No," says Bill, "nothing chronic except malaria and accidents. Why?"

"Then you might turn around," says I, "and have a look behind you."

Bill turns and sees the boy, and loses his complexion and sits down plump on the ground and begins to pluck aimlessly at grass and little sticks. For an hour I was afraid for his mind. And then I told him that my scheme was to put the whole job through immediately and that we would get the ransom and be off with it by midnight if old Dorset fell in with our proposition. So Bill braced up enough to give the kid a weak sort of a smile and a promise to play the Russian in a Japanese war with him as soon as he felt a little better.

I had a scheme for collecting that ransom without danger of being caught by counterplots that ought to commend itself to professional kidnappers. The tree under which the answer was to be left—and the money later on—was close to the road fence with big, bare fields on all sides. If a gang of constables should be watching for any one to come for the note they could see him a long way off crossing the fields or in the road. But no, sirree! At half-past eight I was up in that tree as well hidden as a tree toad, waiting for the messenger to arrive.

Exactly on time, a half-grown boy rides up the road on a bicycle, locates the pasteboard box at the foot of the fencepost, slips a folded piece of paper into it and pedals away again back toward Summit.

I waited an hour and then concluded the thing was square. I slid down the tree, got the note, slipped along the fence till I struck the woods, and was back at the cave in another half an hour. I opened the note, got near the lantern and read it to Bill. It was written with a pen in a crabbed hand, and the sum and substance of it was this:

Two Desperate Men.
Gentlemen: I received your letter to-day by post, in regard to the ransom you

ask for the return of my son. I think you are a little high in your demands, and I hereby make you a counter-proposition, which I am inclined to believe you will accept. You bring Johnny home and pay me two hundred and fifty dollars in cash, and I agree to take him off your hands. You had better come at night, for the neighbours believe he is lost, and I couldn't be responsible for what they would do to anybody they saw bringing him back.

Very respectfully,

EBENEZER DORSET.

"Great pirates of Penzance!" says I; "of all the impudent—"

But I glanced at Bill, and hesitated. He had the most appealing look in his eyes I ever saw on the face of a dumb or a talking brute.

"Sam," says he, "what's two hundred and fifty dollars, after all? We've got the money. One more night of this kid will send me to a bed in Bedlam. Besides being a thorough gentleman, I think Mr. Dorset is a spendthrift for making us such a liberal offer. You ain't going to let the chance go, are you?"

"Tell you the truth, Bill," says I, "this little he ewe lamb has somewhat got on my nerves too. We'll take him home, pay the ransom and make our get-away."

We took him home that night. We got him to go by telling him that his father had bought a silver-mounted rifle and a pair of moccasins for him, and we were going to hunt bears the next day.

It was just twelve o'clock when we knocked at Ebenezer's front door. Just at the moment when I should have been abstracting the fifteen hundred dollars from the box under the tree, according to the original proposition, Bill was counting out two hundred and fifty dollars into Dorset's hand.

When the kid found out we were going to leave him at home he started up a howl like a calliope and fastened himself as tight as a leech to Bill's leg. His father peeled him away gradually, like a porous plaster.

"How long can you hold him?" asks Bill.

"I'm not as strong as I used to be," says old Dorset, "but I think I can promise you ten minutes."

"Enough," says Bill. "In ten minutes I shall cross the Central, Southern and Middle Western States, and be legging it trippingly for the Canadian border."

And, as dark as it was, and as fat as Bill was, and as good a runner as I am, he was a good mile and a half out of summit before I could catch up with him.

—by O. Henry

Day 2

Story Analysis

In this short study unit, you will be working with the elements of story: setting, character, plot, point of view, and theme. This story by O. Henry lends itself well to a study of the way authors portray character.

An author creates an impression in us about a character indirectly through physical description; the character's thoughts, feelings, and words; the comments and reactions of others; and the actions of the character. We learn directly about the character when the author explicitly states his opinion of the character. Find places in the story where the author uses each of the indirect methods of developing the character of Red Chief, Sam, and Bill. Record them on the chart below.

	Red Chief	Bill	Sam
Physical description			
Character's own thoughts, feelings, and words			
Comments and reactions of others			
Actions			

Writing

Write a quick "thumbnail" sketch of each of the characters (Red Chief, Sam, and Bill). This quick sketch should be no more than one paragraph long for each character but gives the reader a good picture of his character.

Day 3

Story Analysis

To analyze the characters further, think about the following aspects of "character" in a story.

The main character is the person around whom the central conflict of the story revolves. We say that the character in a story *develops* if he changes from the beginning of the story to the end. Characterization is the way the authors shows his readers the character (directly or indirectly as discussed on Day 2). When a character has a change in attitude in a story, the character is said to be *dynamic* or *round*. If the attitude stays the same, the character is said to be *static* or *flat*.

The main character who is faced with a conflict is the *protagonist* while the person who causes the conflict is the *antagonist*. A character's *motive* is the reason behind his actions. A *dialogue* is a conversation between two or more people in the story. The *dialect* is the way characters speak in the story to show that they are from different parts of the country.

Exercise A
Think about the characters in the story "Ransom of Red Chief" and decide which characters fit in the chart. Jot in the chart your reasons for your choices.

Main character(s)	
Dynamic character	
Static character	
Protagonist	
Antagonist	

Exercise B

Answer the following questions about the story.

1. What is the motive behind each of the characters in the story?

2. In what places does the author show the dialect of the characters?

3. What is the main conflict of the story? How is the conflict mixed up with the characterization of the characters?

4. Why is Dorset concerned about the "desperate men" bringing the child back during the day?

Writing

Notice the punctuation of the dialogue of the story. Find places in the story where the dialogue is broken up by other words. Copy three different ways that O. Henry punctuates his dialogue.

Write a dialogue between Red Chief and his father after Red Chief is returned home, In your dialogue, break the dialogue at least two times showing the proper way to punctuate the dialogue. Remember to start a new paragraph each time the speaker changes.

Day 4

Writing

Write the story of "The Ransom of Red Chief" in your own words. (You do not have to include dialogue unless you want to.)

Parsing

Parse the following sentence.
1. Identify the part of speech of each word.
2. Identify the parts of the sentence (As you tell the parts of the sentence give the case, number and gender of nouns and the tense, mood, and voice of verbs. Tell whether verbs are transitive or intransitive.)
3. Identify subordinate clauses and their subjects, predicates, and complements. (When labeling the words on your paper, label the subject, verb, and complement of the subordinate clause *under* the sentence so that it's not confused with the subject and verb of the main clause.)
4. Identify verbals and phrases and their objects and modifiers and tell how they are used.
5. Explain the modifiers.

(Remember that a clause may be inside a phrase and a phrase inside a clause.)

It was a sling that Red Chief had pulled out of his pocket, and he was whirling it around his head.

Week 29

Day 1

Read the following short story and think about it. As you read, highlight particularly descriptive passages or anything that catches your attention as an especially effective piece of writing.

To Build a Fire

Day had broken cold and gray, exceedingly cold and gray, when the man turned aside from the main Yukon trail and climbed the high earth-bank, where a dim and little-travelled trail led eastward through the fat spruce timberland. It was a steep bank, and he paused for breath at the top, excusing the act to himself by looking at his watch. It was nine o'clock. There was no sun nor hint of sun, though there was not a cloud in the sky. It was a clear day, and yet there seemed an intangible pall over the face of things, a subtle gloom that made the day dark, and that was due to the absence of sun. This fact did not worry the man. He was used to the lack of sun. It had been days since he had seen the sun, and he knew that a few more days must pass before that cheerful orb, due south, would just peep above the sky-line and dip immediately from view.

The man flung a look back along the way he had come. The Yukon lay a mile wide and hidden under three feet of ice. On top of this ice were as many feet of snow. It was all pure white, rolling in gentle undulations where the ice-jams of the freeze-up had formed. North and south, as far as his eye could see, it was unbroken white, save for a dark hair-line that curved and twisted from around the spruce-covered island to the south, and that curved and twisted away into the north, where it disappeared behind another spruce-covered island. This dark hair-line was the trail—the main trail—that led south five hundred miles to the Chilcoot Pass, Dyea, and salt water; and that led north seventy miles to Dawson, and still on to the north a thousand miles to Nulato, and finally to St. Michael on Bering Sea, a thousand miles and half a thousand more.

But all this—the mysterious, far-reaching hair-line trail, the absence of sun from the sky, the tremendous cold, and the strangeness and weirdness of it all—made no impression on the man. It was not because he was long used to it. He was a newcomer in the land, a *chechaquo*, and this was his first winter. The trouble with him was that he was without imagination. He was quick and alert in the things of life, but only in the things, and not in the significances. Fifty degrees below zero meant eighty-odd degrees of frost. Such fact impressed him as being cold and uncomfortable, and that was all. It did not lead him to meditate upon his frailty as a creature of temperature, and upon man's frailty in general, able only to live within certain narrow limits of heat and cold; and from there on it did not lead him to the conjectural field of immortality and man's place in the universe. Fifty degrees below zero stood for a bite of frost that hurt and that must be guarded against by the use of mittens, ear-flaps, warm moccasins, and thick socks. Fifty degrees below zero was to him just precisely fifty degrees below zero. That there should be anything more to it than that was a thought that never entered his head.

As he turned to go on, he spat speculatively. There was a sharp, explosive crackle that startled him. He spat again. And again, in the air, before it could fall to the snow, the spittle crackled. He knew that at fifty below spittle crackled on the snow, but this spittle had crackled in the air. Undoubtedly it was colder than fifty below—how much colder he did not know. But the temperature did not matter. He was bound for the old claim on the left fork of Henderson Creek, where the boys were already. They had come over across the divide from the Indian Creek country, while he had come the roundabout way to take a look at the possibilities of getting out logs in the spring from the islands in the Yukon. He would be in to camp by six o'clock; a bit after dark, it was true, but the boys would be there, a fire would be going, and a hot supper would be ready. As for lunch, he pressed his hand against the protruding bundle under his jacket. It was also under his shirt, wrapped up in a handkerchief and lying against the naked skin. It was the only way to keep the biscuits from freezing. He smiled agreeably to himself as he thought of those biscuits, each cut open and sopped in bacon grease, and each enclosing a generous slice of fried bacon.

He plunged in among the big spruce trees. The trail was faint. A foot of snow had fallen since the last sled had passed over, and he was glad he was without a sled, travelling light. In fact, he carried nothing but the lunch wrapped in the handkerchief. He was surprised, however, at the cold. It certainly was cold, he concluded, as he rubbed his numb nose and cheek-bones with his mittened hand. He was a warm-whiskered man, but the hair on his face did not protect the high cheek-bones and the eager nose that thrust itself aggressively into the frosty air.

At the man's heels trotted a dog, a big native husky, the proper wolf-dog, gray-coated and without any visible or temperamental difference from its brother, the wild wolf. The animal was depressed by the tremendous cold. It knew that it was no time for travelling. Its instinct told it a truer tale than was told to the man by the man's judgment. In reality, it was not merely colder than fifty below zero; it was colder than sixty below, than seventy below. It was seventy-five below zero. Since the freezing-point is thirty-two above zero, it meant that one hundred and seven degrees of frost obtained. The dog did not know anything about thermometers. Possibly in its brain there was no sharp consciousness of a condition of very cold such as was in the man's brain. But the brute had its instinct. It experienced a vague but menacing apprehension that subdued it and made it slink along at the man's heels, and that made it question eagerly every unwonted movement of the man as if expecting him to go into camp or to seek shelter somewhere and build a fire. The dog had learned fire, and it wanted fire, or else to burrow under the snow and cuddle its warmth away from the air.

The frozen moisture of its breathing had settled on its fur in a fine powder of frost, and especially were its jowls, muzzle, and eyelashes whitened by its crystalled breath. The man's red beard and mustache were likewise frosted, but more solidly, the deposit taking the form of ice and increasing with every warm, moist breath he exhaled. Also, the man was chewing tobacco, and the muzzle of ice held his lips so rigidly that he was unable to clear his chin when he expelled the juice. The result was that a crystal beard of the color and solidity of amber was increasing its length on his chin. If he fell down it would shatter itself, like glass, into brittle fragments. But he did not mind the appendage. It was the penalty all tobacco-chewers paid in that country, and he had been out before in two cold snaps. They had not been so cold as this, he knew, but by the spirit thermometer at Sixty Mile he knew they had been registered at fifty below and at fifty-five.

He held on through the level stretch of woods for several miles, crossed a wide flat of niggerheads, and dropped down a bank to the frozen bed of a small stream. This was

Henderson Creek, and he knew he was ten miles from the forks. He looked at his watch. It was ten o'clock. He was making four miles an hour, and he calculated that he would arrive at the forks at half-past twelve. He decided to celebrate that event by eating his lunch there. The dog dropped in again at his heels, with a tail drooping discouragement, as the man swung along the creek-bed. The furrow of the old sled-trail was plainly visible, but a dozen inches of snow covered the marks of the last runners. In a month no man had come up or down that silent creek. The man held steadily on. He was not much given to thinking, and just then particularly he had nothing to think about save that he would eat lunch at the forks and that at six o'clock he would be in camp with the boys. There was nobody to talk to; and, had there been, speech would have been impossible because of the ice-muzzle on his mouth. So he continued monotonously to chew tobacco and to increase the length of his amber beard.

Once in a while the thought reiterated itself that it was very cold and that he had never experienced such cold. As he walked along he rubbed his cheek-bones and nose with the back of his mittened hand. He did this automatically, now and again changing hands. But rub as he would, the instant he stopped his cheek-bones went numb, and the following instant the end of his nose went numb. He was sure to frost his cheeks; he knew that, and experienced a pang of regret that he had not devised a nose-strap of the sort Bud wore in cold snaps. Such a strap passed across the cheeks, as well, and saved them. But it didn't matter much, after all. What were frosted cheeks? A bit painful, that was all; they were never serious.

Empty as the man's mind was of thoughts, he was keenly observant, and he noticed the changes in the creek, the curves and bends and timber-jams, and always he sharply noted where he placed his feet. Once, coming around a bend, he shied abruptly, like a startled horse, curved away from the place where he had been walking, and retreated several paces back along the trail. The creek he knew was frozen clear to the bottom,—no creek could contain water in that arctic winter,—but he knew also that there were springs that bubbled out from the hillsides and ran along under the snow and on top the ice of the creek. He knew that the coldest snaps never froze these springs, and he knew likewise their danger. They were traps. They hid pools of water under the snow that might be three inches deep, or three feet. Sometimes a skin of ice half an inch thick covered them, and in turn was covered by the snow. Sometimes there were alternate layers of water and ice-skin, so that when one broke through he kept on breaking through for a while, sometimes wetting himself to the waist.

That was why he had shied in such panic. He had felt the give under his feet and heard the crackle of a snow-hidden ice-skin. And to get his feet wet in such a temperature meant trouble and danger. At the very least it meant delay, for he would be forced to stop and build a fire, and under its protection to bare his feet while he dried his socks and moccasins. He stood and studied the creek-bed and its banks, and decided that the flow of water came from the right. He reflected awhile, rubbing his nose and cheeks, then skirted to the left, stepping gingerly and testing the footing for each step. Once clear of the danger, he took a fresh chew of tobacco and swung along at his four-mile gait. In the course of the next two hours he came upon several similar traps. Usually the snow above the hidden pools had a sunken, candied appearance that advertised the danger. Once again, however, he had a close call; and once, suspecting danger, he compelled the dog to go on in front. The dog did not want to go. It hung back until the man shoved it forward, and then it went quickly across the white, unbroken surface. Suddenly it broke through, floundered to one side, and got away to firmer footing. It had wet its forefeet and legs, and almost immediately the water that clung to it turned to ice. It made quick efforts to lick the ice off its legs, then dropped down in the snow and began to bite out the ice that had formed between the toes. This was a matter of instinct. To permit the ice to remain would mean sore feet. It did not know this. It merely obeyed the mysterious prompting that arose from the deep crypts of its being. But the man knew, having achieved a judgment on the subject, and he removed the mitten from his right hand and helped tear out the ice-particles. He did not expose his fingers more than a minute, and was astonished at the swift numbness that smote them. It certainly was cold. He pulled on the mitten hastily, and beat the hand savagely across his chest.

At twelve o'clock the day was at its brightest. Yet the sun was too far south on its winter journey to clear the horizon. The bulge of the earth intervened between it and Henderson Creek, where the man walked under a clear sky at noon and cast no shadow. At half-past twelve, to the minute, he arrived at the forks of the creek. He was pleased at the speed he had made. If he kept it up, he would certainly be with the boys by six. He unbuttoned his jacket and shirt and drew forth his lunch. The action consumed no more than a quarter of a minute, yet in that brief moment the numbness laid hold of the exposed fingers. He did not put the mitten on, but, instead, struck the fingers a dozen sharp smashes against his leg. Then he sat down on a snow-covered log to eat. The sting that followed upon the striking of his fingers against his leg ceased so quickly that he was startled. He had had no chance to take a bite of biscuit. He struck the fingers repeatedly and returned them to the mitten, baring the other hand for the purpose of eating. He tried to take a mouthful, but the ice-muzzle prevented. He had forgotten to build a fire and thaw out. He chuckled at his foolishness, and as he chuckled he noted the numbness creeping into the exposed fingers. Also, he noted that the stinging which had first come to his toes when he sat down was already passing away. He wondered whether the toes were warm or numb. He moved them inside the moccasins and decided that they were numb.

He pulled the mitten on hurriedly and stood up. He was a bit frightened. He stamped up and down until the stinging returned into the feet. It certainly was cold, was his thought. That man from Sulphur Creek had spoken the truth when telling how cold it sometimes got in the country. And he had laughed at him at the time! That showed one must not be too sure of things. There was no mistake about it, it *was* cold. He strode up and down, stamping his feet and threshing his arms, until reassured by the returning warmth. Then he got out matches and proceeded to make a fire. From the undergrowth, where high water of the previous spring had lodged a supply of seasoned twigs, he got his fire-wood. Working carefully from a small beginning, he soon had a roaring fire, over which he thawed the ice from his face and in the protection of which he ate his biscuits. For the moment the cold of space was outwitted. The dog took satisfaction in the fire, stretching out close enough for warmth and far enough away to escape being singed.

When the man had finished, he filled his pipe and took his comfortable time over a smoke. Then he pulled on his mittens, settled the ear-flaps of his cap firmly about his ears, and took the creek trail up the left fork. The dog was disappointed and yearned back toward the fire. This man did not know cold. Possibly all the generations of his ancestry had been ignorant of cold, of real cold, of cold one hundred and seven degrees below freezing-point. But the dog knew; all its ancestry knew, and it had inherited the knowledge. And it knew that it was not good to walk abroad in such fearful cold. It was the time to lie snug in a hole in the snow and wait for a curtain of cloud to be drawn across the face of outer space whence this cold came. On the other hand, there was no keen intimacy between the dog and the man. The one was the toil-slave of the other, and the only caresses it had ever received were the caresses of the whip-lash and of harsh and menacing throat-sounds that threatened the whip-lash. So the dog made no effort to communicate its apprehension to the man. It was not concerned in the welfare of the man; it was for its own sake that it yearned back toward the fire. But the man whistled, and spoke to it with the sound of whip-lashes, and the dog swung in at the man's heels and followed after.

The man took a chew of tobacco and proceeded to start a new amber beard. Also, his moist breath quickly powdered with white his mustache, eyebrows, and lashes. There did not seem to be so many springs on the left fork of the Henderson, and for half an hour the man saw no signs of any. And then it happened. At a place where there were no signs, where the soft, unbroken snow seemed to advertise solidity beneath, the man broke through. It was not deep. He wet himself halfway to the knees before he floundered out to the firm crust. He was angry, and cursed his luck aloud. He had hoped to get into camp with the boys at six o'clock, and this would delay him an hour, for he would have to build a fire and dry out his foot-gear. This was imperative at that low temperature—he knew that much; and he turned aside to the bank, which he climbed. On top, tangled in the underbrush about the trunks of several small spruce trees, was a high-water deposit of dry fire-wood—sticks and twigs, principally, but also larger portions of seasoned branches and fine, dry, last-year's grasses. He threw down several large pieces on top of the snow. This served for a foundation and prevented the young flame from drowning itself in the snow it otherwise would melt. The flame he got by touching a match to a small shred of birch-bark that he took from his pocket. This burned even more readily than paper. Placing it on the foundation, he fed the young flame with wisps of dry grass and with the tiniest dry twigs.

He worked slowly and carefully, keenly aware of his danger. Gradually, as the flame grew stronger, he increased the size of the twigs with which he fed it. He squatted in the snow, pulling the twigs out from their entanglement in the brush and feeding directly to the flame. He knew there must be no failure. When it is seventy-five below zero, a man must not fail in his first attempt to build a fire—that is, if his feet are wet. If his feet are dry, and he fails, he can run along the trail for half a mile and restore his circulation. But the circulation of wet and freezing feet cannot be restored by running when it is seventy-five below. No matter how fast he runs, the wet feet will freeze the harder.

All this the man knew. The old-timer on Sulphur Creek had told him about it the previous fall, and now he was appreciating the advice. Already all sensation had gone out of his feet. To build the fire he had been forced to remove his mittens, and the fingers had quickly gone numb. His pace of four miles an hour had kept his heart pumping blood to the surface of his body and to all the extremities. But the instant he stopped, the action of the pump eased down. The cold of space smote the unprotected tip of the planet, and he, being on that unprotected tip, received the full force of the blow. The blood of his body recoiled before it. The blood was alive, like the dog, and like the dog it wanted to hide away and cover itself up from the fearful cold. So long as he walked four miles an hour, he pumped that blood, willy-nilly, to the surface; but now it ebbed away and sank down into the recesses of his body. The extremities were the first to feel its absence. His wet feet froze the faster, and his exposed fingers numbed the faster, though they had not yet begun to freeze. Nose and cheeks were already freezing, while the skin of all his body chilled as it lost its blood.

But he was safe. Toes and nose and cheeks would be only touched by the frost, for the fire was beginning to burn with strength. He was feeding it with twigs the size of his finger. In another minute he would be able to feed it with branches the size of his wrist, and then he could remove his wet foot-gear, and, while it dried, he could keep his naked feet warm by the fire, rubbing them at first, of course, with snow. The fire was a success. He was safe. He remembered the advice of the old-timer on Sulphur Creek, and smiled. The old-timer had been very serious in laying down the law that no man must travel alone in the Klondike after fifty below. Well, here he was; he had had the accident; he was alone; and he had saved himself. Those old-timers were rather womanish, some of them, he thought. All a man had to do was to keep his head, and he was all right. Any man who was a man could travel alone. But it was surprising, the rapidity with which his cheeks and nose were freezing. And he had not thought his fingers could go lifeless in so short a time. Lifeless they were, for he could scarcely make them move together to grip a twig, and they seemed remote from his body and from him. When he touched a twig, he had to look and see whether or not he had hold of it. The wires were pretty well down between him and his finger-ends.

All of which counted for little. There was the fire, snapping and crackling and promising life with every dancing flame. He started to untie his moccasins. They were coated with ice; the thick German socks were like sheaths of iron halfway to the knees; and the moccasin strings were like rods of steel all twisted and knotted as by some conflagration. For a moment he tugged with his numb fingers, then, realizing the folly of it, he drew his sheath-knife.

But before he could cut the strings, it happened. It was his own fault or, rather, his mistake. He should not have built the fire under the spruce tree. He should have built it in the open. But it had been easier to pull the twigs from the brush and drop them directly on the fire. Now the tree under which he had done this carried a weight of snow on its boughs. No wind had blown for weeks, and each bough was fully freighted. Each time he had pulled a twig he had communicated a slight agitation to the tree—an imperceptible agitation, so far as he was concerned, but an agitation sufficient to bring about the disaster. High up in the tree one bough capsized its load of snow. This fell on the boughs beneath, capsizing them. This process continued, spreading out and involving the whole tree. It grew like an avalanche, and it descended without warning upon the man and the fire, and the fire was blotted out! Where it had burned was a mantle of fresh and disordered snow.

The man was shocked. It was as though he had just heard his own sentence of death. For a moment he sat and stared at the spot where the fire had been. Then he grew very calm. Perhaps the old-timer on Sulphur Creek was right. If he had only had a trail-mate he would have been in no danger now. The trail-mate could have built the fire. Well, it was up to him to build the fire over again, and this second time there must be no failure. Even if he succeeded, he would most likely lose some toes. His feet must be badly frozen by now, and there would be some time before the second fire was ready.

Such were his thoughts, but he did not sit and think them. He was busy all the time they were passing through his mind. He made a new foundation for a fire, this time in the open, where no treacherous tree could blot it out. Next, he gathered dry grasses and tiny twigs from the high-water flotsam. He could not bring his fingers together to pull them out, but he was able to gather them by the handful. In this way he got many rotten twigs and bits of green moss that were undesirable, but it was the best he could do. He worked methodically, even collecting an armful of the larger branches to be used later when the fire gathered strength. And all the while the dog sat and watched him, a certain yearning wistfulness in its eyes, for it looked upon him as the fire-provider, and the fire was slow in coming.

When all was ready, the man reached in his pocket for a second piece of birch-bark. He knew the bark was there, and, though he could not feel it with his fingers, he could hear its crisp rustling as he fumbled for it. Try as he would, he could not clutch hold of it. And all the time, in his consciousness, was the knowledge that each instant his feet were freezing. This thought tended to put him in a panic, but he fought against it and kept calm. He pulled on his mittens with his teeth, and threshed his arms back and forth, beating his hands with

all his might against his sides. He did this sitting down, and he stood up to do it; and all the while the dog sat in the snow, its wolf-brush of a tail curled around warmly over its forefeet, its sharp wolf-ears pricked forward intently as it watched the man. And the man, as he beat and threshed with his arms and hands, felt a great surge of envy as he regarded the creature that was warm and secure in its natural covering.

After a time he was aware of the first faraway signals of sensation in his beaten fingers. The faint tingling grew stronger till it evolved into a stinging ache that was excruciating, but which the man hailed with satisfaction. He stripped the mitten from his right hand and fetched forth the birch-bark. The exposed fingers were quickly going numb again. Next he brought out his bunch of sulphur matches. But the tremendous cold had already driven the life out of his fingers. In his effort to separate one match from the others, the whole bunch fell in the snow. He tried to pick it out of the snow, but failed. The dead fingers could neither touch nor clutch. He was very careful. He drove the thought of his freezing feet, and nose, and cheeks, out of his mind, devoting his whole soul to the matches. He watched, using the sense of vision in place of that of touch, and when he saw his fingers on each side the bunch, he closed them—that is, he willed to close them, for the wires were down, and the fingers did not obey. He pulled the mitten on the right hand, and beat it fiercely against his knee. Then, with both mittened hands, he scooped the bunch of matches, along with much snow, into his lap. Yet he was no better off.

After some manipulation he managed to get the bunch between the heels of his mittened hands. In this fashion he carried it to his mouth. The ice crackled and snapped when by a violent effort he opened his mouth. He drew the lower jaw in, curled the upper lip out of the way, and scraped the bunch with his upper teeth in order to separate a match. He succeeded in getting one, which he dropped on his lap. He was no better off. He could not pick it up. Then he devised a way. He picked it up in his teeth and scratched it on his leg. Twenty times he scratched before he succeeded in lighting it. As it flamed he held it with his teeth to the birch-bark. But the burning brimstone went up his nostrils and into his lungs, causing him to cough spasmodically. The match fell into the snow and went out.

The old-timer on Sulphur Creek was right, he thought in the moment of controlled despair that ensued: after fifty below, a man should travel with a partner. He beat his hands, but failed in exciting any sensation. Suddenly he bared both hands, removing the mittens with his teeth. He caught the whole bunch between the heels of his hands. His arm-muscles not being frozen enabled him to press the hand-heels tightly against the matches. Then he scratched the bunch along his leg. It flared into flame, seventy sulphur matches at once! There was no wind to blow them out. He kept his head to one side to escape the strangling fumes, and held the blazing bunch to the birch-bark. As he so held it, he became aware of sensation in his hand. His flesh was burning. He could smell it. Deep down below the surface he could feel it. The sensation developed into pain that grew acute. And still he endured it, holding the flame of the matches clumsily to the bark that would not light readily because his own burning hands were in the way, absorbing most of the flame.

At last, when he could endure no more, he jerked his hands apart. The blazing matches fell sizzling into the snow, but the birch-bark was alight. He began laying dry grasses and the tiniest twigs on the flame. He could not pick and choose, for he had to lift the fuel between the heels of his hands. Small pieces of rotten wood and green moss clung to the twigs, and he bit them off as well as he could with his teeth. He cherished the flame carefully and awkwardly. It meant life, and it must not perish. The withdrawal of blood from the surface of his body now made him begin to shiver, and he grew more awkward. A large piece of green moss fell squarely on the little fire. He tried to poke it out with his fingers, but his shivering frame made him poke too far, and he disrupted the nucleus of the little fire, the burning grasses and tiny twigs separating and scattering. He tried to poke them together again, but in spite of the tenseness of the effort, his shivering got away with him, and the twigs were hopelessly scattered. Each twig gushed a puff of smoke and went out. The fire-provider had failed. As he looked apathetically about him, his eyes chanced on the dog, sitting across the ruins of the fire from him, in the snow, making restless, hunching movements, slightly lifting one forefoot and then the other, shifting its weight back and forth on them with wistful eagerness.

The sight of the dog put a wild idea into his head. He remembered the tale of the man, caught in a blizzard, who killed a steer and crawled inside the carcass, and so was saved. He would kill the dog and bury his hands in the warm body until the numbness went out of them. Then he could build another fire. He spoke to the dog, calling it to him; but in his voice was a strange note of fear that frightened the animal, who had never known the man to speak in such way before. Something was the matter, and its suspicious nature sensed danger—it knew not what danger, but somewhere, somehow, in its brain arose an apprehension of the man. It flattened its ears down at the sound of the man's voice, and its restless, hunching movements and the liftings and shiftings of its forefeet became more pronounced; but it would not come to the man. He got on his hands and knees and crawled toward the dog. This unusual posture again excited suspicion, and the animal sidled mincingly away.

The man sat up in the snow for a moment and struggled for calmness. Then he pulled on his mittens, by means of his teeth, and got upon his feet. He glanced down at first in order to assure himself that he was really standing up, for the absence of sensation in his feet left him unrelated to the earth. His erect position in itself started to drive the webs of suspicion from the dog's mind; and when he spoke peremptorily, with the sound of whip-lashes in his voice, the dog rendered its customary allegiance and came to him. As it came within reaching distance, the man lost his control. His arms flashed out to the dog, and he experienced genuine surprise when he discovered that his hands could not clutch, that there was neither bend nor feeling in the fingers. He had forgotten for the moment that they were frozen and that they were freezing more and more. All this happened quickly, and before the animal could get away, he encircled its body with his arms. He sat down in the snow, and in this fashion held the dog, while it snarled and whined and struggled.

But it was all he could do, hold its body encircled in his arms and sit there. He realized that he could not kill the dog. There was no way to do it. With his helpless hands he could neither draw nor hold his sheath-knife nor throttle the animal. He released it, and it plunged wildly away, with tail between its legs, and still snarling. It halted forty feet away and surveyed him curiously, with ears sharply pricked forward. The man looked down at his hands in order to locate them, and found them hanging on the ends of his arms. It struck him as curious that one should have to use his eyes in order to find out where his hands were. He began threshing his arms back and forth, beating the mittened hands against his sides. He did this for five minutes, violently, and his heart pumped enough blood up to the surface to put a stop to his shivering. But no sensation was aroused in the hands. He had an impression that they hung like weights on the ends of his arms, but when he tried to run the impression down, he could not find it.

A certain fear of death, dull and oppressive, came to him. This fear quickly became poignant as he realized that it was no longer a mere matter of freezing his fingers and toes, or of losing his hands and feet, but that it was a matter of life and death with the chances against him. This threw him into a panic, and he turned and ran up the creek-bed along the old, dim trail. The dog joined in behind and kept up with him. He ran blindly, without intention, in fear such as he had never known in his life. Slowly, as he ploughed and floundered through the snow, he began to see things again—the banks of the creek, the old timber-jams, the leafless aspens, and the sky. The running made him feel better. He did not shiver. Maybe, if he ran on, his feet would thaw out; and, anyway, if he ran far enough, he would reach camp and the boys. Without doubt he would lose some fingers and toes and some of his face; but the boys would take care of him, and save the rest of him when he got there. And at the same time there was another thought in his mind that said he would never get to the camp and the boys; that it was too many miles away, that the freezing had too great a start on him, and that he would soon be stiff and dead. This thought he kept in the background and refused to consider. Sometimes it pushed itself forward and demanded to be heard, but he thrust it back and strove to think of other things.

It struck him as curious that he could run at all on feet so frozen that he could not feel them when they struck the earth and took the weight of his body. He seemed to himself to skim along above the surface, and to have no connection with the earth. Somewhere he had once seen a winged Mercury, and he wondered if Mercury felt as he felt when skimming over the earth.

His theory of running until he reached camp and the boys had one flaw in it: he lacked the endurance. Several times he stumbled, and finally he tottered, crumpled up, and fell. When he tried to rise, he failed. He must sit and rest, he decided, and next time he would merely walk and keep on going. As he sat and regained his breath, he noted that he was feeling quite warm and comfortable. He was not shivering, and it even seemed that a warm glow had come to his chest and trunk. And yet, when he touched his nose or cheeks, there was no sensation. Running would not thaw them out. Nor would it thaw out his hands and feet. Then the thought came to him that the frozen portions of his body must be extending. He tried to keep this thought down, to forget it, to think of something else; he was aware of the panicky feeling that it caused, and he was afraid of the panic. But the thought asserted itself, and persisted, until it produced a vision of his body totally frozen. This was too much, and he made another wild run along the trail. Once he slowed down to a walk, but the thought of the freezing extending itself made him run again.

And all the time the dog ran with him, at his heels. When he fell down a second time, it curled its tail over its forefeet and sat in front of him, facing him, curiously eager and intent. The warmth and security of the animal angered him, and he cursed it till it flattened down its ears appeasingly. This time the shivering came more quickly upon the man. He was losing in his battle with the frost. It was creeping into his body from all sides. The thought of it drove him on, but he ran no more than a hundred feet, when he staggered and pitched headlong. It was his last panic. When he had recovered his breath and control, he sat up and entertained in his mind the conception of meeting death with dignity. However, the conception did not come to him in such terms. His idea of it was that he had been making a fool of himself, running around like a chicken with its head cut off—such was the simile that occurred to him. Well, he was bound to freeze anyway, and he might as well take it decently. With this new-found peace of mind came the first glimmerings of drowsiness. A good idea, he thought, to sleep off to death. It was like taking an anesthetic. Freezing was not so bad as people thought. There were lots worse ways to die.

He pictured the boys finding his body next day. Suddenly he found himself with them, coming along the trail and looking for himself. And, still with them, he came around a turn in the trail and found himself lying in the snow. He did not belong with himself any more, for even then he was out of himself, standing with the boys and looking at himself in the snow. It certainly was cold, was his thought. When he got back to the States he could tell the folks what real cold was. He drifted on from this to a vision of the old-timer on Sulphur Creek. He could see him quite clearly, warm and comfortable, and smoking a pipe. "You were right, old hoss; you were right," the man mumbled to the old-timer of Sulphur Creek.

Then the man drowsed off into what seemed to him the most comfortable and satisfying sleep he had ever known. The dog sat facing him and waiting. The brief day drew to a close in a long, slow twilight. There were no signs of a fire to be made, and, besides, never in the dog's experience had it known a man to sit like that in the snow and make no fire. As the twilight drew on, its eager yearning for the fire mastered it, and with a great lifting and shifting of forefeet, it whined softly, then flattened its ears down in anticipation of being chidden by the man. But the man remained silent. Later, the dog whined loudly. And still later it crept close to the man and caught the scent of death. This made the animal bristle and back away. A little longer it delayed, howling under the stars that leaped and danced and shone brightly in the cold sky. Then it turned and trotted up the trail in the direction of the camp it knew, where were the other food-providers and fire-providers.

—by Jack London
First published in *The Century Magazine*, v. 76, August 1908

Day 2

Story Analysis

In this week's lessons you'll focus on setting as an element of storytelling. The portrayal of the setting in the story is essential to the development of the plot. Obviously, a story about the Ititarod dog sled race must be set in Alaska; it wouldn't make sense anywhere else. But, the author must describe the setting such that the reader feels as though he is there: wind whipping, dogs barking, the smell of sweat, the icy cold.

As the author portrays the setting (conveying the time and the place of the story), he uses vivid imagery. All the senses can be involved. The author also uses figurative language to bring the setting to life. Review the kinds of figurative language in Week 15.

"To Build a Fire" is a good example of the author's use of setting to create his story. His images are sharp and effective. You can feel the man getting colder and more panicked as the icy wilderness defeats him.

Find at least one example of each of the following kinds of figurative language in the story and write it on the chart below. Then in the second chart, make a list of some of the details from the story that involve the senses.

Figurative Language

metaphor	
simile	
personification	
apostrophe	

Imagery

Sight	
Sound	
Taste	
Touch	
Smell	

Writing

Imitate the first paragraph of the story "To Build Fire" to write the description of a setting. First choose the place and close your eyes to imagine it in your mind. Think about the tone of the place you are describing. Then write your paragraph. Use vivid imagery (involving the senses).

In addition, write a thumbnail sketch of the character of the man in the story.

Day 3

Story Analysis

To analysis the use of setting further, think about the main problem of the story. What is the man's problem? How is the setting intertwined with his problem? Isn't the setting, in fact, part of his problem? Often in tales of wilderness survival, the setting works against the efforts of the protagonist, almost becoming an antagonist itself.

The creation of the setting in a story is also the main way an author portrays mood or atmosphere, so it is very important to the theme of the story.

Stories have two types of settings: chronological and physical (time and place). An author may purposely be vague about either one of those to create an effect in the story. To make the story more universal, he may make the setting so nondescript that it could be anywhere, or so specific that the story could not have taken place anywhere else.

Here are the various ways setting is used in a story:

Backdrop setting: The setting is unimportant for the story and the story could take place in any setting.

Integral setting: The setting influences the action, character, or theme. A character's action are determined by the place and time in which he is placed.

Setting as antagonist: Characters must resolve conflict created by the setting.

Setting that illuminates character: The particular nature of the setting helps the characters learn and grow and is essential to the "development" of the character as was discussed in Week 28.

Setting as symbolism: The setting can represent another level of meaning in the story. For example, sunlight may symbolize hope, red color may symbolize anger.

Exercise A
Answer the following questions about the setting of the story.

1. Think carefully about each one and decide which one *best* describes the way setting is used in "To Build a Fire." Explain your answer (give reasons for your choice).

2. What is the chronological and physical setting of this story.

3. Find as many places as you can in the story where the author talks about it being cold. Record the phrase or sentence in which the cold is mentioned or described.

4. Think of the mood of the story. What specifically creates that mood in this story?

Exercise B
Answer the following questions about the story.

1. Think about the 4 ways an author reveals his main character that were discussed in Week 28. Which of those does this author use to portray the man?

2. Why do you think the author does not give the man a name?

3. Of all the things that the man did, what do you think was his most important mistake?

Writing

Describe the setting of the camp to which the man was headed, the camp the dog was running to at the end of the story. Use action verbs as much as possible and include sensory (5 senses) details.

Day 4

Writing

Write the story of "To Build a Fire" in your own words. Before you write, make a quick list of the events in order so that you may include them in your retelling.

Parsing

Parse the following sentence.
1. Identify the part of speech of each word.
2. Identify the parts of the sentence (As you tell the parts of the sentence give the case, number and gender of nouns and the tense, mood, and voice of verbs. Tell whether verbs are transitive or intransitive.)
3. Identify subordinate clauses and their subjects, predicates, and complements. (When labeling the words on your paper, label the subject, verb, and complement of the subordinate clause *under* the sentence so that it's not confused with the subject and verb of the main clause.)
4. Identify verbals and phrases and their objects and modifiers and tell how they are used.
5. Explain the modifiers.

(Remember that a clause may be inside a phrase and a phrase inside a clause.)

He kept his head to one side to escape the strangling fumes, and held the blazing bunch to the birch-bark.

Week 30

Day 1

Read the following short story and comment on it.

Br'er Rabbit and Tar Baby

One day Brer Fox and Brer Wolf, Brer Bear and Brer Possum, and all the other animals gathered together. "We shall dig a well," they declared.

So all the animals set to digging, and they dug and they dug and they dug. All except Brer Rabbit. He wasn't going to dig a well! He ran about and played in the bushes and had a good time.

"Brer Rabbit, if you aren't going to dig the well, what will you do when you need water?" said the other animals, watching him.

"Oh, I shall just go and get it and drink it," said Brer Rabbit, and he ran about and played in the bushes some more.

After a while, when the well was dug, all the animals gathered together and said, 'We shall plough the field and plant some corn.'

So Brer Fox and Brer Wolf, Brer Bear and Brer Possum, and all the other animals began ploughing the field and planting corn. All except Brer Rabbit. He wasn't going to plough the field! He wasn't going to plant the corn! He ran about and played in the bushes and had a good time.

"Brer Rabbit, if you aren't going to plough the field and plant the corn, what will you do when you need corn?" said the other animals, watching him.

"Oh, I shall just go and get it and eat it," said Brer Rabbit, and he ran about and played in the bushes some more.

And so, when Brer Fox and Brer Wolf and Brer Bear and Brer Possum had dug the well, Brer Rabbit came along and helped himself to the water. And when Brer Fox and Brer Wolf and Brer Bear and Brer Possum and all the rest had ploughed the field and planted the corn and cut it, Brer Rabbit came along and helped himself to it.

Then Brer Fox and Brer Wolf and Brer Bear and Brer Possum and all the other animals got together and made up their minds to catch Brer Rabbit so he could not steal their water and their corn any more. But Brer Rabbit was very clever, and nobody could catch him.

But Brer Wolf said, "I have to catch him'" He took some straw and made it into a baby with a head, arms, legs, a body, and he covered it with sticky black tar till the tar baby looked just like a real human baby. Then he sat Tar Baby right next to the well and went away.

By and by, Brer Rabbit came along. He saw Tar Baby and stopped. He thought it was a real person sitting there. But he needed the water, so he said politely as he could, "Good evening, sir. Fine weather we are having, sir!" But the Tar Baby made no reply. Brer Rabbit came a little closer and still being as polite as polite, said, "How is your mother, sir? And your grandmother? And your children? And all the rest of your family?" But still the Tar Baby made no reply.

Brer Rabbit came closer and still Tar Baby did nothing and said nothing. Then Brer

Rabbit felt very brave, and dropping his party manners, said, "You there! Get out of my way!" But still Tar Baby said nothing.

"You there!" said Brer rabbit again. "If you don't move out of my way, I'll hit you with this paw!" And he held up his right paw. Tar Baby still said nothing, did nothing. So Brer Rabbit hit him a great big crack on the head, and Brer Rabbit's paw got stuck in the tar and he couldn't pull it loose!

Then Brer Rabbit began to shout, "Let me go, let me go!" But Tar Baby wouldn't let him go. So Brer Rabbit hit him with his left paw, and with his right foot, and with his left foot—and they all got stuck in the tar! Now Brer Rabbit was really angry, and butted Tar Baby with his head—and his head got stuck tight in the tar!

Brer Rabbit shouted and yelled and pulled, but he couldn't get loose, and there he had to stay till the morning, when Brer Wolf came by to see what he had caught.

"Good morning, Brer Rabbit," said Brer Wolf. "How are you this morning? You seem to be a little stuck today!" And Brer Wolf laughed till his tummy hurt. Brer Rabbit said nothing because he knew what was coming.

Brer Wolf picked up Brer Rabbit and said, "It seems you wanted water. So let me throw you into the well."

"Yes, Brer Wolf, throw me into the well, but please don't throw me into that briar patch!" cried Brer Rabbit.

Brer Wolf looked surprised. Brer Rabbit wanted to be thrown into the well?

"Well then, I will light a fire and roast you and eat you," said Brer Wolf.

"Yes, Brer Wolf. Light a fire and roast me and eat me, but please don't throw me into the briar patch!"

Brer Wolf looked thoughtful. "Hmm," he thought. "Brer Rabbit doesn't mind the well, he doesn't mind the fire. But he minds the briar patch!" And Brer Wolf pulled Brer Rabbit loose from Tar Baby and threw him straight into the briar patch. "There now! The briars will poke him and jab him and hurt him!" he said.

Brer Wolf waited for Brer Rabbit's howls, but instead he heard Brer Rabbit laughing. "Thank you Brer Wolf, thank you for sending me back home," cried Brer Rabbit. "I and all my family grew up in this briar patch!"

And off ran Brer Rabbit through the brambles.

—Adapted From Uncle Remus Stories
by Joel Chandler Harris

Write your first response to the story.

Story Analysis

Uncle Remus and Brer Rabbit is a book of African American folktales about a wily, prankish character, Brer Rabbit, and his relationship with the other animals. The stories were collected and compiled by Joel Harris and published in 1907. The original text included the dialect in which Mr. Harris heard the stories. Here is a sample of one of the original stories:

> Now, den, you done hear what I say. Dar wuz Mr. Man, yander wuz de gyarden, an' here wuz ol' Brer Rabbit." Uncle Remus made a map of this part of the story by marking in the sand with his walking-cane. "Well, dis bein' de case, what you speck gwineter happen? Nothin' in de roun' worl' but what been happenin' sence greens an' sparrer-grass wuz planted in de groun'. Dey look fine an' dey tas'e fine, an' long to 'rds de shank er de mornin', Brer Rabbit 'ud creep thoo de crack er de fence an' nibble at um. He'd take de greens, but leave his tracks, mo' speshually right atter a rain. Takin' an' leavin'—it's de way er de worl'.
>
> —From "The Creeturs Go to the Barbeque" in

This dialect makes the story harder to read, but much more interesting. As in a tall tale, the kind of language used lends to the tone of the piece.

Exercise

1. What can you tell about the character of Brer Rabbit in the story "Brer Rabbit and Tar Baby"?

2. What is the physical and chronological setting of the story? What kind of setting is used (see Week 29 Day 3)?

3. What lesson do you think the original tellers of this story wanted to teach or show about life?

4. In what ways do you think the story is figurative?

Day 2

Story Analysis

This week the lessons focus on the element of storytelling called . The plot of the story is the organization of the events in the work, the relation between the story and the characters, and the structure of the narrative. The plot traces the development of a problem or conflict of some kind and how the main character deals with it. It is the framework of the story, having a beginning, middle, and end.

Exercise A
The plots of all stories follow this progression:

1. **Introduction:** Characters and the setting is revealed. (Sometime the conflict is introduced in the introduction.)
2. **Rising Action:** Events in the story become complicated and the conflict in the story is revealed. Suspense increases and ends in a crisis.
3. **Climax:** The highest point of interest and the turning point of the story. The reader wonders what will happen next; will the conflict be resolved or not?
4. **Falling action:** Events and complications begin to resolve themselves. The reader knows what has happened and whether the conflict was resolved or not.
5. **Denouement (or Resolution):** The final outcome or untangling of events in the story.

In longer stories, there may several repeats of steps 2-4 ending in a final climax and resolution. It is much easier to "plot" the steps in a short story.

For each story you have read so far, fill in the chart on the next page with details from the story for each step in the plot progression.

Exercise B
Plots may be structured in several different ways, and authors use many different techniques to advance the story. Here are some techniques used by authors:

Creating Suspense: excitement or tension.

Foreshadowing: hint or clue about what will happen in story.

Providing Flashback: interrupts the normal sequence of events to tell about something that happened in the past.

Surprise Ending: conclusion that reader does not expect.

Do you find any of these techniques used in the three short stories you have read so far? We'll talk about story structure on Day 3.

Phases of Plot

	Ransom of Red Chief	To Build Fire	Brer Rabbit and Tar Baby
Introduction			
Rising Action			
Climax			
Falling action			
Denouement			

Day 3

Story Analysis

Conflict

The conflict in a story is crucial to the plot. Without it, there really is no story worth telling. There are two kinds of conflict internal (a struggle within one's self, a decision to be made, a virtue to acquire or a vice to overcome) and external (a struggle with a force outside one's self).

There are four *kinds* of conflict:

Man vs. Man or Nature (physical): The leading character struggles with his physical strength against other men, forces of nature, or animals.

Man vs. Circumstances (classical): The leading character struggles against fate, or the circumstances of life facing him/her.

Man vs. Society (social): The leading character struggles against ideas, practices, or customs of other people.

Man vs. Himself/Herself (psychological): The leading character struggles with himself/ herself; with his/her own soul, ideas of right or wrong, physical limitations, choices, etc.

Structure

The author organizes a story in a way he thinks most effective. Some stories are in that the main character ends up at the same place he started. Other stories are in that several somewhat unrelated events are narrated and held loosely together around a common character or time setting. (The series by Laura Ingalls Wilder follows this structure.)

Most stories, however, are , in that the action takes place in a series of cause and effect events. This linear story can be told chronologically, as a series of flashbacks, or it may start right in the middle of the action (the reader has to figure out the information that would normally be in an introduction). The main thing to remember is that no matter what structure is used, plot is the result of *choices* made by characters in a story, especially the main character.

Several writers over time have tried to define and break it down to its basic structure. Aristotle in his book says there are only two kinds of plots: Tragedies (Bad things happen to good people) and Comedies (Good things happen to good people). In Shakespeare's stories, there are seven basic plots: the love story, the revenge story, murder mystery, the history, the tall tale, the coming of age, and the hail and farewell.

Exercise

Think about each of the stories you have read and decide which kind(s) of conflict is included and what structure the story follows. Use the chart on the following page to record your answers.

Story	Kind of Conflict	Structure
Ransom of Red Chief		
To Build a Fire		
Brer Rabbit and Tar Baby		

Writing

Retell the story of "Brer Rabbit and Tar Baby" in your own words.

Day 4

Writing

Today you will write a summary of one of the stories that you have read in this unit so far. A summary is different from a retelling. In a retelling you become the narrator, relating the events in order, adding significant details from the original work. A summary stands outside the story, telling a reader what a story is about.

Opening of a retelling: Brer Rabbit was making all the other animals very angry. Every day, he came along and ate the food that the other animals had worked hard to procure.

Opening of a summary: In the story Brer Rabbit, the life and antics of an irresponsible member of the animal community are described and praised.

A summary does not *have* to relate the story in the order things happened, but gives an overall view of the story. Review the steps for writing a summary in Week 17. These steps refer to a non-fiction work. When writing a summary of a piece of fiction, you can include the techniques the author uses, lessons learned by the characters, the kinds of conflicts, etc. The following sample not only talks about the characters, but the structure of the story and what a person might learn from the story.

Death Comes for the Archbishop by Willa Cather

Death Comes for the Archbishop by Willa Cather is the story of the life of a refined French priest, Fr. Jean LaTour, who is assigned to the new Southwest Territory in the 1800's. He and his valiant assistant, Fr. Vaillant, take on the rigors of desert frontier life, bringing the sacraments and Catholic ritual to a superstitious yet devout people.

The territory had been evangelized by the Spanish but abandoned when Mexico won its freedom from Spain. So a generation had passed without the benefit of learned churchmen in the region. La Tour has his work cut out for him when he arrives to right the misapplied religious practices of the faithful.

The story is told as a series of vignettes depicting incidences and phases of Archbishop LaTour's life. Through his gentle and timely enforcement of religious life and devotion LaTour wins the respect and regard of the natives and the Europeans alike. Over time, through gentle persistence, he rights the wrong influence of improper priests and learns to serve his people as they need.

There is a great contrast between the rugged life of the frontier and the refined personality of the Archbishop. There is also a contrast between the Archbishop and Fr. Vaillant. Fr. Vaillant is dramatic, aggressive and close to many people, while Archbishop LaTour is much more understated. While he is friendly and endears himself to many people, he remains aloof and has no close friends aside from Fr. Vaillant. Both men are portrayed as exemplary models of the religious vocation and the missionary zeal with which the religious approached the conversion of the American frontier.

Ms. Cather captures both the desert life of the Indian and Mexican cultures as well as the hearts of the Europeans who conquered them.

Since you will be writing a summary of a short story, it may only take a paragraph or two. The more you can condense the story to its essence, the better the summary. Here is a summary of the story Goldilocks and The Three Bears.

Sometimes, a curious nature can get a person into trouble, especially if it turns into trespassing. In the story "Goldilocks and the Three Bears," Goldilocks, a young curious girl learns that she shouldn't walk into someone else's house. While a bear family is out walking, letting their porridge cool, Goldilocks comes by and helps herself to the porridge, tasting from each bowl and gobbling up the Little Bear's altogether. She then breaks Little Bear's chair, tries to sleep in everyone's bed and finally falls asleep in Little Bear's bed.

When the bears come home, they find everything amiss and eventually find Goldilocks asleep in Little Bear's bed. They are not happy about this. Goldilocks awakens, and frightened by the bears, runs away. The life of the bears goes on but the reader does not know what happens to Goldilocks. The reader hopes that she has learned her lesson because the next time she trespasses, she might find something less friendly than the bears.

Directions

Decide which story you will summarize. Begin by doing a free-write on your thoughts about the story. You may list events from the story, include your ideas about the characters, the setting, and the plot. Write continuously for at least 10 minutes (longer if you're on a roll).

Then write your summary as concisely as possible. Use a variety of sentence structures so that your summary is interesting to read. When you are done, ask someone to read it and give you some feedback on the effectiveness of the summary.

File the summary in your drafts folder.

Parsing

Parse the following sentence.
1. Identify the part of speech of each word.
2. Identify the parts of the sentence (As you tell the parts of the sentence give the case, number and gender of nouns and the tense, mood, and voice of verbs. Tell whether verbs are transitive or intransitive.)
3. Identify subordinate clauses and their subjects, predicates, and complements. (When labeling the words on your paper, label the subject, verb, and complement of the subordinate clause *under* the sentence so that it's not confused with the subject and verb of the main clause.)
4. Identify verbals and phrases and their objects and modifiers and tell how they are used.
5. Explain the modifiers.

(Remember that a clause may be inside a phrase and a phrase inside a clause.)

Now Brer Rabbit was really angry, and butted Tar Baby with his head—and his head got stuck tight in the tar!

Week 31

Day 1

Read the following short story. After reading, go through and highlight vivid passages, or places where the writing is effective. Identify the steps in plot development: Introduction, rising action, climax, falling action, denouement (resolution).

The Ambitious Guest

One September night a family had gathered round their hearth, and piled it high with the driftwood of mountain streams, the dry cones of the pine, and the splintered ruins of great trees that had come crashing down the precipice. Up the chimney roared the fire, and brightened the room with its broad blaze. The faces of the father and mother had a sober gladness; the children laughed; the eldest daughter was the image of Happiness at seventeen; and the aged grandmother, who sat knitting in the warmest place, was the image of Happiness grown old. They had found the "herb, heart's-ease," in the bleakest spot of all New England. This family were situated in the Notch of the White Hills, where the wind was sharp throughout the year, and pitilessly cold in the winter,— giving their cottage all its fresh inclemency before it descended on the valley of the Saco. They dwelt in a cold spot and a dangerous one; for a mountain towered above their heads, so steep, that the stones would often rumble down its sides and startle them at midnight.

The daughter had just uttered some simple jest that filled them all with mirth, when the wind came through the Notch and seemed to pause before their cottage—rattling the door, with a sound of wailing and lamentation, before it passed into the valley. For a moment it saddened them, though there was nothing unusual in the tones. But the family were glad again when they perceived that the latch was lifted by some traveller, whose footsteps had been unheard amid the dreary blast which heralded his approach, and wailed as he was entering, and went moaning away from the door.

Though they dwelt in such a solitude, these people held daily converse with the world. The romantic pass of the Notch is a great artery, through which the life-blood of internal commerce is continually throbbing between Maine, on one side, and the Green Mountains and the shores of the St. Lawrence, on the other. The stage-coach always drew up before the door of the cottage. The wayfarer, with no companion but his staff, paused here to exchange a word, that the sense of loneliness might not utterly overcome him ere he could pass through the cleft of the mountain, or reach the first house in the valley. And here the teamster, on his way to Portland market, would put up for the night; and, if a bachelor, might sit an hour beyond the usual bedtime, and steal a kiss from the mountain maid at parting. It was one of those primitive taverns where the traveller pays only for food and lodging, but meets with a homely kindness beyond all price. When the footsteps were heard, therefore, between the outer door and the inner one, the whole family rose up, grandmother, children and all, as if about to welcome some one who belonged to them, and whose fate was linked with theirs.

The door was opened by a young man. His face at first wore the melancholy expression, almost despondency, of one who travels a wild and bleak road, at nightfall and alone, but soon brightened up when he saw the kindly warmth of his reception. He felt his heart spring forward to meet them all, from the old woman, who wiped a chair with her apron, to the little child that held out its arms to him. One glance and smile placed the stranger on a footing of innocent familiarity with the eldest daughter.

"Ah, this fire is the right thing!" cried he; "especially when there is such a pleasant circle round it. I am quite benumbed; for the Notch is just like the pipe of a great pair of bellows; it has blown a terrible blast in my face all the way from Bartlett."

"Then you are going towards Vermont?" said the master of the house, as he helped to take a light knapsack off the young man's shoulders.

"Yes; to Burlington, and far enough beyond," replied he. "I meant to have been at Ethan Crawford's to-night; but a pedestrian lingers along such a road as this. It is no matter; for, when I saw this good fire, and all your cheerful faces, I felt as if you had kindled it on purpose for me, and were waiting my arrival. So I shall sit down among you, and make myself at home."

The frank-hearted stranger had just drawn his chair to the fire when something like a heavy footstep was heard without, rushing down the steep side of the mountain, as with long and rapid strides, and taking such a leap in passing the cottage as to strike the opposite precipice. The family held their breath, because they knew the sound, and their guest held his by instinct.

"The old mountain has thrown a stone at us, for fear we should forget him," said the landlord, recovering himself. "He sometimes nods his head and threatens to come down; but we are old neighbors, and agree together pretty well upon the whole. Besides we have a sure place of refuge hard by if he should be coming in good earnest."

Let us now suppose the stranger to have finished his supper of bear's meat; and, by his natural felicity of manner, to have placed himself on a footing of kindness with the whole family, so that they talked as freely together as if he belonged to their mountain brood. He was of a proud, yet gentle spirit—haughty and reserved among the rich and great; but ever ready to stoop his head to the lowly cottage door, and be like a brother or a son at the poor man's fireside. In the household of the Notch he found warmth and simplicity of feeling, the pervading intelligence of New England, and a poetry of native growth, which they had gathered when they little thought of it from the mountain peaks and chasms, and at the very threshold of their romantic and dangerous abode. He had travelled far and alone; his whole life, indeed, had been a solitary path; for, with the lofty caution of his nature, he had kept himself apart from those who might otherwise have been his companions. The family, too, though so kind and hospitable, had that consciousness of unity among themselves, and separation from the world at large, which, in every domestic circle, should still keep a holy place where no stranger may intrude. But this evening a prophetic sympathy impelled the refined and educated youth to pour out his heart before the simple mountaineers, and constrained them to answer him with the same free confidence. And thus it should have been. Is not the kindred of a common fate a closer tie than that of birth?

The secret of the young man's character was a high and abstracted ambition. He could have borne to live an undistinguished life, but not to be forgotten in the grave. Yearning desire had been transformed to hope; and hope, long cherished, had become like certainty, that, obscurely as he journeyed now, a glory was to beam on all his pathway,— though not, perhaps, while he was treading it. But when posterity should gaze back into the gloom of what was now the present, they would trace the brightness of his footsteps, brightening as meaner glories faded, and confess that a gifted one had passed from his cradle to his tomb with none to recognize him.

"As yet," cried the stranger—his cheek glowing and his eye flashing with enthusiasm—"as yet, I have done nothing. Were I to vanish from the earth to-morrow, none would know so much of me as you: that a nameless youth came up at nightfall from the valley of the Saco, and opened his heart to you in the evening, and passed through the Notch by sunrise, and was seen no more. Not a soul would ask, 'Who was he? Whither did the wanderer go?' But I cannot die till I have achieved my destiny. Then, let Death come! I shall have built my monument!"

There was a continual flow of natural emotion, gushing forth amid abstracted reverie, which enabled the family to understand this young man's sentiments, though so foreign from their own. With quick sensibility of the ludicrous, he blushed at the ardor into which he had been betrayed.

"You laugh at me," said he, taking the eldest daughter's hand, and laughing himself. "You think my ambition as nonsensical as if I were to freeze myself to death on the top of Mount Washington, only that people might spy at me from the country round about. And, truly, that would be a noble pedestal for a man's statue!"

"It is better to sit here by this fire," answered the girl, blushing, "and be comfortable and contented, though nobody thinks about us."

"I suppose," said her father, after a fit of musing, "there is something natural in what the young man says; and if my mind had been turned that way, I might have felt just the same. It is strange, wife, how his talk has set my head running on things that are pretty certain never to come to pass."

"Perhaps they may," observed the wife. "Is the man thinking what he will do when he is a widower?"

"No, no!" cried he, repelling the idea with reproachful kindness. "When I think of your death, Esther, I think of mine, too. But I was wishing we had a good farm in Bartlett, or Bethlehem, or Littleton, or some other township round the White Mountains; but not where they could tumble on our heads. I should want to stand well with my neighbors and be called Squire, and sent to General Court for a term or two; for a plain, honest man may do as much good there as a lawyer. And when I should be grown quite an old man, and you an old woman, so as not to be long apart, I might die happy enough in my bed, and leave you all crying around me. A slate gravestone would suit me as well as a marble one--with just my name and age, and a verse of a hymn, and something to let people know that I lived an honest man and died a Christian."

"There now!" exclaimed the stranger; "it is our nature to desire a monument, be it slate or marble, or a pillar of granite, or a glorious memory in the universal heart of man."

"We're in a strange way, to-night," said the wife, with tears in her eyes. "They say it's a sign of something, when folks' minds go a wandering so. Hark to the children!"

They listened accordingly. The younger children had been put to bed in another room, but with an open door between, so that they could be heard talking busily among themselves. One and all seemed to have caught the infection from the fireside circle, and were outvying each other in wild wishes, and childish projects of what they would do when they came to be men and women. At length a little boy, instead of addressing his brothers and sisters, called out to his mother.

"I'll tell you what I wish, mother," cried he. "I want you and father and grandma'm, and all of us, and the stranger too, to start right away, and go and take a drink out of the basin of the Flume!"

Nobody could help laughing at the child's notion of leaving a warm bed, and dragging them from a cheerful fire, to visit the basin of the Flume,—a brook, which tumbles over the precipice, deep within the Notch. The boy had hardly spoken when a wagon rattled along the road, and stopped a moment before the door. It appeared to contain two or three men, who were cheering their hearts with the rough chorus of a song, which resounded, in broken notes, between the cliffs, while the singers hesitated whether to continue their journey or put up here for the night.

"Father," said the girl, "they are calling you by name."

But the good man doubted whether they had really called him, and was unwilling to show himself too solicitous of gain by inviting people to patronize his house. He therefore did not hurry to the door; and the lash being soon applied, the travellers plunged into the Notch, still singing and laughing, though their music and mirth came back drearily from the heart of the mountain.

"There, mother!" cried the boy, again. "They'd have given us a ride to the Flume."

Again they laughed at the child's pertinacious fancy for a night ramble. But it happened that a light cloud passed over the daughter's spirit; she looked gravely into the fire, and drew a breath that was almost a sigh. It forced its way, in spite of a little struggle to repress it. Then starting and blushing, she looked quickly round the circle, as if they had caught a glimpse into her bosom. The stranger asked what she had been thinking of.

"Nothing," answered she, with a downcast smile. "Only I felt lonesome just then."

"Oh, I have always had a gift of feeling what is in other people's hearts," said he, half seriously. "Shall I tell the secrets of yours? For I know what to think when a young girl shivers by a warm hearth, and complains of lonesomeness at her mother's side. Shall I put these feelings into words?"

"They would not be a girl's feelings any longer if they could be put into words," replied the mountain nymph, laughing, but avoiding his eye.

All this was said apart. Perhaps a germ of love was springing in their hearts, so pure that it might blossom in Paradise, since it could not be matured on earth; for women worship such gentle dignity as his; and the proud, contemplative, yet kindly soul is oftenest captivated by simplicity like hers. But while they spoke softly, and he was watching the happy sadness, the lightsome shadows, the shy yearnings of a maiden's nature, the wind through the Notch took a deeper and drearier sound. It seemed, as the fanciful stranger said, like the choral strain of the spirits of the blast, who in old Indian times had their dwelling among these mountains, and made their heights and recesses a sacred region. There was a wail along the road, as if a funeral were passing. To chase away the gloom, the family threw pine branches on their fire, till the dry leaves crackled and the flame arose, discovering once again a scene of peace and humble happiness. The light hovered about them fondly, and caressed them all. There were the little faces of the children, peeping from their bed apart and here the father's frame of strength, the mother's subdued and careful mien, the high-browed youth, the budding girl, and the good old grandam, still knitting in the warmest place. The aged woman looked up from her task, and, with fingers ever busy, was the next to speak.

"Old folks have their notions," said she, "as well as young ones. You've been wishing and planning; and letting your heads run on one thing and another, till you've set my mind a wandering too. Now what should an old woman wish for, when she can go but a step or two before she comes to her grave? Children, it will haunt me night and day till I tell you."

"What is it, mother?" cried the husband and wife at once.

Then the old woman, with an air of mystery which drew the circle closer round the fire, informed them that she had provided her graveclothes some years before,—a a nice linen shroud, a cap with a muslin ruff, and everything of a finer sort than she had worn since her wedding day. But this evening an old superstition had strangely recurred to her. It used to be said, in her younger days, that if anything were amiss with a corpse, if only the ruff were not smooth, or the cap did not set right, the corpse in the coffin and beneath the clods would strive to put up its cold hands and arrange it. The bare thought made her nervous.

"Don't talk so, grandmother!" said the girl, shuddering.

"Now,"—continued the old woman, with singular earnestness, yet smiling strangely at her own folly,—"I want one of you, my children—when your mother is dressed and in the coffin—I want one of you to hold a looking-glass over my face. Who knows but I may take a glimpse at myself, and see whether all's right?"

"Old and young, we dream of graves and monuments," murmured the stranger youth. "I wonder how mariners feel when the ship is sinking, and they, unknown and undistinguished, are to be buried together in the ocean—that wide and nameless sepulchre?"

For a moment, the old woman's ghastly conception so engrossed the minds of her hearers that a sound abroad in the night, rising like the roar of a blast, had grown broad, deep, and terrible, before the fated group were conscious of it. The house and all within it trembled; the foundations of the earth seemed to be shaken, as if this awful sound were the peal of the last trump. Young and old exchanged one wild glance, and remained an instant, pale, affrighted, without utterance, or power to move. Then the same shriek burst simultaneously from all their lips.

"The Slide! The Slide!"

The simplest words must intimate, but not portray, the unutterable horror of the catastrophe. The victims rushed from their cottage, and sought refuge in what they deemed a safer spot—where, in contemplation of such an emergency, a sort of barrier had been reared. Alas! they had quitted their security, and fled right into the pathway of destruction. Down came the whole side of the mountain, in a cataract of ruin. Just before it reached the house, the stream broke into two branches—shivered not a window there, but overwhelmed the whole vicinity, blocked up the road, and annihilated everything in its dreadful course. Long ere the thunder of the great Slide had ceased to roar among the mountains, the mortal agony had been endured, and the victims were at peace. Their bodies were never found.

The next morning, the light smoke was seen stealing from the cottage chimney up the mountain side. Within, the fire was yet smouldering on the hearth, and the chairs in a circle round it, as if the inhabitants had but gone forth to view the devastation of the Slide, and would shortly return, to thank Heaven for their miraculous escape. All had left separate tokens, by which those who had known the family were made to shed a tear for each. Who has not heard their name? The story has been told far and wide, and will forever be a legend of these mountains. Poets have sung their fate.

There were circumstances which led some to suppose that a stranger had been received into the cottage on this awful night, and had shared the catastrophe of all its inmates. Others denied that there were sufficient grounds for such a conjecture. Woe for the high-souled youth, with his dream of Earthly Immortality! His name and person utterly unknown; his history, his way of life, his plans, a mystery never to be solved, his death and his existence equally a doubt! Whose was the agony of that death moment?

—Nathaniel Hawthorne

Thompson Falls and Saco Valley by Benjamin Champney

Day 2

Story Analysis

This week our study of the elements of story will focus on *theme*. The theme of a story is the underlying truth or main idea of the story. It differs from the subject or topic in that it involves a judgement about the topic. So the subject might be love, but the theme might be that love is essential to good health. The theme is inferred from the events and other elements of story and often evolves through the experiences of the main character.

There are four ways a theme is related by the author.

1. **By emotions**: The feelings and thoughts of the main character are revealed and evoke emotions in the reader.
2. **By the thoughts and conversations of the characters**: Dialogue not only lets the reader find out about the personality of a character but also develops the story's themes. Themes may appear in thoughts that are repeated throughout the story.
3. **By the lessons learned by the main character**: The main character usually illustrates the most important theme of the story. A good way to get at this theme is to ask yourself the question: What does the main character learn in the course of the story?
4. **By the actions or events in the story**: Characters express ideas and feelings through their actions.

Each reader brings his own experiences to bear on the story, and so different readers will often find varying themes in the same story. Think about each of the stories that you have read in this unit and decide on a theme for the story. Ask yourself these questions about the stories as you make your decision:

*   What is the story's central purpose?
*   What view of life does it support or what insight into life does it reveal?
*   What is the central insight, the one that explains the greatest number of elements in the story and relates them to each other?
*   In what way(s) does the main character(s) change in the course of the story and what, if anything, has the character(s) learned before its end?
*   What is the central conflict of the story and how is it resolved? What information does the title reveal?

Your theme should be a complete sentence *about* the subject, not merely an identification of the subject. It should be a generalization and not include specifics from the story.

For example, when writing the theme for Little Red Riding Hood, you would not write:

Red Riding Hood learns she should not walk in the forest with wolves.

But instead, write:

Children should obey their parents.

You would not say: *The theme of this story is obedience.* That is to merely identify the subject. You want to say something *about* the subject, such as, *Disobedience can lead to dangerous situations, even death.*

Decide on a theme for each of the following stories. Fill in the chart below with your theme statement. Then decide which of the four methods of conveying theme are most used in this story.

Story	Theme statement	Main methods author uses to convey theme.
Ransom of Red Chief		
To Build a Fire		
Brer Rabbit		
The Ambitious Guest		

Writing

Retell (narrate) the story of The Ambitious Guest.

Day 3

Thoughts about Theme for Catholic Readers

In some stories the theme might be very obviously represented as a moral or lesson. Even if an author has no theme in mind and is simply telling a story for its own sake, themes can be drawn out of the story. Even though Tolkein says he had no particular theme in mind with his Lord of the Rings trilogy, the reader certainly takes away truths about the value of sacrifice, loyalty, and courage. In contemporary or modern stories, however, the themes are often purposely obscured. This may be an attempt on the part of the author to say that nothing in life is "black and white" or that truth is subjectively interpreted differently by different people and therefore cannot be known. You must know that that in itself is a theme in an author's work. As Catholics we believe that truth can be known and should be wary of authors who propose otherwise.

An author will use many techniques to craft an imaginative story to convey his theme.

Foreshadowing

Although a part of plot really, foreshadowing is often used to let the reader know where the author is going thematically with a story. Foreshadowing is quite simply a hint or clue given early in a story about the events that will happen later in a story. It may make a story more believable by partially preparing the reader for events which are to follow.

Irony

Irony is Irony is the contrast between what is expected or what appears to be and what actually is; a contrast or discrepancy between one thing and another. There are four kinds of irony in storytelling.

- **Verbal irony:** The reader understands the opposite of what the speaker says.
- **Irony of Circumstance or Situational Irony:** When one event is expected to occur but the opposite happens.
- **Dramatic Irony:** Discrepancy between what characters know and what readers know.
- **Ironic Vision:** An overall tone of irony that pervades a work, suggesting how the writer views the characters.

Exercise A

Discuss these questions about *The Ambitious Guest* with you teacher.

1. What is the conflict in the story?

2. Who is the main character? Is there more than one main character?

3. What is the setting of the story?

4. What foreshadowing do you find in the story?

5. What instances of irony do you find in the story? What kind of irony is each one?

Writing

Prewriting Literary Analysis

This week you will write a literary analysis of one of the stories you have read in this unit. In a literary analysis paper, you make a claim about a story or piece of literature and then prove it in the body of your essay using the text itself as evidence for your opinion. The goal of analysis writing is to demonstrate understanding of the text. When you use quotes from the text, be sure to explain them.

Here is the outline of a literary analysis paper:

I. Introduction: describe the story setting and characters
Give your thesis statement.
   II. Body
      A. Evidence from story that supports your thesis.
      B. Another example from the story that supports your thesis.
      C. Another example from the story that supports your thesis.
   III. Conclusion
Tie together your support and connect it back to you thesis statement

Today you will begin the prewriting phase. In this analysis paper, you will be discussing the theme of your chosen story.

1. Decide upon the theme of your chosen story (review you chart from Day 2).
2. Do a free-write on the topic of your theme. Write continuously for 15-20 minutes about your theme and the story making connections and exploring the ideas in your head about the story.

3. Use the chart below to take notes for each section of the essay.

Introduction
Thesis Statement:
First evidence/reason from story: How does this evidence support the thesis?
Second evidence/reason from story: How does this evidence support the thesis?
Third evidence/reason from story: How does this evidence support the thesis?
Conclusion:

Save your free-write and chart for Day 4

Day 4

Writing

Today you will write the first draft of your literary analysis theme paper. Reread your free-write from Day 3 to remind yourself what you think of the theme and the story. Then review the chart you made.

Using the chart, write your essay. Each box of the chart becomes one paragraph in your paper. The chart only provided space for three pieces of support for your thesis, but if you have more than three ways to support your thesis, use as many paragraphs as you have evidence. Use one paragraph for each idea about the thesis.

Some writing teachers instruct their students to write a thesis statement that has three parts that can be neatly discussed in three paragraphs. That way the reader can follow the thesis more easily. If you think that will help you, make sure your thesis has three parts and that you discuss each of those three parts in three subsequent paragraphs. However, you may be ready for more sophisticated writing at this point in the year. You can demonstrate control of your paper and support your thesis well by using good transitions and continually tying your support back to your thesis.

Share your draft with your teacher and discuss how effectively you analyzed the story. Did you keep tight control of the paper by effective transitions? Does the introduction adequately set up the story for the reader? Does the conclusion tie the support back to the thesis?

Parsing

Parse the following sentence.
1. Identify the part of speech of each word.
2. Identify the parts of the sentence (As you tell the parts of the sentence give the case, number and gender of nouns and the tense, mood, and voice of verbs. Tell whether verbs are transitive or intransitive.)
3. Identify subordinate clauses and their subjects, predicates, and complements. (When labeling the words on your paper, label the subject, verb, and complement of the subordinate clause *under* the sentence so that it's not confused with the subject and verb of the main clause.)
4. Identify verbals and phrases and their objects and modifiers and tell how they are used.
5. Explain the modifiers.

(Remember that a clause may be inside a phrase and a phrase inside a clause.)

With quick sensibility of the ludicrous, he blushed at the ardor into which he had been betrayed.

Week 32

Day 1

Study this picture and write a description of what you think is happening.

Dust Storm, Texas 1935

Point of View

Point of view in fiction refers to the narrative voice of the storyteller. In other words, from whose perspective is the story told? The tone and feel of the story, and even its meaning, can change depending on who the narrator is. And, the credibility of the story will depend on the how reliable the reader perceives the narrator to be. The narrator could be either *objective* (detached) or *subjective* (biased). An objective narrator's tale is more readily believed than that of a subjective narrator.

Traditionally there are two distinct types of point of view used in stories and two variations of each of those.

1. **First Person** (subjective): The story is told by someone within the story with firsthand knowledge of the events.

a. *The narrator is the main character or protagonist.* In first person narratives, the trustworthiness of narrator should be evaluated. It is possible that what the narrator is recounting might not be the objective truth. For instance, a first person narrator might try to justify his actions or present himself in a favorable light to the reader.

b. *The narrator is a secondary character.* A famous example of this is in Sir Conan Doyle's Sherlock Holmes stories: Dr. Watson is the narrator.

2. **Third Person or Omniscient** (objective): The author is the narrator, moving from character to character, event to event, having free access to the thoughts, feelings, and motivations of his characters. This is the most common method used by short story authors.

a. *Limited:* The author tells the story in third person (using pronouns they, she, he, it, etc). We know only what the character knows and what the author allows him/her to tell us. We can see the thoughts and feelings of characters if the author chooses to reveal them to us.

b. *Objective:* The author tells the story in the third person. It appears as though a camera is following the characters, going anywhere, and recording only what is seen and heard. There is no comment on the characters or their thoughts. No interpretations are offered. The reader is placed in the position of spectator without the author there to explain. The reader has to interpret events on his own.

In modern stories you may also find two other varieties of point of view

1. ***Innocent Eye:*** The story is told through the eyes of a child (his/her judgment being different from that of an adult) or bystander outside the story.

2. ***Stream of Consciousness:*** The story is told so that the reader feels as if he is "inside the head" of one character and knows all his thoughts and reactions.

Exercise A

For each of the stories you have read in this unit, decide from what point of view the story is told. Use the chart on the next page to record your findings.

Story	Point of View
Ransom of Red Chief	
To Build a Fire	
Brer Rabbit	
The Ambitious Guest	

Exercise B

Using the story *Ransom of Red Chief*, answer the following questions.

1. How does the point of view affect your response to the story, to the characters and the theme?

2. Is the narrator reliable? Give your reasons.

3. Are the plot and the point-of-view of the story linked? If so, how?

Day 2

Writing

Look again at the photograph reprinted on Day 1. It shows a dust storm approaching a small town in Texas during the dust bowl era. Today you will write about this dust storm from three different points of view.

1. First person: imagine that you are standing in the town watching the storm approach. Narrate what happens.

2. Third Person, Limited Omniscient: you are the narrator and reveal only the reactions of certain characters without revealing the whole scene.

3. Third Person, Objective Omniscient: you are the narrator and narrate the action as though you are holding a camera watching the event unfold. Nothing is withheld from the reader.

After you write the three pieces, decide which of these three points of view you like the best for this narrative and explain why you think it is the best.

Day 3

The narrative voice can be the most important of all the elements of story we've discussed so far. It's the vehicle in which the story is delivered: it's what makes the story believable to the reader and it sets the tone. It isn't so much what is said . . . as how. Skilled writers will adjust voice for the intended audience and purpose of the story and will use it to intentionally evoke emotion in the reader.

In the story *My Antonia* by Willa Cather, the author uses the first person point of view of a secondary character. In fact, the narrator only figures in a small way in the story; he is mostly telling about his firsthand experience of his friend Antonia and her family. This is a good example of how the narrator is different from the author. Another great example is *Huckleberry Finn* by Mark Twain. Twain chose Huck to be the narrator, and life is so much more exciting from Huck's first-person point of view.

Today you will begin to write a paper about a person you know well by narrating some events you have witnessed. You reader should get a clear picture of the person you have chosen. You must not merely *tell* the reader about this person, but *show* something about him (or her) by *telling a story* about him. Think of some trait that person possesses that you will show in the story. For example, if you think your chosen person is brave, tell a story about him that shows his bravery. If you think the person is generous, tell a story that shows his generosity. Even though you are writing about someone real and so it may seem biographical, you are telling a story of only one or two events. (Don't forget the attributes of *show*ing writing: action verbs, specific nouns, and descriptive language.)

Here is the general outline you should follow:

Introduction: General statements about the kind of person who would . . . .
    End the introduction letting the reader know what story or what kind of story you're going to tell.

Body: Narrate the story about your person using *show*ing language.

Conclusion: Include some reflection about this person or what you learned from the story.

Prewriting
Think of what you want to show about the person you have chosen. Make a list possible events that illustrate what you want to show. Choose the best one to write about, the one that

you can elaborate into a well told story. List the order in which you will tell the story, jotting notes to yourself.

Write your first draft without worry about grammar and spelling; just get the story out. Read over your draft and check the verbs you chose. If any are weak, replace them with stronger, more expressive verbs. Save your draft for Day 4

Day 4

Writing

Reread the story that you wrote about someone that you know well. Today you will make some improvements in the story.

Sentence Variety

Count how many simple, complex, and compound sentences you used. Short simple sentences can be used for effect to create a mood.

> *She turned the key not knowing what to expect. Her heart thumped.*
> *The clock ticked. Every nerve in her body was stretched.*

But if you use too many simple sentences without that purpose in mind, your writing can be dull. If you find sentences that can be combined by adding coordinating conjunctions to make complex sentences, combine them. Check for run-on sentences. Sentences with a series of events can also be used to create an effect.

> *Sam didn't know whether to laugh or cry; whether to run or fall to her knees;*
> *whether to shout or shake with relief.*

Be sure to use the proper punctuation if you make a long sentence. Check for parallel structure whenever you used a conjunction. (See Week 25)

To increase the variety of your sentences, see if you can include each of the following grammatical forms in your story:

Adverb clause beginning a sentence
Adjective clause
Participle phrase beginning a sentence
Gerund
Compound sentence
Appositive phrase
Figurative language (metaphor, simile, personification, etc.)

Elements of Voice

Review the elements of voice:

Diction: Word choice is the most basic and important element.

Details: Facts, individual incidents.

Imagery: Brings the senses to life in words.

Syntax: Syntax is the grammatical structure of a sentence, the way words are arranged. Various sentence structures pace the writing and determine the focus.

Tone: Tone is the attitude of the speaker or writer as revealed in the choice of vocabulary or the intonation of speech.

Check your paper for these 5 elements. In what ways do you employ them?

Make changes in your paper to improve the elements of voice in your story (for example, include more vivid images; change any words that could be made more specific). Think about what in your story sets the tone. Then file the paper in your drafts folder.

Parsing

Parse the following sentence.
1. Identify the part of speech of each word.
2. Identify the parts of the sentence (As you tell the parts of the sentence give the case, number and gender of nouns and the tense, mood, and voice of verbs. Tell whether verbs are transitive or intransitive.)
3. Identify subordinate clauses and their subjects, predicates, and complements. (When labeling the words on your paper, label the subject, verb, and complement of the subordinate clause *under* the sentence so that it's not confused with the subject and verb of the main clause.)
4. Identify verbals and phrases and their objects and modifiers and tell how they are used.
5. Explain the modifiers.

(Remember that a clause may be inside a phrase and a phrase inside a clause.)

The Plains winds whipped across the fields raising billowing clouds of dust to the sky.

Week 33

Day 1

Read the following story and write your first reaction to it. What did you enjoy in it? What did you find surprising? What is your opinion of the ending? As you read, note places where you find vivid imagery.

The Bride Comes to Yellow Sky

The great Pullman was whirling onward with such dignity of motion that a glance from the window seemed simply to prove that the plains of Texas were pouring eastward. Vast flats of green grass, dull-hued spaces of mesquite and cactus, little groups of frame houses, woods of light and tender trees, all were sweeping into the east, sweeping over the horizon, a precipice.

A newly married pair had boarded this coach at San Antonio. The man's face was reddened from many days in the wind and sun, and a direct result of his new black clothes was that his brick-colored hands were constantly performing in a most conscious fashion. From time to time he looked down respectfully at his attire. He sat with a hand on each knee, like a man waiting in a barber's shop. The glances he devoted to other passengers were furtive and shy.

The bride was not pretty, nor was she very young. She wore a dress of blue cashmere, with small reservations of velvet here and there and with steel buttons abounding. She continually twisted her head to regard her puff sleeves, very stiff, straight, and high. They embarrassed her. It was quite apparent that she had cooked, and that she expected to cook, dutifully. The blushes caused by the careless scrutiny of some passengers as she had entered the car were strange to see upon this plain, under-class countenance, which was drawn in placid, almost emotionless lines.

They were evidently very happy. "Ever been in a parlor-car before?" he asked, smiling with delight.

"No," she answered, "I never was. It's fine, ain't it?"

"Great! And then after a while we'll go forward to the diner and get a big layout. Finest meal in the world. Charge a dollar."

"Oh, do they?" cried the bride. "Charge a dollar? Why, that's too much - for us - ain't it, Jack?"

"Not this trip, anyhow," he answered bravely. "We're going to go the whole thing."

Later, he explained to her about the trains. "You see, it's a thousand miles from one end of Texas to the other, and this train runs right across it and never stops but four times." He had the pride of an owner. He pointed out to her the dazzling fittings of the coach, and in truth her eyes opened wider as she contemplated the sea-green figured velvet, the shining brass, silver, and glass, the wood that gleamed as darkly brilliant as the surface of a pool of oil. At one end a bronze figure sturdily held a support for a separated chamber, and at convenient places on the ceiling were frescoes in olive and silver.

To the minds of the pair, their surroundings reflected the glory of their marriage that morning in San Antonio. This was the environment of their new estate, and the man's face in particular beamed with an elation that made him appear ridiculous to the negro porter. This individual at times surveyed them from afar with an amused and superior grin. On other occasions he bullied them with skill in ways that did not make it exactly plain to them that they were being bullied. He subtly used all the manners of the most unconquerable kind of snobbery. He oppressed them, but of this oppression they had small knowledge, and they speedily forgot that infrequently a number of travelers covered them with stares of derisive enjoyment. Historically there was supposed to be something infinitely humorous in their situation.

"We are due in Yellow Sky at 3:42," he said, looking tenderly into her eyes.

"Oh, are we?" she said, as if she had not been aware of it. To evince surprise at her husband's statement was part of her wifely amiability. She took from a pocket a little silver watch, and as she held it before her and stared at it with a frown of attention, the new husband's face shone.

"I bought it in San Anton' from a friend of mine," he told her gleefully.

"It's seventeen minutes past twelve," she said, looking up at him with a kind of shy and clumsy coquetry. A passenger, noting this play, grew excessively sardonic, and winked at himself in one of the numerous mirrors.

At last they went to the dining-car. Two rows of negro waiters, in glowing white suits, surveyed their entrance with the interest and also the equanimity of men who had been forewarned. The pair fell to the lot of a waiter who happened to feel pleasure in steering them through their meal. He viewed them with the manner of a fatherly pilot, his countenance radiant with benevolence. The patronage, entwined with the ordinary deference, was not plain to them. And yet, as they returned to their coach, they showed in their faces a sense of escape.

To the left, miles down a long purple slope, was a little ribbon of mist where moved the keening Rio Grande. The train was approaching it at an angle, and the apex was Yellow Sky. Presently it was apparent that, as the distance from Yellow Sky grew shorter, the husband became commensurately restless. His brick-red hands were more insistent in their prominence. Occasionally he was even rather absent-minded and far-away when the bride leaned forward and addressed him.

As a matter of truth, Jack Potter was beginning to find the shadow of a deed weigh upon him like a leaden slab. He, the town marshal of Yellow Sky, a man known, liked, and feared in his corner, a prominent person, had gone to San Antonio to meet a girl he believed he loved, and there, after the usual prayers, had actually induced her to marry him, without consulting Yellow Sky for any part of the transaction. He was now bringing his bride before an innocent and unsuspecting community.

Of course, people in Yellow Sky married as it pleased them, in accordance with a general custom; but such was Potter's thought of his duty to his friends, or of their idea of his duty, or of an unspoken form which does not control men in these matters, that he felt he was heinous. He had committed an extraordinary crime. Face to face with this girl in San Antonio, and spurred by his sharp impulse, he had gone headlong over all the social hedges. At San Antonio he was like a man hidden in the dark. A knife to sever any friendly duty, any form, was easy to his hand in that remote city. But the hour of Yellow Sky, the hour of daylight, was approaching.

He knew full well that his marriage was an important thing to his town. It could only be exceeded by the burning of the new hotel. His friends could not forgive him. Frequently he had reflected on the advisability of telling them by telegraph, but a new cowardice had been upon him. He feared to do it. And now the train was hurrying him toward a scene of amazement, glee, and reproach. He glanced out of the window at the line of haze swinging slowly in towards the train.

Yellow Sky had a kind of brass band, which played painfully, to the delight of the populace. He laughed without heart as he thought of it. If the citizens could dream of his prospective arrival with his bride, they would parade the band at the station and escort them, amid cheers and laughing congratulations, to his adobe home.

He resolved that he would use all the devices of speed and plains-craft in making the journey from the station to his house. Once within that safe citadel he could issue some sort of a vocal bulletin, and then not go among the citizens until they had time to wear off a little of their enthusiasm.

The bride looked anxiously at him. "What's worrying you, Jack?"

He laughed again. "I'm not worrying, girl. I'm only thinking of Yellow Sky."

She flushed in comprehension.

A sense of mutual guilt invaded their minds and developed a finer tenderness. They looked at each other with eyes softly aglow. But Potter often laughed the same nervous laugh. The flush upon the bride's face seemed quite permanent.

The traitor to the feelings of Yellow Sky narrowly watched the speeding landscape. "We're nearly there," he said.

Presently the porter came and announced the proximity of Potter's home. He held a brush in his hand and, with all his airy superiority gone, he brushed Potter's new clothes as the latter slowly turned this way and that way. Potter fumbled out a coin and gave it to the porter, as he had seen others do. It was a heavy and muscle-bound business, as that of a man shoeing his first horse.

The porter took their bag, and as the train began to slow they moved forward to the hooded platform of the car. Presently the two engines and their long string of coaches rushed into the station of Yellow Sky.

"They have to take water here," said Potter, from a constricted throat and in mournful cadence, as one announcing death. Before the train stopped, his eye had swept the length of the platform, and he was glad and astonished to see there was none upon it but the station-agent, who, with a slightly hurried and anxious air, was walking toward the water-tanks. When the train had halted, the porter alighted first and placed in position a little temporary step.

"Come on, girl," said Potter hoarsely. As he helped her down they each laughed on a false note. He took the bag from the negro, and bade his wife cling to his arm. As they slunk rapidly away, his hang-dog glance perceived that they were unloading the two trunks, and also that the station-agent far ahead near the baggage-car had turned and was running toward him, making gestures. He laughed, and groaned as he laughed, when he noted the first effect of his marital bliss upon Yellow Sky. He gripped his wife's arm firmly to his side, and they fled. Behind them the porter stood chuckling fatuously.

Chapter 2

The California Express on the Southern Railway was due at Yellow Sky in twenty-one minutes. There were six men at the bar of the "Weary Gentleman" saloon. One was a drummer who talked a great deal and rapidly; three were Texans who did not care to talk at that time; and two were Mexican sheep-herders who did not talk as a general practice in the "Weary Gentleman" saloon. The barkeeper's dog lay on the board walk that crossed in front of the door. His head was on his paws, and he glanced drowsily here and there with the constant vigilance of a dog that is kicked on occasion. Across the sandy street were some vivid green grass plots, so wonderful in appearance amid the sands that burned near them in a blazing sun that they caused a doubt in the mind. They exactly resembled the grass mats used to represent lawns on the stage. At the cooler end of the railway station a man without a coat sat in a tilted chair and smoked his pipe. The fresh-cut bank of the Rio Grande circled near the town, and there could be seen beyond it a great, plum-colored plain of mesquite.

Save for the busy drummer and his companions in the saloon, Yellow Sky was dozing. The new-comer leaned gracefully upon the bar, and recited many tales with the confidence of a bard who has come upon a new field.

"— and at the moment that the old man fell down stairs with the bureau in his arms, the old woman was coming up with two scuttles of coal, and, of course—"

The drummer's tale was interrupted by a young man who suddenly appeared in the open door. He cried: "Scratchy Wilson's drunk, and has turned loose with both hands." The two Mexicans at once set down their glasses and faded out of the rear entrance of the saloon.

The drummer, innocent and jocular, answered: "All right, old man. S'pose he has. Come in and have a drink, anyhow."

But the information had made such an obvious cleft in every skull in the room that the drummer was obliged to see its importance. All had become instantly solemn. "Say," said he, mystified, "what is this?" His three companions made the introductory gesture of eloquent speech, but the young man at the door forestalled them.

"It means, my friend," he answered, as he came into the saloon, "that for the next two hours this town won't be a health resort."

The barkeeper went to the door and locked and barred it. Reaching out of the window, he pulled in heavy wooden shutters and barred them. Immediately a solemn, chapel-like gloom was upon the place. The drummer was looking from one to another.

"But, say," he cried, "what is this, anyhow? You don't mean there is going to be a gun-fight?"

"Don't know whether there'll be a fight or not," answered one man grimly. "But there'll be some shootin' - some good shootin'."

The young man who had warned them waved his hand. "Oh, there'll be a fight fast enough if anyone wants it. Anybody can get a fight out there in the street. There's a fight just waiting."

The drummer seemed to be swayed between the interest of a foreigner and a perception of personal danger.

"What did you say his name was?" he asked.

"Scratchy Wilson," they answered in chorus.

"And will he kill anybody? What are you going to do? Does this happen often? Does he rampage around like this once a week or so? Can he break in that door?"

"No, he can't break down that door," replied the barkeeper. "He's tried it three times. But when he comes you'd better lay down on the floor, stranger. He's dead sure to shoot at it, and a bullet may come through."

Thereafter the drummer kept a strict eye upon the door. The time had not yet been called for him to hug the floor, but, as a minor precaution, he sidled near to the wall. "Will he kill anybody?" he said again.

The men laughed low and scornfully at the question.

"He's out to shoot, and he's out for trouble. Don't see any good in experimentin' with him."

"But what do you do in a case like this? What do you do?"

A man responded: "Why, he and Jack Potter -- "

"But," in chorus, the other men interrupted, "Jack Potter's in San Anton'."

"Well, who is he? What's he got to do with it?"

"Oh, he's the town marshal. He goes out and fights Scratchy when he gets on one of these tears."

"Wow," said the drummer, mopping his brow. "Nice job he's got."

The voices had toned away to mere whisperings. The drummer wished to ask further questions which were born of an increasing anxiety and bewilderment; but when he attempted them, the men merely looked at him in irritation and motioned him to remain silent. A tense waiting hush was upon them. In the deep shadows of the room their eyes shone as they listened for sounds from the street. One man made three gestures at the barkeeper, and the latter, moving like a ghost, handed him a glass and a bottle. The man poured a full glass of whisky, and set down the bottle noiselessly. He gulped the whisky in a swallow, and turned again toward the door in immovable silence. The drummer saw that the barkeeper, without a sound, had taken a Winchester from beneath the bar. Later he saw this individual beckoning to him, so he tiptoed across the room.

"You better come with me back of the bar."

"No, thanks," said the drummer, perspiring. "I'd rather be where I can make a break for the back door."

Whereupon the man of bottles made a kindly but peremptory gesture. The drummer obeyed it, and finding himself seated on a box with his head below the level of the bar, balm was laid upon his soul at sight of various zinc and copper fittings that bore a resemblance to armor-plate. The barkeeper took a seat comfortably upon an adjacent box.

"You see," he whispered, "this here Scratchy Wilson is a wonder with a gun - a perfect wonder - and when he goes on the war trail, we hunt our holes - naturally. He's about the last one of the old gang that used to hang out along the river here. He's a terror when he's drunk. When he's sober he's all right - kind of simple - wouldn't hurt a fly - nicest fellow in town. But when he's drunk - whoo!"

There were periods of stillness. "I wish Jack Potter was back from San Anton'," said the barkeeper. "He shot Wilson up once - in the leg - and he would sail in and pull out the kinks in this thing."

Presently they heard from a distance the sound of a shot, followed by three wild yowls. It instantly removed a bond from the men in the darkened saloon. There was a shuffling of feet. They looked at each other. "Here he comes," they said.

Chapter 3

A man in a maroon-colored flannel shirt, which had been purchased for purposes of decoration and made, principally, by some Jewish women on the east side of New York, rounded a corner and walked into the middle of the main street of Yellow Sky. In either hand the man held a long, heavy, blue-black revolver. Often he yelled, and these cries rang through a semblance of a deserted village, shrilly flying over the roofs in a volume that seemed to have no relation to the ordinary vocal strength of a man. It was as if the surrounding stillness formed the arch of a tomb over him. These cries of ferocious challenge rang against walls of silence. And his boots had red tops with gilded imprints, of the kind beloved in winter by little sledding boys on the hillsides of New England.

The man's face flamed in a rage begot of whisky. His eyes, rolling and yet keen for ambush, hunted the still doorways and windows. He walked with the creeping movement of the midnight cat. As it occurred to him, he roared menacing information. The long revolvers in his hands were as easy as straws; they were moved with an electric swiftness. The little fingers of each hand played sometimes in a musician's way. Plain from the low collar of the shirt, the cords of his neck straightened and sank, straightened and sank, as passion moved him. The only sounds were his terrible invitations. The calm adobes preserved their demeanor at the passing of this small thing in the middle of the street.

There was no offer of fight; no offer of fight. The man called to the sky. There were no attractions. He bellowed and fumed and swayed his revolvers here and everywhere.

The dog of the barkeeper of the "Weary Gentleman" saloon had not appreciated the advance of events. He yet lay dozing in front of his master's door. At sight of the dog, the man paused and raised his revolver humorously. At sight of the man, the dog sprang up and walked diagonally away, with a sullen head, and growling. The man yelled, and the dog broke into a gallop. As it was about to enter an alley, there was a loud noise, a whistling, and something spat the ground directly before it. The dog screamed, and, wheeling in terror, galloped headlong in a new direction. Again there was a noise, a whistling, and sand was kicked viciously before it. Fear-stricken, the dog turned and flurried like an animal in a pen. The man stood laughing, his weapons at his hips.

Ultimately the man was attracted by the closed door of the "Weary Gentleman" saloon. He went to it, and hammering with a revolver, demanded drink.

The door remaining imperturbable, he picked a bit of paper from the walk and nailed it to the framework with a knife. He then turned his back contemptuously upon this popular resort, and walking to the opposite side of the street, and spinning there on his heel quickly and lithely, fired at the bit of paper. He missed it by a half inch. He swore at himself, and went away. Later, he comfortably fusilladed the windows of his most intimate friend. The man was playing with this town. It was a toy for him.

But still there was no offer of fight. The name of Jack Potter, his ancient antagonist, entered his mind, and he concluded that it would be a glad thing if he should go to Potter's house and by bombardment induce him to come out and fight. He moved in the direction of his desire, chanting Apache scalp-music.

When he arrived at it, Potter's house presented the same still front as had the other adobes. Taking up a strategic position, the man howled a challenge. But this house regarded him as might a great stone god. It gave no sign. After a decent wait, the man howled further challenges, mingling with them wonderful epithets.

Presently there came the spectacle of a man churning himself into deepest rage over the immobility of a house. He fumed at it as the winter wind attacks a prairie cabin in the North. To the distance there should have gone the sound of a tumult like the fighting of 200 Mexicans. As necessity bade him, he paused for breath or to reload his revolvers.

Chapter 4

Potter and his bride walked sheepishly and with speed. Sometimes they laughed together shamefacedly and low.

"Next corner, dear," he said finally.

They put forth the efforts of a pair walking bowed against a strong wind. Potter was about to raise a finger to point the first appearance of the new home when, as they circled the corner, they came face to face with a man in a maroon-colored shirt who was feverishly pushing cartridges into a large revolver. Upon the instant the man dropped his revolver to the ground, and, like lightning, whipped another from its holster. The second weapon was aimed at the bridegroom's chest.

There was silence. Potter's mouth seemed to be merely a grave for his tongue. He exhibited an instinct to at once loosen his arm from the woman's grip, and he dropped the bag to the sand. As for the bride, her face had gone as yellow as old cloth. She was a slave to hideous rites gazing at the apparitional snake.

The two men faced each other at a distance of three paces. He of the revolver smiled with a new and quiet ferocity.

"Tried to sneak up on me," he said. "Tried to sneak up on me!" His eyes grew more baleful. As Potter made a slight movement, the man thrust his revolver venomously forward. "No, don't you do it, Jack Potter. Don't you move a finger toward a gun just yet. Don't you move an eyelash. The time has come for me to settle with you, and I'm goin' to do it my own way and loaf along with no interferin'. So if you don't want a gun bent on you, just mind what I tell you."

Potter looked at his enemy. "I ain't got a gun on me, Scratchy," he said. "Honest, I ain't." He was stiffening and steadying, but yet somewhere at the back of his mind a vision of the Pullman floated, the sea-green figured velvet, the shining brass, silver, and glass, the wood that gleamed as darkly brilliant as the surface of a pool of oil - all the glory of the marriage, the environment of the new estate. "You know I fight when it comes to fighting, Scratchy Wilson, but I ain't got a gun on me. You'll have to do all the shootin' yourself."

His enemy's face went livid. He stepped forward and lashed his weapon to and fro before Potter's chest. "Don't you tell me you ain't got no gun on you, you whelp. Don't tell me no lie like that. There ain't a man in Texas ever seen you without no gun. Don't take me for no kid." His eyes blazed with light, and his throat worked like a pump.

"I ain't takin' you for no kid," answered Potter. His heels had not moved an inch backward. "I'm takin' you for a damn fool. I tell you I ain't got a gun, and I ain't. If you're goin' to shoot me up, you better begin now. You'll never get a chance like this again."

So much enforced reasoning had told on Wilson's rage. He was calmer. "If you ain't got a gun, why ain't you got a gun?" he sneered. "Been to Sunday-school?"

"I ain't got a gun because I've just come from San Anton' with my wife. I'm married," said Potter. "And if I'd thought there was going to be any galoots like you prowling around when I brought my wife home, I'd had a gun, and don't you forget it."

"Married!" said Scratchy, not at all comprehending.

"Yes, married. I'm married," said Potter distinctly.

"Married?" said Scratchy. Seemingly for the first time he saw the drooping, drowning woman at the other man's side. "No!" he said. He was like a creature allowed a glimpse of another world. He moved a pace backward, and his arm with the revolver dropped to his side. "Is this the lady?" he asked.

"Yes, this is the lady," answered Potter.

There was another period of silence.

"Well," said Wilson at last, slowly, "I s'pose it's all off now."

"It's all off if you say so, Scratchy. You know I didn't make the trouble." Potter lifted his valise.

"Well, I 'low it's off, Jack," said Wilson. He was looking at the ground. "Married!" He was not a student of chivalry; it was merely that in the presence of this foreign condition he was a simple child of the earlier plains. He picked up his starboard revolver, and placing both weapons in their holsters, he went away. His feet made funnel-shaped tracks in the heavy sand.

—Stephen Crane

Day 2

Story Analysis

This week we will examine the story considering all the elements of fiction that we have studied so far.

Setting

1. What are the physical settings of the story? In what time period is it set? How is it conveyed to the reader?

2. This story uses quite a lot of figurative language. Review the kinds of figurative language in Week 14. Find at least two instances of figurative language in describing the setting and explain them. (For example, the train is personified as "pouring over the plains.")

Character

Describe each of the characters or classes of characters. For each one say how the reader finds out about the character (physical description, from comments and reactions of other people, from the character's thoughts and feelings, from the character's actions).

1. Jack Potter

2. The Bride

3. The waiters and porters on the train

4. The people in the bar (A drummer is a traveling salesman.)

5. Scratchy Wilson

Plot

1. Make a list of the main events in the story. Is this story circular, episodic, or linear?

2. What is the conflict in this story?

3. What do you think is the climax of the story?

4. Why is Potter so worried about the fact that he is returning from San Anton a married man? (This is alluded to throughout the story.)

5. Why does Scratchy give up his rampage when he hears that Potter is married?

6. Do you find any kinds of irony in this story (review kinds of irony in Week 31 Day 3)?

Day 3

Point of View

1. Describe what kind of point of view is used by the author? (First Person or Omniscient)

2. At what points in the story does the point of view change? What affect does this have on the story?

Theme

Keeping in mind that each reader brings his own experiences to a story, think about the themes that can be found in the story. Think about each of the following possible thematic possibilities. Decide whether you think any of these themes are present in the story and explain how they are present.

Unconditional Love

Change in society

Courage

Then after considering these themes, describe any other themes that you find in the story.

Imagery

1. This story is full of beautiful imagery. Select your two favorite descriptions and explain why you like them best.

2. Do a copy change imitation of the following passage using your own topic.

> The barkeeper's dog lay on the board walk that crossed in front of the door. His head was on his paws, and he glanced drowsily here and there with the constant vigilance of a dog that is kicked on occasion. Across the sandy street were some vivid green grass plots, so wonderful in appearance amid the sands that burned near them in

a blazing sun that they caused a doubt in the mind. They exactly resembled the grass mats used to represent lawns on the stage. At the cooler end of the railway station a man without a coat sat in a tilted chair and smoked his pipe. The fresh-cut bank of the Rio Grande circled near the town, and there could be seen beyond it a great, plum-colored plain of mesquite.

Day 4

Literary Analysis

Today you will begin to write a literary analysis of one of the stories in this unit. Remember that in a literary analysis you make a claim about a piece of literature and then support it with both evidence from the story and your logical explanation. You may choose only one story to write about or you may compare and contrast any of the stories on one of the elements of fiction. For example, you can compare the characters of two stories, compare the use of irony in two stories, compare the themes of two stories, and so on.

Review the stories and make a decision about the focus of your paper. You need to choose a topic narrow enough to easily discuss in a one or two page paper. But the eventual thesis statement needs to be something debatable; that is, something that others might not agree with and will thus require you to make a case for it. Choose one of the essay styles listed below for your paper:

1. Theme Essay
In this essay you make a claim about the theme of the short story. You use examples from the text to show that your theme is correct, always explaining how the quote supports your thesis about the theme of the story.

2. Character Analysis
In this essay, you make a claim about one of the characters in the story. This claim is your opinion, or some thought you have about the character. For example, if you are writing about Goldilocks, your thesis statement might be:

Goldilocks is a brazen child with no sense of manners or courtesy.

Your essay will then be ordered to proving that your opinion or idea about the character is correct by citing example from the story.

3. Analysis of the Devices Used
In this essay, you discuss the effects that one of the devices, such as point of view, setting, or imagery, has on the story. Think of one statement about the effects of the device that you will focus on and find examples in the story to prove it.

General Outline

Here is the general outline you will follow:

Introduction: Introduce and *briefly* summarize the story
                Introduce the topic you will be discussing
                Give your thesis statement

Body: Find support for your thesis in the story and present it.
                Divide the support into logical paragraphs and use transitions to move
                  your reader through the essay.
                Be sure to explain *how* your examples support your thesis.

Conclusion: Remind your reader of your thesis
                (Review writing a conclusion in Week 17 Day 4)

Be sure that you have your thesis statement clearly in mind before you begin!

Today you will create an outline and find the supporting text you need for your paper. Copy the following chart onto your paper and use it to record your textual examples. Once you have completed your chart and created your outline, file them for next week.

Thesis Statement:

Example from story: How this example shows the thesis:
Example from story: How this example shows the thesis:
Example from story: How this example shows the thesis:

Week 34

Day 1

Better than Gold

Better than grandeur, better than gold,
Than rank and titles a thousand fold,
Is a healthy body and a mind at ease,
And simple pleasures that always please
A heart that can feel for another's woe,
With sympathies large enough to enfold
All men as brothers, is better than gold.

Better than gold is a conscience clear,
Though toiling for bread in an humble sphere,
Doubly blessed with content and health,
Untried by the lusts and cares of wealth,
Lowly living and lofty thoughtful,
Adorn and ennoble a poor man's cot;
For mind and morals in nature's plan
Are the genuine test of a gentleman.

Better than gold is the sweet repose
Of the sons of toil when the labors close;
Better than gold is the poor man's sleep,
And the balm that drops on slumbers deep
Bring sleeping draughts on the downy bed,
Where luxury pillows its aching head,
The toiler simple opiate deems
A short route to the land of dreams.

Better than gold is a thinking mind,
That in the realm of books can find
A treasure surpassing Australian ore,
And live with the great and good of yore.
The sage's lore and the poet's lay,
The glories of empires passed away;
The world's great dream will thus unfold
And yield a please better than gold.

Better than gold is a peaceful home
Where all the fireside characters come,
The shrine of love, the heaven of life,
Hallowed by mother, or sister, or wife.
However humble the home may be,
Or tried with sorrow by heaven's decree,
The blessing that never were bought or sold,
And centre there, are better than gold.

—Father Abram Ryan

Write an interpretation of this poem. Begin by writing what you think the overall theme is and then break it down by stanza to say how that theme is conveyed as the poem progresses.

Grammar Study

Unit 1 Review

Exercise A
Answer the following questions. If you don't know the answers, refer to Unit 1.

1. What are the 7 parts of speech?

2. What are the 3 major parts of a sentence?

3. What is a verbal? Name the 3 kinds of verbal phrases

4. What are the 3 types of clauses and how is each kind used.

5. What is the difference between a simple, compound, and complex sentence?

Exercise B

In the passage below from *To Build a Fire*, find the following grammatical forms:

gerund phrase   direct object   adjective clause
adverb clause   infinitive phrase   predicate adjective

After some manipulation he managed to get the bunch between the heels of his mittened hands. In this fashion he carried it to his mouth. The ice crackled and snapped when by a violent effort he opened his mouth. He drew the lower jaw in, curled the upper lip out of the way, and scraped the bunch with his upper teeth in order to separate a match. He succeeded in getting one, which he dropped on his lap. He was no better off. He could not pick it up.

Day 2

Writing

Today you will write a first draft of the literary analysis paper you began last week. Review the chart and the outline you made. Add to it or make changes that improve the flow of your thoughts. Then write you first draft without worrying about spelling and punctuation. You may want to get some initial feedback from your teacher about the draft, but otherwise, set it aside until Day 3.

Grammar

Review of Unit 2

Exercise A

Answer the following questions. If you don't know the answers, refer to Unit 2.

1. Explain the following grammatical forms: concrete noun, abstract noun, collective noun, appositive.

2. Explain the three characteristics of verbs: mood, tense, and voice

3. Name the various kinds of figurative language. Choose 3 and write an example of each one.

4. What is the benefit of sentence combining?

Exercise B

Tell the tense, mood, and voice of each of the underlined verbs below.

1. The children <u>had tried</u> for hours to get out of the basement window.

2. The truck <u>had been hit</u> by the snow plow.

3. If you <u>could</u> see your face, you might think it's funny.

4. I <u>do want</u> to attend the social, but I <u>haven't got</u> a dress to wear.

5. She <u>was turning</u> the door knob slowly, afraid of what she might find.

6. <u>Leave</u> that book on the back table.

Day 3

Writing

Review the paper you wrote on Day 2. Use the following Revision Checklist as you review the essay. After you finish, ask someone to read your paper and ask them these same questions. Make changes in your paper based on your conversation with the reader. Make a second draft if needed.

Revision Checklist

Organization/Structure

- Does the paper seem appropriate to the audience—your peers? (What makes it so?)
- Have the ideas been adequately developed?
- Are all paragraphs unified and coherent?
- Is there an inherent logical order evident in the placement of each paragraph? (Paragraph location is purposeful and logical.)
- Do the paragraphs flow smoothly from one to another?
  Does each paragraph serve a logical purpose?
- Could any of the sentences be written more concisely without losing meaning? Could any of the sentence be combined to introduce more variety?
- Are the sentences clear and complete?
- Are there sentences that announce what you are going to say or that sum up what have already said, *and therefore could be cut*?

Style and Voice

- Minimal use of passive voice
- Use of specific details ("Showing" language with action verbs and concrete nouns)
- Consistency of verb tense (all literary analysis paper must use the present tense)
- Minimal use of forms of "to be" (is, are, was, were)
- Varied sentence structure, rhythm, and length
- Word choice: clear, effective, concise

Grammar, Punctuation, Spelling

- Pronoun-antecedent agreement
- Subject-verb agreement
- No sentence fragments or run-ons
- Quotations places correctly
- No comma splices
- Correct spelling

Grammar

Review of Unit 3

Exercise A
Answer the following questions. If you are unsure of the answers, check Unit 3.

1. Explain how you can tell whether to use the pronoun *who* or the pronoun *whom*.

2. What is meant by the two terms: misplaced modifier and a dangling modifier?

3. How can you tell what case to use when using pronouns?

4. What is the proper way to use the words *good* and *well*?

Exercise B
Explain the proper usage that each of these sentences demonstrates.

1. I hope I did as well as he.
2. It was George who saw you and whom I saw.
3. I wanted to read the book myself.

4. Neither of her books was lying on the desk.
5. There was a conflict between him and me.
6. John likes skiing, skateboarding, and bicycling.
7. Does either of you know where the manual is?
8. The door's being locked created problems.
9. Don't just try to do it; be sure to do it.
10. Running along the curb, he tripped.

Day 4

Writing

Today you will make a final copy of your literary analysis paper. When you finish it, fill out the Final Paper Reflection (below) and attach it to your final copy.

Take some time this week to look back over all the writing you have done in this course. Compare your writing from the beginning of the year to the end of the year. Do you notice any improvements? What paper do you like the best?

Keep in mind that you are progressing toward becoming a great writer. Every year you work on it, you move closer to that goal. So keep up the good work!

Final Copy Reflection

1. What I think I did well in this paper:

2. What I tried to improve on in this paper:

3. What I liked least about my writing on this paper:

4. What I want the teacher to address when reviewing my paper:

5. What I want to work on in my next paper:

6. The most important thing to me about my writing right now is:

Parsing

Demonstrate what you have learned in grammar this year, but parsing the following sentence.

1. Identify the part of speech of each word.
2. Identify the parts of the sentence (As you tell the parts of the sentence give the case, number and gender of nouns and the tense, mood, and voice of verbs. Tell whether verbs are transitive or intransitive.)
3. Identify subordinate clauses and their subjects, predicates, and complements. (When labeling the words on your paper, label the subject, verb, and complement of the subordinate clause *under* the sentence so that it's not confused with the subject and verb of the main clause.)
4. Identify verbals and phrases and their objects and modifiers and tell how they are used.
5. Explain the modifiers.

(Remember that a clause may be inside a phrase and a phrase inside a clause.)

The drummer wished to ask further questions which were born of an increasing anxiety and bewilderment; but when he attempted them, the men merely looked at him in irritation and motioned him to remain silent.

Appendix

Grammar Information

Basic Parts of Speech

1. **Noun**: a noun is a word used as the name of a person, place, thing, or idea. A common noun is a word used as the name of any one of a class of persons, places, or things. A proper noun is a word used as the name of a particular person, place or thing.

   Virtue is accomplished by practicing good habits. (noun)

   A *puppy* lay sleeping on the sun-filled porch. (common noun)

   Rex lay sleeping on the sun-filled porch. (proper noun)

2. **Pronoun**: A pronoun is a word used in place of a noun. See a complete list on page of this Appendix.

   He lay sleeping on the sun-filled porch. (pronoun "He" takes the place of *Rex*)

3. **Adjective**: An adjective is a word used to modify a noun or pronoun. Articles (a, an, the) are included as adjectives.

   A *golden* puppy lay sleeping on the sun-filled porch.

4. **Verb**: A verb is a word used to express action or state of being. A transitive verb passes its action to an object. An intransitive verb has no object receiving the action. A linking verb, or *copulative* verb, connects the subject with another noun, pronoun, or adjective. A noun or adjectives linked to the subject through the copulative is called the subject complement. A noun complement is the predicate nominative and the adjective complement is known as the predicate adjective.

   Sam *threw* the ball. (transitive action verb with the object *ball* receiving the action)

   Sam's ability *matured* as he grew older. (intransitive verb)

   Sam *is* a great ball player. (copulative verb with *great ball player* being the complement linked to the subject)

5. **Adverb**: An adverb is a word that modifies a verb, an adjective, or another adverb.

   Sam threw the ball *quite quickly*. (*quickly* modifies "threw" and *quite* modifies "quickly")

6. **Preposition**: A preposition is a word used to introduce a phrase that shows the relation between the principal word of the phrase and some other word in the sentence. It is best to memorize the common prepositions. (See page in the Appendix)
   In the barn, *over* the door Sally saw a rusty farm tool *with* many dents.

7. **Conjunction**: A conjunction is a word used to connect words or groups of words.

We wanted to play baseball, *but* we ended up playing football.

Sally *and* Susan went to the state competition, *for* they had won our local meet.

8. **Interjection**: An interjection is a word used to express sudden or strong feeling.

Wow! That is a large piece of cake.

Parts of a Sentence

Subject: The *subject* of a sentence or clause is the part of the sentence or clause about which *something* is being said. It can be a noun, pronoun, or clause.

Predicate: That which is said about the subject is the **predicate**. It makes an assertion about the subject, telling what it is, or what it does.

Direct Object: A **direct object** is a noun or pronoun that receives the action of a verb or shows the result of the action. It answers the question "What?" or "Whom?" after an action verb. An action verb with a direct object is called a **transitive verb**.

Indirect Object: An indirect object precedes the direct object and tells **to whom** or **for whom** the action of the verb is done and who is receiving the direct object. There must be a direct object to have an indirect object. Indirect objects are usually found with verbs of giving or communicating like *give, bring, tell, show, take,* or *offer.* An indirect object is always a noun or pronoun which is not part of a prepositional phrase.

Predicate Nominative: A **predicate nominative** is a *noun* or *pronoun* which follows the verb and describes or renames the subject. It is another *way* of naming the subject. It follows a linking verb.

Predicate Adjective: A **predicate adjective** is an adjective that is used to predicate an attribute of the subject.

Prepositions

about	behind	from	on	toward
above	below	in	on top of	under
across	beneath	in front of	onto	underneath
after	beside	inside	out of	until
against	between	instead of	outside	up
along	by	into	over	upon
among	down	like	past	with
around	during	near	since	within
at	except	of	through	without
before	for	off	to	

Pronouns

Pronouns are words used to replace a noun.
Here is a chart of the personal pronouns:

	Subject Pronouns	Object Pronouns	Possessive Adjectives	Possessive Pronouns	Reflexive Pronouns
1st person	I	me	my	mine	myself
2nd person	you	you	your	yours	yourself
3rd person (m)	he	him	his	his	himself
3rd person (f)	she	her	her	hers	herself
3rd person (n)	it	it	its	(not used)	itself
1st person (pl.)	we	us	our	ours	ourselves
2nd person (pl.)	you	you	your	yours	yourselves
3rd person (pl)	they	them	their	theirs	themselves

Here are all the pronouns—personal, demonstrative, indefinite, intensive, interrogative, and reflexive—in alphabetical order.

all	its	something
another	itself	that
any	many	their
anybody	me	theirs
anyone	mine	them
anything	my	themselves
both	myself	these
each	neither	they
either	nobody	this
everybody	none	this
everyone	no one	us
everything	nothing	we
few	one	what
he	others	which
her	our	who
hers	ours	whom
herself	ourselves	whose
him	several	you
himself	she	your
his	some	yours
I	somebody	yourself
it	someone	yourselves

Verb Tenses

What do each of the tenses indicate?

Simple

Present tense: Present tense expresses an unchanging, repeated, or reoccurring action or situation that exists only now. It can also represent a widespread truth.

Past Tense: Past tense expresses an action or situation that was started and finished in the past. Most past tense verbs end in **-ed**. The irregular verbs have special past tense forms which must be memorized.

Future Tense: Future tense expresses an action or situation that will occur in the future. This tense is formed by using *will/shall* with the *simple form* of the verb. It also uses *could* in the conditional mood.

Perfect

Present perfect: Present perfect tense describes an action that happened at an indefinite time in the past or that began in the past and continues in the present. This tense is formed by using *has/have* with the *past participle* of the verb. Most past participles end in "-ed." Irregular verbs have special past participles that must be memorized. **Passive form**: *has been* with past participle.

Past perfect: Past perfect tense describes an action that took place in the past before another past action. This tense is formed by using *had* with the *past participle* ("-ed") of the verb. **Passive form**: *had been* with the past participle.

Future perfect: Future perfect tense describes an action that will occur in the future before some other action. This tense is formed by using *will have* with the *past participle* of the verb. **Passive form**: *will have been* with the past participle.

Progressive

Present progressive: Present progressive tense describes an ongoing action that is happening at the same time the statement is written. This tense is formed by using **am/is/are** with the verb form ending in **-ing**.

Past progressive: Past progressive tense describes a past action which was happening when another action occurred. This tense is formed by using **was/were** with the verb form ending in **-ing**.

Future Progressive: Future progressive tense describes an ongoing or continuous action that will take place in the future. This tense is formed by using **will be** or **shall be** with the verb form ending in **-ing**.

Perfect Progressive

Present perfect progressive: Present perfect progressive tense describes an action that began in the past, continues in the present, and may continue into the future. This tense is formed by using **has/have been** and the **present participle** of the verb (the verb form ending in **-ing**).

Past perfect progressive: Past perfect progressive tense describes a past, ongoing action that was completed before some other past action. This tense is formed by using **had been** and the **present perfect** of the verb (the verb form ending in **-ing**).

Future perfect progressive: Future perfect progressive tense describes a future, ongoing action that will occur before some specified future time. This tense is formed by using **will have been** and the **present participle** of the verb (the verb form ending in **-ing**).

Emphatic

The two **emphatic** tenses receive their name because they are used for emphasis. More commonly, however, they are used with the negative **not** and with questions when the normal order is inverted and part of the verb comes before the subject.

Present Emphatic: Formed by adding the simple present form of the verb to the present tense of the verb **to do** or **Past Emphatic** tense is formed by adding the basic present form of the verb to the simple past tense of the verb **to do**

Passive Voice Verbs
Simple Tenses

Present tense

Person	Singular	Plural
1st	I am struck	We are struck.
2nd	You are struck.	You are struck.
3rd	He/She/It is struck	They are struck

(Simple) Past Tense

Person	Singular	Plural
1st	I was struck.	We were struck
2nd	You were struck.	You were struck.
3rd	He/She/It was struck.	They were struck.

Future

Person	Singular	Plural
1st	I will be struck.	We will be struck
2nd	You will be struck.	You will be struck
3rd	He/She/It will be struck.	They will be struck.

Transition Toolbox

Alternative
Either . . or . .
Instead
Rather than
Alternatively
Otherwise

Assumption
needless to say
It goes without saying
Assuming
of course
Obviously

Cause
Because
Since
For

Comparison
Similarly,
In the same way
Likewise
By contrast
On the one hand
On the other hand
Just as "X," so does "Y"

Contingency
If
Assuming
On the conviction that
Unless
Until

Overcoming Contingency
Even
Even so
Regardless,
nonetheless,
Despite
In spite of
Though
Even though
Although

Concession/Exception
Of course
Admittedly
Besides
Albeit
To be sure
Yes
Not "X" perhaps, but
In saying this, I do not mean to suggest
Which is not to say

Except for
With the exception of
I acknowledge
Granted
It is true that
There is no denying

Expert Testimony
According to "So and so"
As "So and so" has written
 "So and so" has put it well
Listen to "So and so"
Supporting this viewpoint, so and so has said
Refuting this viewpoint, so and so has said
In the words of "so and so"

Example
For example,
For instance
Including
Like
Such as
To illustrate
Specifically
One kind of

Instances are too numerous
Let me name a few
In one case,
As in
Witness
I have in mind such . . . as . . .
I think of the time when

Limiting
In general
Insofar as
At least in the case of
Where "X" is concerned
All other things being equal
To the extent that
Quite apart from
Not "X" but "Y"
Among other things

Equivalence
By which I mean to say
Which is to say
That is
In other words
To put the matter simply
Simply put,

Logical Extension
With this in mind
Accordingly
In light of
Therefore
Consequently
It follows that
As a result
Predictably

Speculation
For all we know
Possibly
Perhaps
It may be that
We cannot rule out

List
To begin with	For openers
First, second . . .	Besides that
Too	Also
Additionally	In addition
Furthermore	Moreover
Finally	Last, but not least

Not only "X" but "Y"
As if this were not enough
The following: _____

Time
Then	Eventually
Slowly	gradually
While	As time passed
Meanwhile,	Suddenly,
Overnight,	By *(time or date)*
Since	In *(month or year)*
Until	On *(date)*
Next	Before
After	Subsequently
Finally,	At last,

No sooner did . . . then . . . .

Contradiction
Contradiction
But	However
And yet	That being said
At the same time	On the other hand
On the contrary	Actually
In point of fact	

Short one sentence paragraphs:
You would be wrong.
Not likely.
Unfortunately, there is more to the story.
Nothing could be further from the truth.

Telegraphing

Supposedly
Conventional wisdom tells us
One might think that
To hear "so and so" tell of it,
　you'd think
It is an article of faith [in many
　quarters] that
Or so the argument runs

Place
Here
There
At
Near
Facing
Across from

Purpose
In order to
so that
Explanatory phrase
beginning with a verbal.
For example: "determined
to be heard." "seeking

Emphasis
In fact
Moreover
More/most importantly
Especially
Of special important/interest
In particular

Within (*specific distance*)   *the first place trophy*   Particularly
   Of   Above all

Sentence placement for emphasis

Placement of emphasized thing at the end of a sentence. Three common means:

       Inversion, as in, *In walked Joan*

       "But" clause, as in, *Most of us turned a deaf hear to these problems, but Joan cared.*

       Passive voice, as in, *The situation was resolved by Joan.*

Dramatic pause: *No one favored the new regulations . . . no one except Joan.*

Repetition with variation: *Ask not what your country can do for you; ask what you can do for your country*

Underlining or italics

Punctuation!

Variety in Sentence Type

True Questions: What should the US do in response to threats of terrorism?

Rhetorical Questions: How we claim to be responsible human beings when we lay waste to the environment daily?

Overstatement: I have in my time, collected enough lost golf balls to fill Lake Michigan.

Understatement: When the king advocated change, violent revolution against his own regime was not precisely what he had in mind.

Imperatives: Do not let the media lead you into frivolous desires.

"Transition Toolbox" adapted from *Writing at the Threshold* by Larry Weinstein (NCTE, 2001). Used by permission

CPSIA information can be obtained
at www.ICGtesting.com
Printed in the USA
LVOW06s2315070817

544195LV00031B/2077/P